THE 15-MINUTE
SINGLE GOURMET

PAULETTE MITCHELL

▼ ▼ ▼

Color photography by Kelly Shields
Illustrations by James Garrison

MACMILLAN • USA

Macmillan
A Simon & Schuster Macmillan Company
1633 Broadway
New York, NY 10019

MACMILLAN is a registered trademark of Macmillan, Inc.

Library of Congress Cataloging-in-Publication Data
Mitchell, Paulette.
  The 15-minute single gourmet/Paulette Mitchell.
    p.   cm.
  ISBN 0-02-860997-2
  1. Cookery for one. 2. Quick and easy cookery. I. Title.
  II. Title: Fifteen minute single gourmet.
  TX652.M565   1994
  641.5'61—dc20   93-38178
                                              CIP

10 9 8 7 6 5 4 3
Printed in the United States of America

Design by Laura Hammond Hough

CONTENTS

▼ ▼ ▼

ACKNOWLEDGMENTS V

PREFACE VII

INTRODUCTION 1

Shopping for One   Methods for the 15-Minute Single Gourmet

Equipping Your Kitchen   The Health-Conscious Cook   Recipe Analyses

PASTA 17

Warm Pastas   Chilled Pastas

ETHNIC AND VEGETARIAN ENTRÉES 39

Pizzas   Ethnic Entrées—Mostly Vegetables   Grains   Eggs

FISH AND SHELLFISH 71

Sautéed Fish and Shellfish   Broiled Fish and Shellfish   Poached Fish

Baked Fish and Shellfish   Steamed Fish   Fish and Shellfish with Pasta   Fish Soups

Fish in Wrappers

CHICKEN 115

Sautéed and Stir-Fried Chicken   Broiled Chicken   Baked Chicken

Chicken Salads

SOUPS 145

Chilled Soups   Puréed Soups   Chunky Soups

SALADS 175

The Mixed Green Salad   Basic Salad Dressings   Vegetable Salads   Bean Salads
Grain Salads   Fruit Salads

ACCOMPANIMENTS 207

Grains and Starches   Vegetable Accompaniments   Breads

DESSERT AND FRUITS 221

Dessert Basics   Puréed Desserts   Fresh Fruits with Sauces, Toppings, and Dips
Cooked Fruits

THIS BOOK IS DEDICATED WITH LOVE TO MY MOM

who privately reminds me that a 9 to 5 job would be easier
than writing cookbooks,
but publicly expresses her pride in me and my work

▼ ▼ ▼

ACKNOWLEDGMENTS

▼ ▼ ▼

Writing a book, especially a cookbook, is a long and arduous process. Having great meals along the way helped, but the long hours at the computer were eased by the encouragement and support from my extraordinary friends and colleagues. Each played a special role in the completion of this project.

Thank you to:

Brett Mitchell—my son, for being such an open-minded 10-year-old as he tasted and honestly evaluated each and every recipe in this book. He never complained until I offered him three cucumber soups for dinner one night! Brett, I apologize for saying "Be quiet" so many times. Life without you would be like food without flavor!

Darryl Trones—my soulmate, who also plays a special role in my life. His enthusiasm for my recipes (and me) led him to design and create our restaurant, Tray Café. As a companion, he provided me much-needed diversion and fun during the intense periods of this project.

Elliott, my cat—for her companionship as I cooked, and for curling up by my side as I typed into the night.

Mary Brindle—for her cheerful and efficient assistance with computer work until the final hour before my deadline.

Patrick Nolan—for his late night calls to check my progress and for advising me to get some sleep!

Linda Platt and Pam Abrams—for turning solitary recipe testing days into an "occasion" when they arrived unexpectedly for lunch now and then!

Fran LeBahn and Barb Kennedy—for cooking inspiration and friendship!

Carla Waldemar—my most literate friend, for her professional advice.

Nancy Lewis, Peggy Struble, Beth Malmgren, Sandra Christianson, Kathlyn Ignacio, Sue Langseth, Tina Shepard, Anne Riemer, and Ann Ulrich—for keeping in touch with encouragement when I rarely had time to get together.

Mary Evans, Mary Frame, the staff at Byerly's School of Culinary Arts, and all of my cooking class students—for affirming the success of my recipes.

Sam Kaplan—for his advice.

Victoria Larrea, Bill Wavrin, and my other friends at Rancho La Puerta—for sharing their corner of the world with me, a special place where I am spiritually and physically inspired.

Kelly Shields, my food photographer, and his assistant, B. Brandenberg—for turning our tedious task into fun!

Stuart Lorenz, my portrait photographer—for his good-natured spirit.

James Garrison—for his excellence as an artist.

Pam Hoenig and Justin Schwartz, my editors—for their guidance during the writing of this book and their patience with the too-lengthy manuscript.

And to all the cooks who have purchased my two previous books.

PREFACE

▼ ▼ ▼

Lifestyles change. Back in the seventies I was a typical bride who cooked a hearty dinner every night—or felt guilty if I didn't. When exercise and nutritional information began to make an impact on our way of thinking and eating, I found myself abandoning a reliance on red meat and experimenting with grains, pastas, legumes—and, yes, tofu—back in those militantly dedicated days. I adapted our favorite ethnic recipes, from lasagna to chili, and found that we not only did not miss the meat, but felt healthy and content with our new diet.

After my son was born—a whole new dimension was added to my cooking—*time.* Between teaching classes in cooking and aerobics and tending a toddler, I found fewer and fewer moments to spare on elaborate preparations. I developed a whole new repertoire of shortcuts that celebrated freshness and flavor without paying for it in time.

The nineties brought another change—a new life as a single. I discovered a whole new world of people eating solo (or not eating, as the case may be), making a meal of popcorn, eating frozen dinners, or straining their paychecks in restaurants because they couldn't imagine taking the time to cook for themselves. And recipe books with instructions that serve "from 6 to 8" provided little encouragement. I saw many singles squeezing health club workouts and time for jogging into their busy schedules; but on the way home they picked up fast food for dinner.

I adapted many of my favorite recipes to suit my need for shopping and preparing food in smaller quantities. And in the revisions I took into account my increasing concern for low-fat, high-carbohydrate, healthful eating. I added these recipes to my cooking class repertoire and found my classes in quick, healthful cooking for singles to be among the most in demand—as well as the most appreciated!

Here, then, is your antidote to junk food and monotony. *The 15-Minute Single Gourmet* will solve the dilemma of cooking for one, for everyone from college students to busy professionals to retirees. Monotony, time pressures, health and fitness concerns, and high cost are addressed by paring fat, salt, sugar, and even preparation time from a sumptuous array of recipes including fish, shellfish, and chicken, in addition to vegetarian meals. In just 15 minutes, you'll be dining well!

Along with new and exciting soups, salads, entrées, and desserts, I've provided nutritional information, suggestions for smart shopping, staples and cooking utensils to have on hand. The recipes are simple enough to appeal to an inexperienced cook or even a "noncook," yet varied enough to satisfy a true gourmet. I have used these recipes in demonstration cooking classes, participation cooking classes, private in-home classes, health spa demonstrations, for catered parties, and in my own home where I have feasted on them and have shared them with guests. The responses have been overwhelmingly positive. Each of the more than 100 recipes includes a breakdown of nutritional information as well as suggested substitutions and an abundance of variations, and a few personal memories. Please enjoy!

Paulette Mitchell

INTRODUCTION

...

Whether single or part of a family with conflicting schedules, all adults eat alone some of the time. Perhaps you've just moved to your first apartment without a roommate. Or maybe your last child just left for school. If your spouse travels for business, your meal patterns can change weekly. Whatever the circumstances, cooking for one means thinking differently about shopping and cooking. But dining alone does not mean you need to deny yourself the pleasures and benefits of eating well. You can cook high-style, healthful food for one. And in only 15 minutes, start to finish!

How many times, after a long day, do you arrive home, devour large quantities of whatever food is on hand, and then feel dissatisfied with yourself for having eaten high-calorie junk rather than nourishing your body with a wholesome dinner? If you routinely stuff yourself with empty calories but neglect your basic needs, this book will help you to build not only a better dinner, but also a stronger, trimmer, healthier body.

Maybe we're coming full circle in our use of unprocessed foods. Our ancestors used fresh almost entirely because that was all they had available. The arrival of processed foods seemed to be the solution to eating amid a frenzied work schedule and other time commitments. But now many of us are demanding freshness because we know it is more healthful and more appealing.

Eating flavorful and interesting food does not need to be reserved for the meals you eat in restaurants. Cooking for one may seem like a big effort with little reward, but in my cooking classes for singles, I see the excitement of students who have been missing out on the sensuous pleasures of handling food and the joy of creation. They realize that eating well alone is essential to their good health, happiness, and well-being.

But how to begin? The prospect of slaving for hours over a hot stove is less than exciting, and many recipes seem to require the resources of time, skill, and energy. Another problem is that conventional cookbooks just aren't right for people like us. Reducing recipes designed for 4 to 6 servings often doesn't work; proportions of ingredients frequently change when you divide a recipe, and cooking times change, too. The alternative—making the entire recipe—results in endless days of leftovers. And most books designed for singles rely heavily on convenience foods, which eliminates many of the advantages of cooking from scratch in the first place.

The good news is that *The 15-Minute Single Gourmet* makes it possible to have it all—convenience, speed, nutrition, variety, and home-cooked flavor with a gourmet flair. You won't need to wait until you are having company to eat well at home! This book will show you how to plan with organization, shop with practicality, cook with creativity, and dine on a small scale with ease. These recipes are realistic and easy to follow; they require little patience, no elaborate techniques, and only 15 minutes each! Also, they have all been tested a minimum of four times to ensure success.

Instead of the traditional dinner of three separate dishes of protein, vegetables, and starch, I often combine these elements in one dish. The recipes borrow the exciting flavors from many cuisines, along with their cooking techniques. Though this is not a diet book, the recipes call for no salt and little added fat; high-flavor ingredients like herbs, spices, and garlic supply assertive taste. Each of the recipes provides a generous serving for one (in some cases two) and can be prepared using readily available in-gredients and a minimum of equipment. Unnecessary and time-consuming procedures have been pared down or eliminated. The steps are taken in order, often telling you how to consolidate your time by doing two things at once. Cleanup is easy and left-overs are kept to a minimum.

Use the original recipes as a guide. Variations are suggested so that you can make a recipe suit your taste and allow you to use what you have on hand. Some may add a little extra preparation time or calories, but they will provide you with innumerable meal ideas. Most recipes also include suggestions for garnishes. Though important for eye appeal, garnishes will do more than just decorate your food; they will add a bit of unexpected flavor and texture, creaminess or crunch. Pick one or two from the suggestions or choose your own. Tips are included which answer the types of questions posed by students in my cooking classes. A nutritional analysis has been provided for all recipes; see page 14 for an explanation of my methods.

The recipes are so simple, they will build confidence in the kitchen. (I always tell my students, there is really no such thing as a mistake in cooking, just an alteration in the recipe!) Once you become comfortable with the recipes, don't be obsessed with following them exactly. Use them as a guide as you improvise using your own ideas for culinary innovation. Your taste buds may be more advanced than your cooking techniques, so rely on your own nose and taste buds to adjust seasonings and ingredients to suit you. Some flavorings, especially those which add hotness like curry powder, chili powder, and pepper, are specified to be added "to taste"; actually that consideration applies to the addition of nearly all the herbs, spices, and ingredients. And don't hesitate to write in your book, starring your favorite variations and inserting your own. The margins of the cookbooks I use are filled with notes and comments for future reference.

One of the pleasures of single cooking is that you never have to cook or eat something you do not like. Let's face it, when you're alone, you need only to please yourself. If you crave soup for breakfast, eggs for dinner, or pancakes at midnight, who cares? You may eat a substantial lunch away from home and choose a light entrée for dinner. There is nothing sacred about three meals a day, so this book is not divided into the traditional chapters of breakfast, lunch, and dinner, but rather, is split into food categories which can fit into your schedule where they may. Although some of the recipes can be made in advance to be ready when you get home, most are designed to be prepared and eaten right away. If you choose, many of the recipes may be doubled if you are having a guest, or to provide a second meal for yourself a day or two later. (When doubled, assembly, preparation, and cooking may take slightly more time.) Because they adapt so well to this idea, the soup recipes all make 2 servings, and so do several of the salads. Some even improve in flavor by mellowing in the refrigerator a day or so. I do not make extra food with freezing in mind. The quality and texture nearly always deteriorate after being frozen and thawed, and these steps diminish the benefits of cooking with fresh ingredients.

Servings are designed to be generous, so if you do have unintentional leftovers, you'll find that most dishes reheat well. Some, like Rainbow Rotini with Parsley-Walnut Pesto (page 23), are equally delicious eaten cold. Some leftovers can be stirred into rice or used as a topping for pasta. Be inventive!

Several of the chapters contain meatless recipes; vegetarian foods do lend themselves easily to quick preparation since vegetables are at their best when they are not overcooked. Not having meat as the focus of a meal may be new to you, but try these recipes and I'm sure you will find them surprisingly satisfying. Since total vegetarianism may not be for everyone, I have also included recipes with shellfish, fish, and chicken. Low-fat cooking techniques have been used so don't hesitate to add these recipes to your menu plans. I have eliminated the use of beef and pork since these foods are not a part of my own diet.

It _is_ possible to dine well alone. After your meal is created, eat quickly if you must. But when time permits, do it in style. Don't stand by your kitchen sink as you eat—a confession made by many of my single students!

I sincerely hope these recipes will satisfy your appetite as they have mine—and that they will reintroduce or introduce home cooking and good eating into your complex schedule. Allow these recipes to liberate you from the boredom of cooking for one. I hope you will discover pleasure in your kitchen as a "15-Minute Single Gourmet."

▼ ▼ ▼

I always appreciate the comments on my recipes and ideas that I receive from cooking class students and clients. If you'd like to share your thoughts, write me c/o

Macmillan General Reference
15 Columbus Circle
New York, NY 10023

▼ ▼ ▼

SHOPPING FOR ONE

First of all, plan your shopping so that your kitchen is well stocked with wholesome foods. Some singles I know think shopping means a trip up and down the frozen food aisle, but good shopping is the key to good eating, and you are more likely to eat better if nutritious fresh foods are readily available and easy to prepare.

Choose the recipes for a couple of meals and make a list of the ingredients you will need. Check the variations, too, so you can plan to use seasonal fresh foods.

The more you cook, the more basics you will have on hand. Keep an ongoing list of staples to buy, and add to the list when you get low on an item. This means fewer trips to the store and more efficient shopping for the basics. Using a combination of fresh seasonal ingredients and staples, you will be able to create fabulous meals.

The ingredients used in my recipes are readily available in most supermarkets; yet my pantry is certainly more interesting than it was ten years ago. Some ingredients, like couscous, basmati rice, and black beans, once were considered exotic or regional foods; today they are commonplace. And at one time it was thought that buying healthful food required a trip to a health food store. Now it simply requires a strategy to find the ethnic and healthful foods among the 15,000 items in a typical large supermarket. Most of my weekly shopping is done in the outer perimeter of the store, where the fresh fruits, fresh vegetables, breads, dairy products, fish, and chicken are stocked. For staples (like pasta and canned tomatoes) and packaged or canned ethnic foods, I venture inward. And, if time permits, once every couple of months, I purchase some of my staples (like a variety of rices) in bulk at a food co-op.

Smart shopping for one avoids waste, so purchasing food in small quantities is best. Economy-size items will not save you money if they go unused and spoil. And even if the extra food could be frozen, fresh food is always better in taste and quality.

TIP

▼ Since fresh herbs are milder
than dried and contain more
moisture, a rule of thumb is to
triple the quantity when using
fresh herbs as opposed to dried
herbs; in some cases, for single
servings, I multiply them by
four.

Look for small size in everything. Most markets will divide
packages of fish and chicken. And many stores, aware of the increasing number of single cooks, package products like chicken,
fish, and produce in smaller quantities. When canned products
are necessary, I have tried to limit them to ingredients available
in small-size cans to eliminate leftovers that may never be used.

Arrive at the store with an open mind and be flexible when
you are shopping, adapting purchases for recipes to suit your
preferences or to make use of regional seasonal produce. A variety of vegetables, fruits, fish, herbs, and other ingredients can be
substituted in most of my recipes. Improvise! Don't be afraid to
try variations and substitutions beyond my suggestions.

In general, think in terms of buying foods that are naturally
low in fat—fresh fruits and vegetables, whole grain bread and
cereal products, poultry without skin, and fish. You can buy
low-fat dairy products, which I have specified in my recipes, but
substitute nonfat if they suit you better.

I use fresh ingredients whenever possible because they are
tastiest. Luckily, fresh produce is easier to purchase in small
quantities than frozen or canned. As staples, I do keep some
frozen vegetables, such as corn and peas. Buy them in bags
rather than in boxes so you can easily remove what you need.
Some stores carry single servings of frozen vegetables, too. For
my recipes you will want to purchase plain frozen vegetables;
check the labels to avoid added butter and sauces.

Eliminating salt is a blessing in disguise. Using garlic, lemon
juice, and herbs will more than compensate for the absence of
salt as a way to perk up the tastes in your recipes. (If salt-free
cooking is new to you, add just a pinch if you feel it is necessary.) I prefer fresh herbs—they are undoubtedly superior, especially for uncooked recipes. But their quick spoilage makes them
impractical for most single cooks. To save time, money, and to
avoid waste, I have tested all of my recipes using herbs in dried
form, too, and have specified when dried herbs are unacceptable.

One bit of advice—when you are improvising, be careful not
to overflavor your food. Fresh herbs can be used more abun-

dantly; dried herbs can easily overwhelm. Begin with small quantities of herbs, then taste. You can always add more. There is a fine line, especially with hot seasonings (like hot pepper sauce, chili powder, cayenne pepper, and pepper), between just right and too much; when it comes to single-serving recipes, sometimes 1/8 teaspoon extra may be too much!

For convenience, chopped garlic packaged in a jar with oil works just fine. Tomato paste can be purchased in tubes, ideal for the small quantities needed for many single-serving recipes. And I always keep on hand small cans of tomatoes, tomato sauce, and several kinds of beans.

Since you will be purchasing some packaged items, you will be faced with package labeling. It seems that every box, bottle, and carton these days comes with nutritional claims aimed at making you feel better about buying and eating what is inside. These labels are often confusing and misleading because strict definitions do not exist for many aspects of labeling in spite of major breakthroughs in scientific knowledge about health and nutrition. A little well-deserved skepticism on your part may be the best defense.

In general, remember, the integrity of the food you produce is totally dependent on the quality of ingredients you purchase.

METHODS FOR THE 15-MINUTE SINGLE GOURMET

After making wise choices at the supermarket, preparing those foods in a healthful and efficient manner is the next step. The secret to preparing a perfect meal in 15 minutes lies in doing away with time-consuming procedures. That is one reason why my recipes rely more on an imaginative use of fresh ingredients than on elaborate techniques.

Fast meals are simplified meals. Instead of thinking of your main course as composed of three separate dishes (a protein, a vegetable, and a starch), plan your entrée to combine all three. Pasta dishes are ideal, providing protein and vegetables atop the noodles. Many of the fish and chicken entrées contain vegeta-

TIPS

▼ Ingredients on labels are listed in order by decreasing weight, with the largest quantity first.

▼ Some ingredients, such as sugar, go by several names (such as sucrose, fructose, dextrose, honey, corn syrup, etc.).

▼ "Light" or "lite" on labels may refer to color, texture, calories, or weight.

▼ "No cholesterol" is not synonymous with "no fat" or "low calorie."

▼ "Organic" and "natural" have come to mean nothing at all.

▼ Natural products may contain coconut or palm oil, both very high in saturated fats.

▼ Some packaged foods simply may contain no nutrients at all!

bles, needing only to be accompanied by pasta or rice. Sometimes a substantial rice or pasta dish, such as Stir-Fried Rice (pages 55–57) or Rainbow Rotini with Parsley-Walnut Pesto (page 23), can be the focus of your meal, accompanied with simply broiled fish or chicken.

Use a variety of cooking procedures during the week. Broiling, boiling, sautéing, stir-frying, steaming, poaching, baking in parchment, and microwaving are the best techniques for quick meals, and these low-fat techniques will enhance freshness, retain nutrients, and enable each ingredient to keep its individual flavor.

If my recipes require some fat, I use a minimal amount of olive oil or safflower oil. Oil sprays can be used in some recipes, or pans can be brushed lightly with oil using a paper towel or pastry brush; nonstick pans will also help to prevent food from sticking. In true "spa cuisine," sautéing is done in vegetable stock, eliminating oil entirely. If your goal is to reduce fats to that degree, try this method in any of the sautéed recipes.

For single cooks, microwaves seem to be especially popular; so, in these recipes, vegetable steaming is done in a microwave. (But, if you prefer, use a vegetable steamer in a saucepan.) Keep in mind that not all microwaves are alike, so cooking times may vary from the timing suggested in my recipes according to the wattage of the oven. Small quantities meant to be cooked only until crisp-tender consistently require very minimal cooking time, usually less than the suggestions on manufacturers' charts. Microwaves are well designed to heat leftovers; I nearly always use my microwave for this purpose.

In general, think of my suggested cooking times as estimates. As you become familiar with my recipes, you will be able to tell if a step is completed by the way the food looks, smells, or tastes. Though I prefer cooking with gas, my recipes were developed using an electric stove. Cooking times may actually be reduced if you are using a gas stove where temperature controls are usually more precise. Keep in mind that the type of pan used may affect not only the amount of oil needed but also cooking times. Whatever method you are using, always taste the food before

TIPS

- ▼ To prolong the lifespan of non-stick cookware, cook over low to medium heat. Also, always use nonabrasive utensils for cooking as well as for cleanup.
- ▼ Buy good quality knives; with proper care, they will last a lifetime.
- ▼ Find knives which are comfortable in your hand.
- ▼ Learn proper techniques for the use of your knives.
- ▼ Buy a sharpening steel; use it often, using the proper technique.
- ▼ Have your knives professionally sharpened once a year.
- ▼ Wash knives by hand soon after they are used and dry them immediately. Do not soak wooden handles in water; do not put knives in the dishwasher.

serving it; check for doneness and adjust the intensity of flavorings to suit you.

Be frugal with your time. Before beginning to cook, read each recipe and select accompaniments, if any, so that you can assemble ingredients, cooking utensils, and equipment, and, if necessary, preheat the oven or place a pot of water on the stove to boil. Clean all vegetables; rinse and dry fish or chicken. As you proceed, remember that is not necessary to complete one step before going on to another. In the kitchen it seems that I always do two things at once. For example, my pasta recipes will instruct you to prepare the sauce as the pasta cooks or to whisk together dressings as vegetables are sautéed. Follow the directions in an organized manner and you will achieve amazing results with minimum effort—and your entire meal will be ready to serve at one time.

Some recipes can either be partially or completely made in advance to be reheated or served chilled later without losing any flavor. Advance preparation is not recommended for those recipes where this information is not included.

Put away ingredients and wash utensils, bowls, and pots as they are used, if time permits—another savings of time and effort. And add to your ongoing list any staple grocery items which need to be replenished.

Most important, enjoy the process of creation. Read the variations and create your own. Taste as you cook to check seasonings and texture.

EQUIPPING YOUR KITCHEN

The size of your kitchen does not matter; the way you make it work for you does.

A 15-minute meal can be prepared in a small kitchen with minimal equipment. While it may be fun to have a wide variety of gadgets, they really are not necessary. But trying to cook if you don't have the proper utensils is frustrating, and owning the basics will make you feel more capable and relaxed in the kitchen. I laugh when I recall a friend whose kitchen was

▼ Store knives in a knife rack, not loosely in a drawer.

▼ The cutting surface, rather than foods, dulls knives. Soft surfaces, such as wooden or molded polyethylene cutting boards, are easier on the blades than very hard surfaces.

equipped so minimally that I witnessed him using bananas as potholders to remove a hot pan from the oven!

When purchasing equipment, buy the best you can afford. Food cooks more evenly in high-quality cookware, and superb pans will last you a lifetime. Be certain you select pans of the proper size to suit your needs as a single cook. If a pan is too large, liquids tend to evaporate too quickly and sauces may burn. Small pans and those with heavy bottoms which distribute heat evenly will enable you to use a minimum of oil. So will nonstick pans; include at least one nonstick skillet and one nonstick saucepan in your collection.

A food processor may seem to be an expensive luxury, but it makes short work out of procedures like shredding. In my kitchen, my food processor has not totally replaced my blender, which I prefer for puréeing soups.

Once you have purchased your equipment, the way to make it work for quick cooking is organization. Most cooking involves three work centers: the refrigerator, the range area, and the counter near the sink. Try to store utensils near where you will use them the most to prevent the frustration that comes with not being able to find what you're looking for.

THE HEALTH-CONSCIOUS COOK

Making a conscious decision to eat healthfully is a step in the right direction. But with the bombardment of contradictory nutritional information in our newspapers and magazines, learning how to do so isn't always easy. Most health professionals agree that the ideal diet is composed of 60 percent or more complex carbohydrates (as opposed to simple carbohydrates such as table sugar which deliver only empty calories), 30 percent or less fat, and 10 percent protein.

In selecting your recipes and planning your menus, keep these health findings in mind, too:

▼ Limit the amount of salt in your diet. The daily sodium requirement is about 1/10 teaspoon, but the average consumption is 1 to 4 teaspoons! Herbs, spices, garlic, and lemon juice can take the place of sodium to perk up flavor.

▼ Fiber has been cited as playing an important role in the prevention of heart disease and cancer. Eating a high-fiber diet also helps to keep you satisfied on a low-fat diet. Experts recommend that we consume 25 to 30 grams daily. Fruits, vegetables, whole wheat products, and brown rice are excellent sources of fiber.

▼ Sugar contains none of the 44 nutrients needed to sustain human life, yet the average American consumes 120 pounds per year—that's 1 pound every 3 days! Sugar often is a hidden ingredient in many of the same processed foods which are high in fat and low in nutrition. It does fulfill a useful role as a sweetener in certain recipes—but use sugar in moderation! What about artificial sweeteners? Personally, I choose to consume sugar in moderation because it is a natural product rather than resort to an artificial and chemical-laden substitute.

▼ Water is the element your body needs most; drink 6 to 8 glasses of water daily, more if you exercise. Ideally it should be pure; this may mean buying bottled water or installing a water purification system.

As I developed these recipes, I implemented a computer diet analysis program (Nutritionist III) to check each for nutrients and dietary composition. My goal was for each recipe to achieve the 60-30-10 guidelines. This meant using minimal fat per serving and the use of low-fat ingredients. (If you wish to reduce the fat even further, in many recipes, a light spraying of oil can substitute for the liquid oil.)

The results of my analyses are included with each recipe. Nearly all derive 30 percent or fewer of their calories from fat. Some, however, do not fall so neatly within the guidelines. For example, dressings and sauces, when analyzed on their own, contain a high percentage of fat even if the number of grams is low. But remember: these recipes are never served alone; the proportion of fat will be reduced when the base for the dressing or sauce is added. (Greens, of course, contain virtually no calories, so even ½ teaspoon of fat in the dressing elevates the fat percentage of a simple green salad to well over 30 percent.) Recipes including salmon do not fall within the guidelines either. I have included some salmon recipes since it contains the "right" kind of fat, plus omega-3 fatty acids; however, its percent of fat is higher than 50 percent. I have also included a couple of personal favorites which are over 30 percent fat.

What really counts is the recommended daily balance of nutrients, from three meals and a snack. In a given day, this means that occasionally I may eat some foods which are over 50 percent in fat, while others may be nearly fat free. My goal is that the average overall composition of my diet adheres to a maximum of 30 percent fat.

Of course, good flavor is always very important to me. Fortunately, with the right choice of ingredients and methods, my goals for healthful food and good flavor can go hand in hand.

RECIPE ANALYSES

Calories and a nutrient breakdown per serving accompany each recipe:

▼ The primary nutrients analyzed are protein, carbohydrates, and fat; cholesterol, sodium, and calcium are also included. All categories are included with each recipe even if the value is "0."
▼ Calories per serving and percent fat are included to help you calculate your daily dietary balance.
▼ Food exchanges are provided to show how the recipe fits into the Food Guide Pyramid and for other dietary purposes. If a category is omitted, this means the value is "0."
▼ When a range is given for an ingredient (for example, 4 to 5 ounces), the lesser amount is calculated.
▼ When a marinade is called for, only the amount absorbed by the food (not discarded) is calculated.

- ▼ Recipes including sauces and dressings have been analyzed in total. The nutrients for the sauces and dressings are also listed separately in the quantity in which they are used as variations in other recipes. (Most are used in the total quantity; others are used by tablespoon.) In all recipes, the amount of salad dressings and sauces is controlled.
- ▼ Regarding sodium, the products used for analysis include low-sodium soy sauce, unsalted vegetable stock powder, and unsalted (and defatted) chicken stock. All canned or frozen products, such as peas, corn, beans, tomatoes, and tomato paste were analyzed using the regular varieties which do contain salt. (If you prefer to reduce sodium further, rinse these products before adding them to your recipes, or purchase products marked "low sodium" or "no sodium.") I do not use added salt as an ingredient in my recipes.
- ▼ Garnishes, variations, and other optional ingredients are not calculated.

PASTA

Long before "pasta" was added to the American vocabulary, we had been consuming mushy "spaghetti with meatballs" and processed-cheese "macaroni and cheese." But thanks to a proliferation of trendy restaurants and the highly acclaimed importance of complex carbohydrates in our diets, pasta has risen to a new level. Though once considered strictly Italian, pasta is now recognized as being multi-ethnic, too.

Pasta is the mainstay of my dinners at least twice a week, all year long. The topping is prepared as the pasta cooks, and my protein, vegetables, and complex carbohydrates are all in one dish. Recipes for pasta dishes always allow for flexibility, so by combining pasta with many foods already in my pantry or refrigerator, I can create a tasty and nutritious meal that is ready in minutes, and cleanup is simple. When time is at an absolute minimum, I don't use a recipe at all; I simply prepare a quick-cooking pasta like capellini. While it is cooking, I chop odds and ends of vegetables which I microwave or lightly sauté. When the pasta is cooked and drained, I toss it with extra-virgin olive oil, fresh or dried basil, pepper, freshly grated Parmesan cheese, and the cooked vegetables. Presto! A great entrée in about 5 minutes!

Weight-watchers once considered pasta an enemy, but we now know it was the rich, heavy toppings loaded with butter, oil, cream, and cheese that turned pasta into high-calorie—as well as high-sodium and high-fat—dishes. A satisfying 2-ounce serving of pasta provides only 200 calories. Pasta is high in fiber, a good source of B vitamins, and low in sodium, cholesterol, and fat (just 4 percent). The toppings in this chapter are low in fat, too, using just the minimum of olive oil to keep the dishes moist. These are some of my most frequently used and enjoyed recipes.

Basic pastas are inexpensive staples found in every supermarket. They're made from a dough of semolina flour and water, kneaded, and then formed into one of more than 600 shapes. Eggs are sometimes added to produce a delicate richness. Vegetable purées of spinach, tomatoes, carrots, and beets can be included to add color, eye appeal, and a hint of flavor. Pastas are also made from whole wheat flour, buckwheat flour, lupini beans, corn, and a variety of other ingredients. For each recipe, I have suggested the shape I most often use with each sauce, but you may use others that you have on hand. There are no strict rules.

Commercially dried pastas will keep almost indefinitely when stored in a cool, dry place. Once a package has been opened, transfer what remains to an airtight container. Many markets also sell fresh pasta, but it must be used quickly because it keeps for only 2 or 3 days in the refrigerator. Both contain the same high-energy nutrition.

For most recipes, I allow 2 to 3 ounces dry pasta (or 3 to 4 ounces fresh pasta) per serving. To determine this amount, you can use a kitchen scale. For long strands like spaghetti, you can use a pasta sizer, a kitchen gadget with a series of graduated openings used to measure pasta bundles; 2 ounces is a ½- to ¾-inch bundle. When applicable, I have given cup measurements. Or simply guess! Exact measurements are rarely necessary when it comes to pasta.

Begin the preparation of your pasta dinners by bringing a pot of water to a full boil over high heat. The pot should be deeper than it is wide. For small quantities, a saucepan will do. For larger quantities, I usually use a pasta pot with a built-in colander, a stockpot, or a Dutch oven. It is not necessary to add salt or oil to the cooking water. Simply add the pasta to plenty of boiling water, enough to allow the pasta to move freely as it cooks to prevent sticking. Do not allow the water to stop boiling when you add the pasta. If the pasta is too long to fit into the pot, do not break it; stand it upright until the submerged ends soften enough to bend. Stir the pasta just once and begin timing. Keeping the pan uncovered, reduce the heat to medium-high, being certain to keep the water at a rapid boil throughout the cooking period.

TIP

▼ To reheat plain cooked pasta, immerse it briefly in a pot of boiling water; then drain in a colander.

Cooking time depends on the shape and thickness of the pasta. Because it contains more water, fresh pasta can be ready in as little as 5 to 10 seconds or up to 2 or 3 minutes. Watch closely so it doesn't become mushy. Dried packaged pasta cooks in 5 to 12 minutes, depending on thickness. Use the package directions and my suggested timing as a guideline; rely on your own testing to tell when the pasta is done. Begin checking for doneness after the minimum cooking time. If you pinch a strand and see a white dot in the center, it is not cooked. Taste the pasta. Perfectly cooked pasta should be *al dente*, firm but not hard, and evenly cooked, so it offers some resistance to the teeth, yet is cooked through. Drain the pasta in a colander the moment it is just tender. There is no need to rinse the pasta unless you need to chill it quickly for use in a cold pasta salad. Ideally, have the sauce ready so you can serve the pasta at once. If the pasta is done before your sauce, don't let it stand in the colander, but return it to the hot cooking pan, cover, and set on a cool burner.

All of the pasta toppings in this chapter can be made in 15 minutes or less, while the pasta is cooking. Advance preparations are given for some of the sauces. Some of the recipes can be made entirely in advance, refrigerated, and reheated for serving. But most often the pasta (except for pasta salads) should be cooked just before you are ready to sit down to eat.

I usually serve these generous portions of pasta in a shallow bowl with crusty bread and a green salad followed by a fruit dessert. In addition, I enjoy many of the dishes, particularly Parmesan Pasta with Herbs and Plum Tomatoes (pages 22–23), in a smaller portion as an accompaniment to broiled fish or chicken.

PARMESAN PASTA WITH HERBS AND PLUM TOMATOES

▼ ▼ ▼

This pasta entrée, which is pictured on the jacket of the book, is the simplest of all.

▼ ▼ ▼

ADVANCE PREPARATION
Toss the warm pasta with the toppings; refrigerate and serve later the same day chilled or at room temperature.

▼ ▼ ▼

TIPS
▼ Always buy freshly grated Parmesan cheese (or grate your own from a block of Parmesan, using a hand grater or your food processor). Kept in a tightly closed container, freshly grated Parmesan will keep in the refrigerator for about a week; it may be frozen although the flavor and texture do deteriorate somewhat.
▼ Pine nuts (also called pignoli nuts or piñons) are the seeds

1½ cups penne (4½ ounces)
1 teaspoon olive oil
2 tablespoons freshly grated Parmesan cheese
2 tablespoons minced fresh basil or ¾ teaspoon dried
1 tablespoon minced fresh parsley
⅛ teaspoon freshly ground black pepper, or to taste
1 plum tomato, at room temperature, cut into ½-inch cubes (½ cup)

GARNISH: *freshly ground black pepper, freshly grated Parmesan cheese, toasted pine nuts (page 36), sprig fresh basil or parsley*

Bring a medium-size saucepan of water to a boil over high heat. Reduce the heat to medium-high; add the penne, and cook until *al dente*, 10 to 12 minutes. When the pasta is done, drain well.

Return the noodles to the saucepan; toss with the olive oil. Add Parmesan, basil, parsley, and pepper; toss. Add the plum tomato; toss again. Taste; adjust seasonings. Transfer to a serving plate and garnish.

Calories 593 (16% from fat)/Protein 22.8g/Carb 101.5g/Fat 10.6g/Chol 10mg/Sodium 439mg/Calcium 233mg/Food Exchanges: Veg 1.0/Bread 6.3/Meat 0.7/Fat 1.1

VARIATIONS
▼ along with the Parmesan cheese, toss in 1 or 2 tablespoons toasted wheat germ

obtained from the cone of certain pine trees. Their natural oil turns rancid very quickly, so they should be refrigerated for no more than 1 month or frozen for 2 to 3 months. Like other nuts, they are high in fat—use them in moderation.

▼ ▼ ▼

▼ for the basil, substitute other herbs such as marjoram, oregano, or tarragon
▼ add sautéed mushroom slices or your choice of steamed vegetables
▼ for *Tomato Pistou*, in a food processor, puree the olive oil, Parmesan, basil, parsley, pepper, and plum tomato; also add 1 tablespoon chopped marinated sun-dried tomatoes and ½ teaspoon minced garlic. Toss with the cooked penne.

RAINBOW ROTINI WITH PARSLEY-WALNUT PESTO

▼ ▼ ▼

1 cup rainbow (multicolor) rotini (2 ounces)

FOR THE PARSLEY-WALNUT PESTO
1 tablespoon walnut pieces
1 teaspoon olive oil
¼ teaspoon minced garlic
½ cup tightly packed fresh parsley sprigs
1 tablespoon freshly grated Parmesan cheese
2 teaspoons minced fresh basil or ½ teaspoon dried
⅛ teaspoon freshly ground black pepper

GARNISH: *freshly ground black pepper, freshly grated Parmesan cheese, plum tomato wedges, chopped walnuts*

Over high heat, bring water to a boil in a medium-size saucepan. Reduce the heat to medium-high, add the rotini, and cook until *al dente*, 8 to 10 minutes.

To make the pesto, while the pasta is cooking, in a blender or food processor whirl together the pesto ingredients to form a chunky purée; use a rubber scraper to push down the sides occasionally.

When the pasta is done, drain well; return to the cooking pan. Toss in the pesto. Spoon onto a serving plate and garnish.

Calories 332 (32% from fat)/Protein 12g/Carb 44.5g/Fat 11.7g/Chol 5mg/Sodium 123mg/Calcium 110mg/Food Exchanges: Veg 0.1/Bread 2.8/Meat 0.3/Fat 1.9

VARIATIONS

- ▼ for part of the parsley sprigs, substitute fresh basil leaves
- ▼ toast the walnuts for the pesto (and garnish): place the nuts on a baking sheet in a preheated 375°F. oven for 8 to 10 minutes; remove from the sheet immediately so they do not continue to brown
- ▼ for the walnuts, substitute pine nuts
- ▼ for the parsley, substitute fresh spinach leaves
- ▼ choose any or all of these tasty additions: ½ cup cubed poached or sautéed chicken, ½ cup steamed cut asparagus, 1 tablespoon coarsely chopped marinated sun-dried tomatoes, sautéed strips of sweet red pepper

PENNE WITH BASIL PESTO

▼ ▼ ▼

1 cup penne (3 ounces)
¼ cup Basil Pesto (recipe follows)
1 plum tomato, at room temperature, halved lengthwise and
   cut into ¼-inch slices (½ cup)

GARNISH: *freshly ground black pepper and freshly grated*
   Parmesan cheese

Bring a medium-size saucepan of water to a boil over high heat. Reduce the heat to medium-high, add the penne, and cook until *al dente*, 10 to 12 minutes.

- ▼ Air and moisture are the biggest enemies of fresh cheese. Wrapped tightly in plastic wrap, a block of Parmesan cheese will keep 2 to 4 weeks in the refrigerator.
- ▼ In most recipes, Romano cheese may be substituted for Parmesan; it has a drier, sharper flavor.

▼ ▼ ▼

ADVANCE PREPARATION
Toss the Basil Pesto with freshly cooked hot penne; refrigerate for several hours and serve later chilled or at room temperature.

▼ ▼ ▼

- ▼ When used in cold pasta salads and other chilled dishes, the pesto should always be tossed with hot pasta or other ingredients and then chilled.
- ▼ Fresh herbs will stay fresh longer if you do not wash them before storage. Refrigerate them in a covered jar with their stems sitting in 1 inch of water. Every few days trim ½ inch from the stems. Or, wrap the stems with a moist paper towel and refrigerate in a sealed plastic bag. For the best flavor, try to use the fresh herb within a few days; but they will be usable for about a week.

You will find plenty of reasons, in addition to this pasta recipe, to keep Basil Pesto on hand in your freezer. For variety, it can be tossed with cooked rice, used as a spread on crusty bread, added to sandwiches and pizzas, stuffed into cherry tomatoes as an appetizer, and used as a flavoring for soups.

Prepare the pesto. When the pasta is done, drain well and return to the saucepan; toss with the pesto. Add the tomato slices; toss again. Transfer to a serving plate and garnish.

Calories 535 (30% from fat)/Protein 17.4g/Carb 76.2g/Fat 17.7g/Chol 0/Sodium 227mg/Calcium 146mg/Food Exchanges: Veg 1.2/Bread 4.2/Fat 3.1

VARIATIONS

- ▼ add or substitute other vegetables such as steamed cut asparagus or coarsely chopped marinated sun-dried tomatoes
- ▼ add ½ cup cubed cooked chicken breast
- ▼ refrigerate the pasta after it has been tossed with the pesto; serve as a pasta salad

BASIL PESTO
▼ ▼ ▼

MAKES ½ CUP
2 cups loosely packed fresh basil leaves (fresh is essential!)
¼ cup pine nuts
1 teaspoon minced garlic
1 tablespoon extra-virgin olive oil
¼ teaspoon freshly ground black pepper

Place the pesto ingredients in a bowl of a food processor or blender. Process until the mixture is a coarse puree, using a rubber scraper to push down the sides occasionally.

Pesto (1 tbsp): Calories 49 (74% from fat)/Protein 1.4g/Carb 1.9g/Fat 4g/Chol 0/Sodium 6mg/Calcium 25mg/Food Exchanges: Fat 0.7

ADVANCE PREPARATION

May be made in advance.
Spoon it into a jar and pour a
thin film of oil on top to prevent discoloration. Cover; refrigerate for up to 1 week.
Bring to room temperature before tossing with pasta. To
freeze, in ¼ cup quantities,
spoon the mixture into foil-
lined custard cups or muffin
tins. Cover tightly with foil and
freeze. Once frozen, remove the
foil-wrapped packets and
place in a freezer bag for up to
2 months. To use, allow to
thaw in the refrigerator
overnight or thaw quickly in
the microwave.

▼ ▼ ▼

VARIATIONS

- ▼ for *Spinach-Parsley Pesto,* substitute ½ cup chopped fresh spinach and ½ cup chopped fresh parsley for 1 cup of the basil
- ▼ for *Broccoli Pesto,* substitute 2 cups steamed broccoli florets and ¼ cup fresh basil leaves for the basil
- ▼ for the pine nuts, substitute walnuts, hazelnuts, or toasted pecans
- ▼ add ¼ cup freshly grated Parmesan cheese
- ▼ add 1 tablespoon fresh lime juice
- ▼ to make *Pesto-Chevre Sauce:* in a small saucepan, stir together 2 tablespoons chevre, 2 tablespoons skim milk, 2 teaspoons Basil Pesto, and a dash of freshly ground black pepper. Heat over low heat, stirring to melt the chevre. Toss with pasta and vegetables or serve over sautéed or steamed vegetables, cooked fish, or cooked chicken.
- ▼ to make *Creamy Pesto Dressing:* stir together 1 tablespoon Basil Pesto, 1 tablespoon low-fat plain yogurt, 1 tablespoon white rice vinegar, and ⅛ teaspoon freshly ground black pepper, or to taste. Toss with steamed cubed new potatoes, other vegetables such as steamed green beans, or toss with cooked cubes of chicken and chill.

FETTUCINE ALMOST ALFREDO

▼ ▼ ▼

3 ounces fettucine
1 cup cut asparagus (1-inch pieces)

FOR THE ALMOST ALFREDO SAUCE
¼ cup lite ricotta cheese
¼ cup skim milk
2 tablespoons freshly grated Parmesan cheese

1 teaspoon minced fresh parsley
1 teaspoon minced fresh basil or ¼ teaspoon dried
¼ teaspoon minced garlic
Dash of freshly ground black pepper, or to taste

GARNISH: *freshly ground black pepper, freshly grated Parmesan cheese, sliced almonds, halved cherry tomatoes, minced fresh parsley, sprig fresh basil*

Over high heat, bring water to a boil in a medium-size saucepan. Reduce the heat to medium-high, add the fettucine, and cook until *al dente*, 10 to 12 minutes.

While the pasta is cooking, place the asparagus in a 1-quart microwave-proof dish, add about 2 tablespoons water, cover, and cook on high until crisp-tender, about 4 minutes, or steam on the stove in a vegetable steamer.

Meanwhile, in a small saucepan, stir together the sauce ingredients. Place over medium heat, stirring gently, to warm the sauce. Do not allow the mixture to come to a boil.

When the pasta is done, drain well. Return to the saucepan; add the sauce and toss. Add the asparagus and toss again. Taste; adjust the seasonings. Spoon onto a serving plate, garnish, and serve immediately.

Calories 531 (18% from fat)/Protein 30g/Carb 78.7g/Fat 11g/Chol 30mg/Sodium 355mg/Calcium 478mg/Food Exchanges: Milk 0.2/Veg 1.9/Bread 4.2/Meat 1.7/Fat 0.6

VARIATIONS

▼ for asparagus, substitute other steamed vegetables such as peas, broccoli florets, or cut green beans; add sautéed strips of sweet red pepper
▼ when tossing the pasta, add a squeeze of lemon juice and a pinch of grated lemon rind or lemon zest
▼ add sautéed sliced mushrooms and/or a cubed plum tomato
▼ add about ½ cup lightly sautéed cubed chicken breast

▼ ▼ ▼

ADVANCE PREPARATION

The sauce can be made in advance and refrigerated. Bring to room temperature before tossing with hot pasta.

▼ ▼ ▼

TIPS

▼ Ricotta cheese is made from the whey that remains after the production of such cheeses as provolone and mozzarella. The whey is blended with whole or skim milk; ricotta, therefore, is not a true cheese because it is not made from curd.
▼ Regular whole milk ricotta cheese has 60 calories per ounce; part-skim has 35 to 40 calories; "lite" ricotta has 25 calories; and nonfat ricotta has 20 calories per ounce.

PENNE WITH TRIPLE TOMATO PESTO

▼ ▼ ▼

ADVANCE PREPARATION
The pesto will keep for 2 days
in the refrigerator; heat before
tossing with freshly cooked
pasta.

▼ ▼ ▼

FOR THE TRIPLE TOMATO PESTO
½ teaspoon olive oil
1 tablespoon minced onion
¼ teaspoon minced garlic
One 8-ounce can tomatoes with juice
1 plum tomato, cut into ½-inch cubes (½ cup)
1 tablespoon coarsely chopped marinated sun-dried toma-
toes
⅛ teaspoon freshly ground black pepper, or to taste
⅛ teaspoon sugar
1 tablespoon minced fresh parsley
2 teaspoons minced fresh basil or ½ teaspoon dried

TO COMPLETE THE DISH
1 cup penne (3 ounces)

GARNISH: *freshly ground black pepper, freshly grated*
Parmesan cheese, Chevre Cream (page 159), snipped fresh
chives, or sprig fresh basil

Bring a medium-size saucepan of water to boil over high heat.
To make the pesto, heat the olive oil in a medium-size skillet over medium heat. Add the onion; cook, stirring, for 1 minute. Add the garlic; cook 30 seconds longer, stirring to prevent browning. Stir in the canned tomatoes with juice; quarter the tomatoes. Stir in the plum tomato, sun-dried tomatoes, dried basil (if you're using it), pepper, and sugar. Cook over medium-low heat, uncovered, for about 10 minutes, stirring occasionally. Add the parsley (and fresh basil, if using it) during the last minute or two of cooking. Taste; adjust seasonings.
While the sauce is simmering, add the pasta to the saucepan

- ▼ Chives are a delicately flavored member of the onion family. Given a choice, buy potted chives. They are fresher than cut. Use scissors to snip off what you need, cutting off whole blades rather than chopping the tops off all the blades. If you do buy cut chives, wrap in damp paper towels and seal in a plastic bag; refrigerate. Avoid dried chopped chives which have lost the characteristic flavor and aroma of fresh.
- ▼ Pepper is available either as whole berries or ground to varying degrees of fineness. Freshly ground pepper is more flavorful than preground and is worth the investment in a good pepper grinder which has settings for coarse and fine grind.
- ▼ Grind spices, like pepper and nutmeg, onto a small sheet of waxed paper to measure the quantity.

of boiling water. Reduce the heat to medium-high and cook until *al dente*, 10 to 12 minutes.

When the pasta is done, drain well. Pour it into the skillet and toss with the pesto. Taste; adjust seasonings. Spoon into a low-sided bowl; garnish.

Calories 467 (9% from fat)/Protein 16.1g/Carb 90.3g/Fat 4.5g/Chol 0mg/Sodium 590mg/Calcium 138mg/Food Exchanges: Veg 3.1/Bread 4.2/Fat 0.4

Triple Tomato Pesto (entire recipe): Calories 136 (19% from fat/Protein 5.2g/Carb 26.4g/Fat 3.2g/Chol 0/Sodium 584mg/Calcium 123mg/Food Exchanges: Veg 3.0/Fat 0.4

VARIATIONS

- ▼ in the Triple Tomato Pesto, sauté 2 tablespoons minced red bell pepper with the onion and garlic
- ▼ for the basil, substitute ½ teaspoon dried oregano or thyme, or a dash of nutmeg
- ▼ toss in about ½ cup cubed, sautéed chicken breast

PASTA PRIMAVERA WITH SESAME-PEPPER DRESSING

▼ ▼ ▼

2 ounces spaghetti

FOR THE SESAME-PEPPER DRESSING
1 teaspoon dark sesame oil
1 teaspoon low-sodium soy sauce
1 teaspoon white rice vinegar
Pinch of crushed red pepper, or to taste
Dash of freshly ground black pepper, or to taste

TO COMPLETE THE DISH
1 teaspoon safflower oil
½ medium-size carrot, thinly sliced (¼ cup)
4 asparagus spears, cut into 2-inch lengths
¼ medium-size red bell pepper, seeded and cut into 2 by ¼-inch strips
½ small zucchini, cut into 2 by ¼-inch strips
3 medium-size mushrooms, sliced
½ teaspoon minced garlic
¼ cup frozen peas, thawed
1 plum tomato, at room temperature, cut into ½-inch cubes (½ cup)

GARNISH: *toasted sesame seeds (see Tips, left) or chopped unsalted dry-roasted peanuts*

Bring a medium-size saucepan of water to a boil over high heat. Reduce the heat to medium-high; add the spaghetti and cook until *al dente*, 8 to 10 minutes.

Stir together all the dressing ingredients in a measuring cup. Set aside.

While the pasta is cooking, heat the safflower oil in a medium-size skillet over medium-high heat. Add the carrot, as-

▼ ▼ ▼

ADVANCE PREPARATION
May be made in advance, refrigerated, and served later the same or next day chilled or at room temperature.

▼ ▼ ▼

TIPS
▼ Sesame seeds are sold with or without their brownish gray hulls; they are more nutritious if unhulled (these are tan in color). Because they contain oil, they become rancid quickly at room temperature and should be stored in the refrigerator in an airtight container.
▼ *Toasted sesame seeds:* The simplest method is to toast them in a dry nonstick skillet over medium to medium-high heat on the stove for 3 to 5 minutes. Toss constantly and watch closely, removing them from the pan when they are lightly browned. They can also be spread on an ungreased baking

baking sheet and baked in a 350° F. oven. Shake the pan or stir occasionally until lightly browned, about 10 minutes. Either method will give the seeds a nutty flavor. It takes the same amount of time to toast 1 tablespoon or ½ cup, so toast extra seeds, store them in an airtight container, and refrigerate.

▼ Bell peppers are sold in the mature green stage, fully developed but not ripe. As they ripen on the vine, many turn red and become sweeter. Bell peppers are also available in gold, orange, and purple, all mildly flavored.

▼ When buying bell peppers, look for plump, firm, crisp vegetables with no wrinkling or soft spots. Store them in plastic bags in the refrigertor.

▼ Extra bell peppers can be frozen without blanching—simply chop them and freeze in small containers or zip-top bags. The thawed peppers will be limp but can be used in cooked dishes.

paragus, and red bell pepper; stir-fry for 3 minutes. Add the zucchini and mushrooms; stir-fry until the vegetables are crisp-tender, about 2 more minutes. Stir in the garlic; cook for about 30 seconds. Add the peas and tomato; heat for 1 minute, stirring gently. Remove from the heat, cover, and set aside.

When the pasta is done, drain well. Return the pasta to the saucepan. Toss in the sautéed vegetables. Add the dressing; toss again. Taste; adjust seasonings. Spoon onto a serving plate or pasta bowl and garnish.

Calories 476 (22% from fat)/Protein 19.5g/Carb 73.6g/Fat 11.5g/Chol 0/Sodium 458mg/Calcium 144mg/Food Exchanges: Veg 5.1/Bread 3.1/Fat 1.7

Sesame-Pepper Dressing (entire recipe): Calories 45 (91% from fat)/Protein 0.3g/Carb 0.8g/Fat 4.5g/Chol 0/Sodium 200mg/Calcium 1mg/Food Exchanges: Fat 0.8

VARIATIONS

▼ add 1 cup shredded spinach and stir-fry with the zucchini and mushrooms.

▼ in the dressing, substitute 1 teaspoon walnut oil for the sesame oil; add 1 tablespoon chopped walnuts

▼ for the Sesame-Pepper Dressing, substitute 1 tablespoon Sesame-Ginger Dressing (page 186)

▼ substitute or add other vegetables such as steamed broccoli florets, blanched snow peas, or steamed snap peas

▼ add cooked shrimp or strips of cooked chicken

ADVANCE PREPARATION

May be prepared in advance, refrigerated, and served later the same or next day chilled or at room temperature.

▼ ▼ ▼

TIPS

▼ Capers are the unopened pickled buds of a shrub native to the Mediterranean. They are always cured in vinegar and salt, giving them a peppery, briny, piquant taste. Size varies—the largest have the strongest flavor; the smallest, "nonpareil," the more subtle, the more tender, and the most expensive. Buy capers in small jars and refrigerate once opened; beyond 2 to 3 months, they may become mushy and acquire a brownish tint.

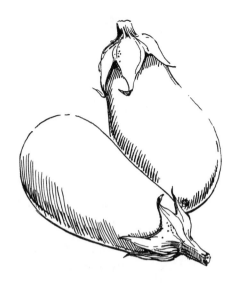

MEDITERRANEAN MOSTACCIOLI

▼ ▼ ▼

1 cup mostaccioli (3 ounces)
2 teaspoons olive oil
1 cup peeled and cubed eggplant (½-inch cubes)
½ cup sliced mushrooms
½ small zucchini, halved lengthwise and cut into ¼-inch slices
  (½ cup)
1 tablespoon minced shallot
1 plum tomato, cut into ½-inch cubes (½ cup)
2 teaspoons capers, drained and rinsed
1½ teaspoons fresh thyme leaves or ½ teaspoon dried
⅛ teaspoon freshly ground black pepper, or to taste
1 tablespoon red wine vinegar
2 tablespoons crumbled mild feta cheese

GARNISH: *freshly ground black pepper, sprig fresh thyme, or chopped fresh Italian flat-leaf parsley*

- Feta cheese is a white Greek cheese made with goat's or sheep's milk, or a combination. Fresh feta is crumbly with whey; when mature it becomes drier and saltier.
- Choose eggplant that is firm, heavy, and not too large. The skin should be smooth and tight, but the flesh should yield slightly to pressure. If it is hard, it's underripe and will not be as flavorful. Store eggplant in a plastic bag in the refrigerator for up to 2 weeks; beyond that it will begin to lose its flavor.
- It is an old wives' tale that eggplant needs to be peeled, sliced, salted, and weighted for a couple of hours to squeeze out the juice. The peel is edible, so it is not even necessary to peel it, unless it is quite tough or you choose to remove it for the sake of appearance.

Bring a medium-size saucepan of water to a boil over high heat. Reduce the heat to medium-high, add the mostaccioli, and cook until *al dente*, 12 to 14 minutes.

While the pasta is cooking heat 1 teaspoon of the olive oil over medium heat in a medium-size skillet. Add the eggplant, mushrooms, and zucchini. Increase the heat to medium-high and cook, stirring, until the eggplant is tender and lightly browned, about 5 minutes. Add the shallot; cook 30 seconds longer. Stir in the tomato; continue to cook, stirring occasionally, until the tomato is softened, 2 more minutes. Stir in the capers, thyme, and pepper. Taste; adjust seasonings. Remove from the heat, cover, and set aside.

When the pasta is done, drain well. Return the pasta to the cooking pan. Add the remaining olive oil and the vinegar; toss. Add the eggplant-tomato mixture; toss. Add the feta cheese; toss again. Spoon onto a serving plate; garnish.

Calories 523 (25% from fat)/Protein 16.8g/Carb 80.8g/Fat 14.7g/Chol 15mg/Sodium 398 mg/Calcium 153mg/Food Exchanges: Veg 2.7/Bread 4.2/Meat 0.3/Fat 2.3

VARIATIONS

- instead of tossing olive oil and red wine vinegar with the cooked pasta, substitute Balsamic Vinaigrette (page 184)
- serve the eggplant mixture with remaining oil, vinegar, and feta tossed in (warm, chilled, or at room temperature) as a side dish—delicious with broiled chicken or fish
- add other vegetables such as steamed cut green beans, sautéed red bell pepper strips, chopped artichoke hearts, or chopped marinated sun-dried tomatoes
- add cooked shrimp

CHILLED PASTAS

Pasta salads can be made in advance; however, because the dressing would soak in as the dishes set, it is usually best to keep the salad and dressing separate, combining them just before serving. Also, if time permits, allow pasta salads to stand at room temperature for at least 15 minutes before serving; the flavors will not be at their best when icy cold.

In addition to the pastas in this section, several of the recipes included in Warm Pastas can be served chilled, too: Parmesan Pasta with Herbs and Plum Tomatoes (page 22), Rainbow Rotini with Parsley-Walnut Pesto (page 23), Penne with Basil Pesto (page 24), Pasta Primavera with Sesame-Pepper Dressing (page 30), Mediterranean Mostaccioli (page 32).

PASTA SALAD PRIMAVERA WITH HERBED TOMATO SAUCE

▼ ▼ ▼

This recipe is a variation of a favorite from one of my previous books, *The 15-Minute Vegetarian Gourmet*. I have often multiplied it for do-ahead entertaining, and since it keeps well and lends itself to improvisation, this recipe can also become your framework for pasta salad for one. The recipe makes 2 servings—one for right away, the other one for the next day—perhaps with a different dressing for variety.

MAKES 2 SERVINGS
1 cup rotini (2 ounces)
1 cup broccoli florets
½ small zucchini, cut into ½-inch cubes (½ cup)

FOR THE HERBED TOMATO SAUCE
⅓ cup water
2 tablespoons tomato paste
1 teaspoon extra-virgin olive oil
1 teaspoon red wine vinegar
½ teaspoon dried basil or 2 teaspoons minced fresh
½ teaspoon dried oregano or 2 teaspoons minced fresh
¼ teaspoon freshly ground black pepper, or to taste
¼ teaspoon minced garlic

Will keep for 2 days in the refrigerator. Because the sauce
tends to be absorbed in the
pasta, refrigerate the sauce
separately; add just before
serving.

▼ ▼ ▼

TIPS

▼ The ridges of rotini and rotelle
help dressings to adhere to the
noodles. Rotini is a small
corkscrew-shaped pasta; rotelle
is a similar shape, only larger.

▼ When doubling recipes, increase the herbs 1½ times; taste
and adjust the seasonings.

▼ Though fresh herbs are nearly
always preferable, some herbs
dry better than others. Sage,
rosemary, thyme, basil, and
oregano are quite effective in
their dried state. Avoid dried
parsley, dried chives, dried
cilantro (coriander), and mixed
"Italian seasonings."

▼ If dried herbs and spices are
stored in a dry and dark area
and in a tightly closed jar
rather than a box, they will remain flavorful for about a year.
Do not store them above your

TO COMPLETE THE DISH
½ cup frozen peas, thawed
1 plum tomato, cut into ½-inch cubes (½ cup)
1 scallion (green parts), chopped
1 tablespoon seeded and chopped red bell pepper

GARNISH: *freshly ground black pepper, freshly grated*
Parmesan cheese, toasted pine nuts, sprig fresh basil

Over high heat, bring water to a boil in a medium-size
saucepan. Reduce the heat to medium-high, add the rotini, and
cook until *al dente*, 10 to 12 minutes

While the pasta is cooking, place the broccoli and zucchini in
a 1-quart microwave-proof dish. Add a small amount of water,
cover, and cook on high until crisp-tender, about 3 minutes, or
steam on the stove in a vegetable steamer.

To make the sauce, stir together the sauce ingredients in a
small bowl. Taste; adjust seasonings.

When the pasta is done, drain, rinse under cold water, then
drain again. In a medium-size bowl toss together the pasta,
broccoli, zucchini, peas, tomato, scallion, and red bell pepper.
Place half of the pasta salad mixture and half of the dressing in
separate refrigerator containers; refrigerate to serve later. Toss
together the remaining pasta salad and dressing. Spoon onto a
serving plate or shallow bowl and garnish.

1 serving: Calories 211 (14% from fat)/Protein 8.7g/Carb 36.5g/Fat
3.3g/Chol 0/Sodium 158mg/Calcium 65mg/Food Exchanges: Veg 1.8/Bread
1.7/Fat 0.4

Herbed Tomato Sauce (1 serving): Calories 54 (43% from fat)/Protein
1.3g/Carb 6.4g/Fat 2.6g/Chol 0/Sodium 108mg/Calcium 24mg/Food Exchanges: Veg 1.1/Fat 0.4

VARIATIONS

▼ substitute or add other steamed vegetables such as chopped
carrots, cauliflower florets, or cut asparagus; or add sliced raw
mushrooms, chopped green bell pepper, or blanched pea pods

stove! When the bright green color of the herbs fades, they probably have lost their effectiveness.

▼ The sweet, mild flavor of pine nuts is enhanced by toasting. Place them in a small skillet over medium heat, stirring constantly and watching carefully; the nuts will brown in 4 to 5 minutes. Pine nuts can be toasted in the oven as well—spread in a single layer on an ungreased baking sheet; bake at 375°F. for 4 to 5 minutes, stirring frequently. Immediately remove the nuts from the pan as soon as they are browned. I usually toast 1 cup at a time, freezing the nuts until I need them.

▼ to add protein, add cubed mozzarella cheese, cubed firm tofu, beans such as chick peas, or strips of cooked chicken
▼ for the Herbed Tomato Sauce, substitute about ¼ cup Balsamic Vinaigrette (page 184) per serving
▼ for the Herbed Tomato Sauce, substitute *Pesto Vinaigrette:* In a measuring cup or small bowl, whisk together 3 tablespoons red wine vinegar, 1 tablespoon fresh lemon juice, 1 tablespoon Basil Pesto (page 25), and a dash of pepper.

Pesto Vinaigrette (1 serving): Calories 49 (54% from fat)/Protein 1.4g/ Carb 6.3g/Fat 4g/Chol 0/Sodium 7mg/Calcium 29mg/Food Exchanges: Fat 0.7

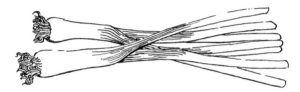

PASTA AND COUSCOUS SALAD WITH SESAME-PEANUT DRESSING

▼ ▼ ▼

1 cup spinach ribbon noodles (2 ounces)
2 tablespoons couscous
2 tablespoons hot water
Dash of vegetable stock powder (optional)
¼ medium-size red bell pepper, cut into 1½ by ¼-inch strips
½ scallion, thinly sliced (green parts)
1 tablespoon minced fresh parsley

After I wrote *The 15-Minute Vegetarian Gourmet*, this recipe became the favorite of several friends. It seemed only appropriate to include a single-serving version in this book!

▼ ▼ ▼

ADVANCE PREPARATION

Toss together the salad ingredients and prepare the dressing up to 1 day in advance; combine the two just before serving.

▼ ▼ ▼

TIPS

▼ Buy natural peanut butter with the oil on top; stir in the oil before using. Many of the processed peanut butters are hydrogenated to prevent separation and have sugar, salt, and stabilizers added.

▼ About half of the composition of peanuts is oil, most of which is unsaturated. Dry roasted, unsalted peanuts are preferable because oil roasted nuts contain even more fat and often salt, as well. As with all nuts, enjoy them in moderation.

FOR THE SESAME-PEANUT DRESSING
1 tablespoon white rice vinegar
1 tablespoon low-fat plain yogurt
1 tablespoon peanut butter
1 teaspoon water
¼ teaspoon dark sesame oil
¼ teaspoon low-sodium soy sauce
¼ teaspoon finely minced garlic
Pinch of crushed red pepper, or to taste

GARNISH: orange slices, mandarin orange segments, pineapple chunks, raisins, unsalted dry-roasted peanuts, sprig cilantro (fresh coriander)

Over high heat, bring water to a boil in a medium-size saucepan. Reduce the heat to medium-high, add the noodles, and cook until *al dente*, 8 to 10 minutes.

While the pasta is cooking, stir together the couscous, hot water, and vegetable stock powder in a small bowl. Let stand, covered, until the liquid is completely absorbed, about 5 minutes. Toss lightly with a fork.

Meanwhile, in a medium-size bowl, toss together the bell pepper, scallion, and parsley.

Whisk together the dressing ingredients in a measuring cup or small bowl. Set aside.

When the pasta is done, drain well and rinse under cold water. Drain well again. Add the pasta and couscous to the bowl of vegetables; toss. Add the dressing; toss again. Taste; adjust seasonings. Arrange the salad on serving plate; garnish.

Calories 355 (26% from fat)/Protein 12.9g/Carb 52.7g/Fat 10.2g/ Chol 1mg/Sodium 152mg/Calcium 80mg/Food Exchanges: Veg 0.3/ Bread 2.9/Meat 0.5/Fat 1.4

Sesame-Peanut Dressing (entire recipe): Calories 125 (67% from fat)/ Protein 4.8g/Carb 5.4g/Fat 9.4g/Chol 1 mg/Sodium 137mg/Calcium 33mg/Food Exchanges: Meat 0.5/Fat 1.4

VARIATIONS

▼ add other vegetables such as cucumber strips, peas, steamed carrot strips, steamed broccoli florets, or blanched snap peas
▼ add cooked garbanzo beans or cubes of tofu
▼ add strips of cooked chicken or fish
▼ for the dressing, substitute Sesame-Ginger Dressing (page 186)

ETHNIC AND VEGETARIAN ENTRÉES

▾ ▾ ▾

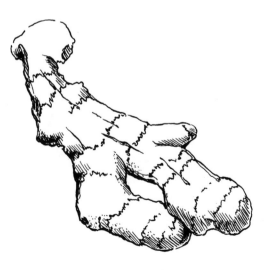

For fifteen years, I followed a lacto-ovo vegetarian diet. It really began as an experiment during a time when I was traveling frequently and studying ethnic cuisines. I learned that in many parts of the world, meat is used sparingly, if at all. These cuisines emphasized alternative protein sources and derived their flavors from interesting combinations of herbs and spices. It was these discoveries that actually led to my reliance on fresh, natural foods and to my passion for cooking. When my focus turned to low-fat cooking, I revised many of my favorite traditional ethnic recipes; to my delight, they were successful because the vibrant flavors predominated even when fat and salt were reduced to a minimum.

Most of the students in my vegetarian cooking classes do not lead a strict vegetarian lifestyle, but many of them are choosing to reduce their red meat intake and prefer not to eat fish and chicken daily. These recipes offer tasty alternatives for those "vegetarian days"; they provide an ethnic flair that will add variety and excitement to your weekly menus.

Some flavors may be new to you, like balsamic vinegar and curry powder, and even some of the ingredients—perhaps hoisin sauce, wasabi powder (Japanese horseradish), couscous, chevre, or tofu. But I have included detailed information on where to find these items and how to work with them. So, be adventuresome! I guarantee you'll be in for some pleasant surprises!

PIZZA

My gourmet pizzas are quite different from those which are commercially prepared, and since the crusts are made from pita bread and flour tortillas, these pizzas can be on the table even sooner than the fastest delivery service can have them at your door.

Typical pizzas derive more than half of their calories from fat, due to the thick layers of cheese. The fat is reduced here and replaced with tantalizing flavors, and there are unlimited possibilities for delicious variations.

Each of the three recipes in this section makes 1 small pizza. Double all ingredients to make 2 pizzas if you're in the mood for a real feast—or if you want to prepare a special treat to share with a friend.

GOAT CHEESE PIZZA WITH FRESH BASIL

▼ ▼ ▼

MAKES ONE 6-INCH PIZZA

Half of a 6-inch pita bread (whole wheat or white), sliced horizontally
½ teaspoon olive oil
2 tablespoons tomato paste
2 teaspoons coarsely chopped marinated sun-dried tomatoes
4 fresh basil leaves or ⅛ teaspoon dried
½ plum tomato, cut into 4 slices
Dash of freshly ground black pepper
2 teaspoons goat cheese (chevre)
2 teaspoons low-fat plain yogurt
¼ teaspoon balsamic vinegar
1 teaspoon freshly grated Parmesan cheese

Adjust the oven broiler rack 4 to 5 inches from the heating element. Preheat the broiler.

Place the pita half, rough side up, on a baking sheet. Lightly brush with the olive oil. Broil for 2 minutes to toast.

Spread the tomato paste on the pita half; sprinkle with the sun-dried tomatoes. Arrange the basil leaves over them (or sprinkle with dried basil), top with the plum tomato slices, and sprinkle lightly with pepper.

In a small bowl, combine the goat cheese, yogurt, and vinegar, stirring until smooth; spoon 3 dollops onto the pizza. Sprinkle with the Parmesan cheese. Place the pizza under the broiler until the Parmesan cheese is melted and the goat cheese is softened, 2 to 3 minutes. Watch closely! Serve immediately.

Calories 206 (26% from fat)/Protein 8.2g/Carb 30g/Fat 6g/Chol 9mg/Sodium 322mg/Calcium 111mg/Food Exchanges: Veg 1.7/Bread 0.7/Meat 0.1/Fat 0.5

TIPS

▼ Sun-dried tomatoes (or just plain dried tomatoes since most of the dried tomatoes today are processed in dehydrators) are an ideal way to add richness and flavor to low-fat soups and sauces. The less expensive dried form must be hydrated first. Pour boiling water over them and allow to set for 5 to 10 minutes; drain, then marinate them in olive oil. Because of their flavor and ease of use, I prefer to purchase the jars of sun-dried tomatoes already marinated in olive oil. The easiest way to chop dried tomatoes is with kitchen shears.

- Plum tomatoes are the same as Italian or Roma tomatoes. They are the ideal cooking tomato because they have thick, meaty walls, small seeds, little juice, and a rich, sweet flavor. Also, they are the perfect size for single-serving recipes.
- Goat cheese, a tangy, mild, and creamy cheese made from goat's milk, is packaged under the names "chevre" and "montrachet." Domestic goat cheese is a fine substitute for the more expensive imported brands. Once opened, wrap tightly in plastic wrap; store it in the refrigerator for 1 to 2 weeks. (Do not confuse chevre with caprini, Italian goat cheese, which is dried, less creamy, and more acidic.)

VARIATIONS

- for the pita bread, substitute a 6- or 7-inch flour tortilla (white or whole wheat); brush both sides of it with olive oil, and prick its surface in several places with a fork. Place the tortilla directly on the oven rack; broil for 1 to 2 minutes on each side to toast before adding toppings. Watch closely when you broil with the pizza toppings.
- for the pita bread, substitute a 6-inch foccacia bread; it is not necessary to add oil when heating it before adding the toppings
- for the basil, substitute other herbs such as oregano or thyme or 2 teaspoons Basil Pesto (page 25); stir the pesto into the tomato paste before it is spread on the crust
- add small pieces of cooked chicken or cooked small shrimp
- add sautéed vegetables such as slivers of onion, minced garlic, shredded carrots, chopped celery, diced red or green bell pepper, sliced zucchini, sliced mushrooms, or shredded spinach
- for the chevre mixture, mix together just the chevre and yogurt, omitting the vinegar
- for the Parmesan and goat cheese, substitute shredded low-fat Cheddar or mozzarella
- top the pizza with a sprinkling of pine nuts

MEXICAN TORTILLA PIZZA

▼ ▼ ▼

Mexicans probably haven't combined their cuisine with Italian pizza or French goat cheese; but in cooking, sometimes traditions beg to be changed for the sake of interesting variety.

TIPS

▼ Taco sauce is made from tomato paste, onions, chilies, vinegar, garlic, and other seasonings. Mild, medium, and hot varieties are available at most supermarkets.

▼ For comparison, 1 ounce of regular Cheddar cheese contains 9 grams fat, 7 grams protein, and .04 gram carbohydrates, totaling 114 calories. One ounce low-fat Cheddar contains 5 grams fat, 9 grams protein, and 1 gram carbohydrates, totaling 82 calories. Even the low-fat variety should be consumed in moderation.

MAKES ONE 6-INCH PIZZA

1 6- or 7-inch flour tortilla (white or whole wheat)
½ teaspoon olive oil
1 tablespoon store-bought taco sauce
2 teaspoons coarsely chopped marinated sun-dried tomatoes
½ plum tomato, cut into 4 slices
¼ teaspoon dried oregano or ½ teaspoon minced fresh
2 teaspoons goat cheese (chevre)
1 teaspoon freshly grated Parmesan cheese

Adjust the oven rack 4 to 5 inches from the broiling element. Preheat the broiler.

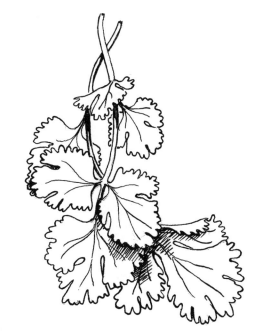

Lightly brush both sides of the tortilla with the olive oil. Prick the surface of the tortilla in several places with a fork. Place directly on the oven rack; broil until lightly browned, 1 to 2 minutes on each side. Watch closely!

Place the tortilla on a baking sheet. Spread the surface with the taco sauce; arrange the sun-dried tomatoes and plum tomato slices over it. Sprinkle with the oregano, dot with the goat cheese, and top with the Parmesan.

Place under the broiler just until the cheese melts, about 2 minutes. Watch closely! Serve warm.

Calories 207 (29% from fat)/Protein 6.2g/Carb 30g/Fat 6.8g/Chol 7mg/Sodium 212mg/Calcium 86mg/Food Exchanges: Veg 0.5/Bread 1.0/Meat 0.1/Fat 0.9

VARIATIONS

▼ as pizza toppings, add other ingredients such as chopped green chilies, thin onion slices, corn, or cooked black or kidney beans

▼ for the oregano, substitute basil before broiling or sprinkle with minced cilantro (fresh coriander) after broiling

▼ for the Parmesan cheese, substitute low-fat shredded Cheddar or Monterey jack cheese

ETHNIC ENTRÉES— MOSTLY VEGETABLES

Early in my vegetarian days, few people seemed to understand how I could be satisfied existing on a vegetable-based diet. My secret was a reliance on Chinese, Indian, Mexican, Italian, and French influences, which enabled me to turn vegetables into something extraordinary, quite different from the overcooked and bland side dishes which most Americans used to accompany their meat entrées at that time.

Serve this over rice, couscous, buckwheat noodles, Chinese wheat noodles, or other pasta.

▼ ▼ ▼

ADVANCE PREPARATION
The Ginger Sauce may be made up to 2 days in advance and re-heated. Serve with freshly stir-fried vegetables.

▼ ▼ ▼

TIPS

▼ Ground ginger is a poor substi-tute for fresh (except in bak-ing). Pickled and crystallized ginger have different roles in cooking; they should not be used in stir-fries.

▼ When buying fresh ginger, look for firm, irregularly shaped rhi-zomes with smooth brown skin and no soft spots. Store at room temperature and use fresh within a few days. What re-mains can be preserved in two ways: Peel, cut it into chunks, place in a jar, and add sherry to cover. (The ginger won't ab-sorb the flavor of the sherry.) Refrigerate for several months. Or, wrap the ginger in alu-minum foil and freeze. Without

VEGETABLE STIR-FRY WITH TOFU AND GINGER SAUCE

▼ ▼ ▼

FOR THE GINGER SAUCE
2 tablespoons white rice vinegar
1 tablespoon sugar
¼ cup plus 1 tablespoon cold water
2 teaspoons low-sodium soy sauce
1 teaspoon cornstarch
1 teaspoon grated fresh ginger

FOR THE STIR-FRY
1 teaspoon safflower oil
1 slice firm or extra-firm tofu, 4 by 2 inches, ½ inch thick
1 medium-size carrot, cut diagonally into ¼-inch slices (about ½ cup)
¼ medium-size red bell pepper, seeded and cut into 2 by ¼-inch strips
1 rib bok choy, thinly sliced diagonally; leaves shredded
One 1½-inch-thick slice onion, separated into rings
½ cup sliced mushrooms
½ teaspoon minced garlic
1 teaspoon low-sodium soy sauce

GARNISH: *toasted sesame seeds (page 30), raw cashews, scallion curls (page 48)*

To prepare the sauce, place the vinegar, sugar, ¼ cup of the water, and the soy sauce in a small saucepan; bring to a boil over high heat. Reduce the heat to medium, cover, and simmer, stir-ring occasionally, for 5 minutes. In a small bowl or measuring cup, combine the cornstarch and the remaining water. Set aside. After the sauce has simmered for 5 minutes, stir the cornstarch mixture and add it to the sauce. Cook, stirring for about 1

thawing, use a fine grater to grate off the amount needed—it isn't even necessary to remove the peel. This method enables you to have fresh ginger on hand at all times; it will keep up to 3 months.

▼ Choose intact, fresh-smelling tofu encased in water. There are several varieties sold according to their firmness and density. "Soft" or "silken" (or Japanese) tofu has a high water content, creamy flavor, and custardlike consistency, and is best for use in creamy products such as blended desserts, salad dressings, or dips. "Firm" (or Chinese) tofu retains its shape when cut and is less apt to fall apart in stir-fries and soups, and will not release extra liquid when cooked or baked. Select the variety appropriate for your recipe. Also check the freshness date printed on the package. Vacuum-packed tofu keeps longer before being opened than tofu in other packaging. Avoid canned tofu.

▼ To make *scallion curls*, slice the green part of the scallion very thinly lengthwise. Drop into ice water. Curls will form in 10 to 15 minutes.

minute, until the sauce is clear and thickened. Remove from the heat; stir in the ginger. Cover and set aside.

While the sauce is simmering, heat ½ teaspoon of the oil in a medium-size skillet over medium-high heat. Add the tofu; cook for 1 minute on each side to warm and lightly brown. Place the tofu on the serving plate; set aside and cover to keep warm.

Also, while the sauce is simmering, heat the remaining oil in the same skillet over medium-high heat. Add the carrots; stir-fry for about 2 minutes. Add the red bell pepper strips, bok choy, and onion; stir-fry for 2 minutes. Add the mushrooms and garlic; stir-fry for 1 more minute. Check to be certain the vegetables are heated through and crisp-tender to a consistency that pleases you. Stir in the soy sauce.

To serve, mound the stir-fried vegetables over the tofu. Drizzle with the sauce; garnish.

Calories 365 (32% from fat)/Protein 23.3g/Carb 38.6g/Fat 13g/Chol 0/Sodium 726mg/Calcium 70mg/Food Exchanges: Veg 3.7/Bread 0.1/ Fat 2.1

Ginger Sauce (entire recipe): Calories 74 (0% from fat)/Protein 0.7g/Carb 17.8g/Fat 0.02g/Chol 0mg/Sodium 401mg/Calcium 4.4mg/ Food Exchanges: Bread 0.1

VARIATIONS

▼ omit the tofu; serve as a vegetable stir-fry; when the vegetables are cooked, stir in the Ginger Sauce rather than drizzling it over

▼ omit the tofu; substitute about 4 ounces medium-size or large shrimp (shelled and deveined). Stir-fry the shrimp until opaque all the way through, about 3 minutes, depending on the size; remove from the pan, keep warm. Stir-fry the vegetables; stir in the shrimp just before serving.

▼ substitute or add other vegetables; the total should be about 2 cups vegetables

▼ serve the Ginger Sauce on poached, broiled, or sautéed fish or chicken, or use it as a sauce for steamed vegetables

ADVANCE PREPARATION

This is best when served immediately, but can be refrigerated for up to 1 day and reheated. The flavor of the curry in a dish often intensifies when allowed to set.

▼ ▼ ▼

TIPS

▼ For the best-flavored carrots, whenever possible, buy those that are sold unbagged with their tops still on. The freshness of the tops will help to determine the quality; they should be green and unwilted. Look for slender, smooth, firm carrots, with no cracks, knobs, or rootlets growing from the sides; roots and a wide diameter indicate carrots which are older and tougher.

▼ If carrots are purchased with greens, the tops should be removed before storing them because they draw out some of the internal juices of the carrots. (The greens can be added to soups.) Keep raw, unwashed carrots refrigerated in a tightly closed plastic bag or airtight container where they will keep

CALCUTTA CURRY

▼ ▼ ▼

1 teaspoon olive oil
1 medium-size carrot, thinly sliced
4 medium-size mushrooms, sliced
2 tablespoons chopped celery
1 tablespoon chopped onion
1 teaspoon curry powder, or to taste
½ cup skim milk
¼ cup apple juice
½ teaspoon grated fresh ginger
Dash of ground cumin
Dash of freshly ground black pepper, or to taste
1 tablespoon cold water
2 teaspoons cornstarch
½ cup frozen peas

GARNISH: *sprig cilantro (fresh coriander) or mint*

Heat the olive oil in a medium-size skillet over medium heat. Add the carrot, mushrooms, celery, and onion; cook, stirring, until the carrot slices are crisp-tender, about 3 minutes. Stir in the curry powder. Add the milk, apple juice, ginger, cumin, and pepper. Increase the heat to medium-high. When the mixture begins to simmer, reduce the heat to medium; stir occasionally.

Meanwhile, in a small bowl or measuring cup, combine the water and cornstarch, mixing well to dissolve the cornstarch. Stir into the curry mixture. Stir constantly until thickened, about 3 minutes. Stir in the peas; heat through. Taste; adjust seasonings. Spoon onto a serving plate, garnish, and serve with accompaniments.

Calories 253 (20% from fat)/Protein 10.1g/Carb 40.7g/Fat 5.6g/Chol 2mg/Sodium 175mg/Calcium 214mg/Food Exchanges: Milk 0.4/Veg 1.9/Fruit 0.4/Bread 1.0/Fat 0.9

for about 2 weeks. Fresh carrots don't need peeling; just scrub them before using.

▼ Cornstarch, a fine, white flour obtained from corn, is used as a thickener in many Asian soups and sauces. Arrowroot, a starch from the tubers of several kinds of tropical plants, can be substituted for cornstarch; use 2½ teaspoons of arrowroot powder for 1 tablespoon of cornstarch. To prevent lumping, either should be mixed with cold water and then added near the end of cooking; the result is a somewhat clear product rather than a soup or sauce with the cloudy appearance provided by flour thickening.

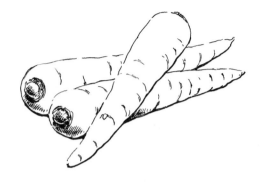

VARIATIONS

▼ substitute or add other vegetables such as thin potato slices, green beans, snap peas, cauliflower florets, broccoli florets, or plum tomato wedges

▼ add cooked beans such as garbanzos; stir in with the peas

▼ add raw cashews; stir in just before serving

▼ add chicken; before sautéing the vegetables, cut a split chicken breast into ½-inch strips; cook the strips, stirring, in ½ teaspoon olive oil heated over medium-high heat; set aside. Stir in with the peas.

▼ add shrimp; before sautéing the vegetables, cook, stirring, 4 ounces shrimp (shelled and deveined) in ½ teaspoon olive oil heated over medium-high heat; set aside. Stir in with the peas.

▼ for the apple juice, substitute pineapple juice

ACCOMPANIMENTS

▼ Traditionally, in addition to being served with rice, curries are accompanied by an assortment of condiments with the purpose of enhancing the flavors and providing a cooling element. I usually select one or two from these suggestions: low-fat plain yogurt, orange slices or mandarin orange segments, pineapple chunks, chutney, raisins, cucumber slices (or Chutney-Yogurt Cucumber Slices—page 132), tomato wedges, or unsalted dry-roasted peanuts.

The topping may be prepared up to 2 days in advance; refrigerate and reheat. Toast the tortilla and assemble the tostada just before serving.

▼ ▼ ▼

TIPS

▼ Zucchini is a summer squash shaped like a tightly ridged cucumber. The most tender and flavorful zucchinis are small and tender. Do not pick zucchinis which are not firm or have skin that is cut, bruised, dull, or shriveled. Like other squashes, zucchinis are 95 percent water, so cook them quickly or they will become mushy.

▼ Spices, such as cumin, allspice, chili powder, cinnamon, and nutmeg, are dried parts of aromatic plants including flowers, seeds, leaves, bark, and roots.

▼ For neat shredding of cheese, oil the shredding disc or grater before using.

VEGETARIAN TOSTADA

▼ ▼ ▼

¼ cup water
1 tablespoon tomato paste
1 teaspoon chili powder, or to taste
⅛ teaspoon ground cumin
Dash of hot pepper sauce, or to taste
1 teaspoon olive oil
½ cup sliced zucchini (halved lengthwise and cut into ¼-inch slices)
½ cup sliced mushrooms
¼ cup coarsely shredded carrot
1 tablespoon chopped onion
¼ teaspoon minced garlic
1 plum tomato, cut into ½-inch cubes (½ cup)
One 6- or 7-inch flour tortilla (white or whole wheat)

GARNISH: on the tostada, shredded low-fat Cheddar or freshly grated Parmesan cheese; on the plate, alfalfa sprouts or shredded lettuce, orange slices

Adjust the oven rack 4 to 5 inches from the broiling element; preheat the broiler.

Stir together the water, tomato paste, chili powder, cumin, and hot pepper sauce in a measuring cup; set aside.

Heat ½ teaspoon of the olive oil in a small skillet over medium heat. Add the zucchini, mushrooms, carrot, and onion. Cook, stirring, until the vegetables are tender, about 4 minutes. Add the garlic; cook 30 seconds longer. Stir in the tomato paste mixture and tomato cubes. Reduce the heat to low, cover, and cook for about 5 minutes, stirring occasionally.

Meanwhile, brush both sides of the tortilla with the remaining olive oil. Prick the surface of the tortilla several places with a fork. Place directly on the oven rack; broil until lightly browned,

1 to 2 minutes on each side. Watch closely! Place on a serving plate.

Taste the topping; adjust seasonings. Mound on the toasted tortilla. Garnish. As a garnish on the plate, place a mound of alfalfa sprouts or shredded lettuce with orange slices arranged on top.

Calories 234 (29% from fat)/Protein 6.7g/Carb 34.9g/Fat 7.5g/Chol 0/Sodium 246mg/Calcium 117mg/Food Exchanges: Veg 3.1/Bread 1.0/Fat 1.1

VARIATIONS:
▼ add or substitute other vegetables such as small broccoli florets or corn
▼ add about 2 tablespoons cooked beans such as black, kidney, or garbanzo beans
▼ add canned chopped green chilies or minced jalapeño pepper
▼ in place of the tortilla, stuff the mixture into 2 taco shells; top each with lettuce and cheese; drizzle with taco sauce
▼ use the Vegetarian Tostada topping as a filling for a Basic Omelet (page 67), as a pita bread filling, or as a topping for toasted English muffins (sprinkle with shredded cheese and place under the broiler for a few minutes until melted)

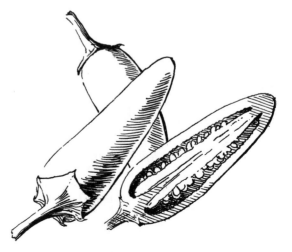

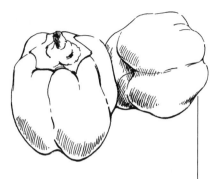

CAPONATA

▼ ▼ ▼

ADVANCE PREPARATION
Will keep, refrigerated, for up
to a week. Serve chilled, at
room temperature, or reheat.

▼ ▼ ▼

TIPS
▼ For very small quantities, herbs
can be minced using kitchen
shears. Mincing herbs and garlic helps to release their flavors
throughout the food.

▼ When mincing fresh parsley,
you can include the thin portion of the stems. Most herbs,
like basil, thyme, and rosemary, have tough stems; pinch
off the leaves and avoid using
the stems.

MAKES 2 CUPS
1 teaspoon olive oil
2½ cups peeled and cubed eggplant (½-inch cubes)
¼ cup seeded and chopped green bell pepper
4 large mushrooms, sliced
1 tablespoon minced onion
¼ teaspoon minced garlic
¼ cup tomato paste
¼ cup water
2 plum tomatoes, cut into ½-inch cubes (1 cup)
1 teaspoon dried basil or 1 tablespoon minced fresh
1 teaspoon dried oregano or 1 tablespoon minced fresh
⅛ teaspoon freshly ground black pepper, or to taste
1 tablespoon minced fresh parsley
1 tablespoon red wine vinegar
2 slices crusty French bread

In a medium-size skillet, heat the olive oil over medium heat.
Add the eggplant, bell pepper, mushrooms, and onion. Cook,
stirring, until the vegetables are tender, about 5 minutes. Add
the garlic; cook 30 seconds longer.

In a measuring cup or small bowl, stir together the tomato
paste and water. Add to the skillet along with the plum tomatoes, basil and oregano (if using dried), and pepper; stir well to
combine. Reduce the heat to low; continue to cook, covered,
until the vegetables are tender, about 10 minutes; add the parsley (and fresh basil and oregano, if using) during the last 2 minutes. Stir in the vinegar. Taste; adjust seasonings. Spoon into a
bowl and serve warm with French bread.

Calories 440 (18% from fat)/Protein 13.9g/Carb 75.7g/Fat 9g/Chol
0/Sodium 828mg/Calcium 188mg/Food Exchanges: Veg 7.1/Bread
2.4/Fat 1.4

▼ along with the tomato cubes, stir in coarsely chopped marinated sun-dried tomatoes and/or 1 teaspoon drained and
rinsed capers
▼ serve Caponata as an accompaniment to broiled fish or
chicken

VEGGIE BURGER
▼ ▼ ▼

½ teaspoon olive oil
2 tablespoons shredded carrot
1 tablespoon seeded and minced green bell pepper
¼ teaspoon minced garlic
2 tablespoons noncholesterol egg product
2 tablespoons drained and rinsed canned black beans
2 tablespoons toasted wheat germ
1 teaspoon minced fresh parsley
½ teaspoon low-sodium soy sauce
⅛ teaspoon ground sage
Dash of freshly ground black pepper
Olive oil spray

Heat the olive oil in a small skillet over medium heat. Add the
carrot and bell pepper; cook, stirring, 3 minutes to soften the
bell pepper. Add the garlic; cook 30 seconds longer. Remove
from the heat.

In a medium-size bowl, stir together the remaining ingredients except the olive oil spray. Stir in the sautéed vegetables.
Form into a burger about ½ inch thick.

Spray olive oil into the skillet; heat over medium heat. Add
the burger. Cook until cooked through and lightly browned,
about 1 minute on each side.

I used to make Nutburgers—delicious but too high in fat for the
way I eat today. This "burger"
also can be served on a bun with
lettuce, tomato, and ketchup.

▼ ▼ ▼

ADVANCE PREPARATION
**The Veggie Burger mixture can
be made a few hours in advance and refrigerated. If
chilled, allow a little extra
cooking time.**

▼ ▼ ▼

▼ Thyme, savory, bay leaf, rosemary, sage, oregano, and marjoram are considered to be "robust herbs" with tough leaves that are resistant to cold weather and to the heat of the sun—and to the heat of cooking. They are strong in aroma and hearty in flavor.

Calories 137 (26% from fat)/Protein 9.1g/Carb 16.2g/Fat 4g/Chol 0/Sodium 147mg/Calcium 25mg/Food Exchanges: Veg 0.5/Bread 0.8/ Meat 0.3/Fat 0.7

VARIATIONS

▼ add or substitute other finely chopped vegetables such as red bell pepper, or other beans such as chopped garbanzos
▼ for the noncholesterol egg product, substitute 1 tablespoon reduced-cholesterol egg product or 1 egg white

GRAINS

In most countries of the world, grains and grain products are the main forms of sustenance. Although the United States is one of the largest producers of grains, these grains contribute just 20 to 25 percent of the calories in the typical American diet. However, that's all changing. For the last few years many Americans with an interest in good health and good-tasting food have been discovering the appetizing versatility of the good grains.

Most of the rice recipes in this chapter call for cooked rice; instructions are provided on pages 211–213 in the Accompaniments chapter, where you will also find an abundance of additional information on grains.

Will keep in the refrigerator
for 2 days; it reheats well.

▼ ▼ ▼

TIPS

▼ It is best to buy mushrooms
loose rather than prepackaged.
The surface should be mostly
white with a few brown flecks.
Because they are very perishable, try to buy them no more
than a couple of days before
using. They will keep for about
a week, but the quality deteriorates. Do not wash before storing in the refrigerator and do
not store them in a tightly
sealed container; they need
cool, moist air to stay fresh.

▼ Before using mushrooms simply
brush or wipe them with a
moist paper towel; because they
are very absorbent, they should
not be allowed to soak in water.

▼ Cook mushrooms quickly; because they are 90 percent
water, they easily become
mushy.

STIR-FRIED RICE

▼ ▼ ▼

1 teaspoon safflower oil
¼ cup noncholesterol egg product
4 medium-size mushrooms, sliced
½ cup coarsely shredded carrot
1 tablespoon seeded and minced red bell pepper
1 tablespoon chopped celery
½ scallion (both green and white parts), chopped
¼ teaspoon minced garlic
½ cup cooked rice—white, brown, basmati, or wild rice
   (pages 211–213)
1 teaspoon low-sodium soy sauce
Dash of ground white pepper, or to taste
¼ cup frozen peas

GARNISH: *red bell pepper strips*

In a medium-size skillet over medium heat, heat ½ teaspoon
of the safflower oil. Add the egg product; scramble until it is almost set. (This will take less than a minute.) Spoon the eggs into
a bowl, cover, and set aside.

In the same pan, heat the remaining safflower oil over
medium-high heat. Add the mushrooms, carrot, red bell pepper,
celery, and scallion; stir-fry until the vegetables are tender, about
3 minutes. Add the garlic; stir-fry 30 seconds longer. Add the
rice; stir-fry for about 3 minutes. Reduce the heat to medium;
stir in the soy sauce and white pepper. Stir in the peas and reserved eggs; cook until heated through, stirring occasionally.
Taste; adjust seasonings. Spoon onto a serving plate; garnish
with red bell pepper strips.

Calories 271 (17% from fat)/Protein 11.6g/Carb 44.6g/Fat 5.2g/Chol
0/Sodium 338mg/Calcium 48mg/Food Exchanges: Veg 1.6/Bread
2.2/Meat 0.6/Fat 0.9

- The fruitiness of olive oil seems to clash with Eastern flavors; in those recipes, I use safflower oil which is blander.
- White pepper is actually the inner portion of the kernels used for black pepper. It is slightly less spicy and sweeter than black pepper.

When beans are included in Mexican rice, it can become a satisfying light lunch. Mexican rice, with or without beans, will add an ethnic touch to a serving of broiled fish or chicken.

▼ ▼ ▼

ADVANCE PREPARATION
Will keep for 2 days in the refrigerator.

▼ ▼ ▼

TIPS
- If garlic browns, it turns bitter. Usually add garlic toward the end of the cooking period when sautéing vegetables unless there is an abundance of moisture in the pan. When cooking in small quantities, I usually sauté garlic for only about one-half minute.

VARIATIONS
- for the noncholesterol egg product, substitute 1 whole egg, lightly beaten, or 2 egg whites, lightly beaten
- substitute or add other vegetables such as cut asparagus, cauliflower florets, broccoli florets, bok choy, jicama, or water chestnuts
- add shredded cooked chicken or cooked small shrimp (or chopped shrimp); stir in with the reserved eggs and heat through

MEXICAN RICE
▼ ▼ ▼

½ teaspoon olive oil
2 tablespoons seeded and chopped green bell pepper
1 tablespoon minced onion
¼ teaspon minced garlic
¼ teaspoon chili powder, or to taste
1 plum tomato, diced into ⅜-inch cubes (½ cup)
¼ cup drained and rinsed canned black beans
½ cup cooked rice—white, brown, or basmati (pages 211–213)
1 teaspoon tomato paste
Dash of freshly ground black pepper, or to taste

In a small skillet, heat the olive oil over medium heat. Add the bell pepper and onion. Cook, stirring, until the vegetables are tender, 5 minutes. Add the garlic; cook 30 seconds longer.

Stir in the chili powder and tomato, stirring until the tomato is softened, about 2 minutes. Stir in the remaining ingredients. Heat, stirring occasionally. Taste; adjust seasonings. Spoon onto a serving plate.

▼ Minced garlic in a jar is an acceptable alternative to using fresh garlic cloves; ½ teaspoon is equivalent to 1 clove of garlic. If clean utensils are used each time the garlic is measured, it will keep for months in the refrigerator. (I store my garlic jar in a ziptop plastic bag to prevent the garlic odor from seeping out into my refrigerator.) Avoid using dried garlic powder which will not lend to your recipes the distinctive flavor, aroma, or healthful benefits of fresh garlic.

Arborio rice is a must for preparing risotto; and the Italian method of cooking it leaves each grain separate and slightly *al dente*—totally different from the rice dishes of other countries. The creaminess that gives risotto its distinctive personality is achieved by sautéing the rice and then adding hot broth as it cooks. Vegetable, cheese, fish, or meat are cooked into the rice making risotto a delicious side dish yet complete enough to stand alone as an entrée.

Calories 255 (12% from fat)/Protein 8.4g/Carb 48g/Fat 3.3g/Chol 0/Sodium 208mg/Calcium 65mg/Food Exchanges: Veg 1.6/Bread 2.5/Fat 0.4

VARIATIONS

▼ add other vegetables such as coarsely shredded carrot or chopped celery
▼ with the rice, stir in 1 tablespoon canned chopped green chilies; or with the vegetables, sauté 1 teaspoon minced fresh jalapeño pepper
▼ for the black beans, substitute other beans as kidney or great northern
▼ omit the beans; use as a lighter side dish with broiled fish or chicken

RISOTTO PRIMAVERA
▼ ▼ ▼

1½ cups water
2 teaspoons vegetable stock powder
1 teaspoon olive oil
1 tablespoon minced shallot
¼ cup uncooked arborio rice
½ cup coarsely shredded carrot
4 medium-size mushrooms, sliced
½ small zucchini, cut into 1½ by ¼-inch strips
¼ cup frozen peas, thawed
¼ cup freshly grated Parmesan cheese
Dash of freshly ground black pepper, or to taste

GARNISH: *sprig fresh Italian flat-leaf parsley*

▼ ▼ ▼

ADVANCE PREPARATION

Risotto is best just after being prepared but may be refrigerated and served the next day. To reheat, add a little water and cook over low heat, stirring constantly, or microwave at medium for 1 to 2 minutes, stirring occasionally.

▼ ▼ ▼

TIPS

▼ Arborio rice is an Italian short-grain rice which can be found in the rice section or among the ethnic foods in most supermarkets and specialty stores. It is the ideal rice for risotto, Spanish paella, and rice puddings because it absorbs liquid without becoming too soft.

Pour the water into a small saucepan over high heat; bring to a boil. Reduce the heat to medium, add the stock powder, and stir to dissolve. Keep the pan covered over medium heat.

Meanwhile, in a medium-size skillet over medium heat, heat the olive oil. Add the shallot; cook, stirring, until tender but not browned, about 30 seconds. Add the rice; stir until each grain is coated with oil, about 1 minute. Pour ¼ cup of hot vegetable stock into the skillet; cook, stirring constantly, until the liquid is absorbed, about 1 minute. (When the liquid is added, it should remain bubbly so it may be necessary to alternate the heat between medium and medium-high.)

Stir the carrot, mushrooms, zucchini, and peas into the rice, and continue adding liquid, ½ cup at a time. Pour it in slowly, adding more only when the previous liquid has been absorbed. (The exact amount of liquid needed may vary with rices—add the liquid only until the rice is tender but still firm to the bite. This process will take about 10 minutes.)

Remove the pan from the heat; add the Parmesan and pepper, stirring until the cheese melts into the rice. Taste; adjust seasonings. Serve immediately, garnished with parsley.

Calories 396 (29% from fat)/Protein 17.4g/Carb 52.9g/Fat 12.7g/Chol 20mg/Sodium 525mg/Calcium 391mg/Food Exchanges: Veg 1.6/Bread 2.8/Meat 1.4/Fat 1.4

VARIATIONS

▼ for the vegetable stock, substitute chicken broth (preferably low-sodium and defatted)
▼ substitute or add other vegetables such as red bell pepper strips, coarsely chopped marinated sun-dried tomatoes, or cooked cut asparagus
▼ add cooked fish, shrimp, or chicken

TIPS
▼ Protein is made of twenty-two
amino acids, eight of which our
bodies cannot produce on their
own; we must get them from
the food we eat. Most legumes
contain all eight amino acids,
but not in the right proportions, so they are called "in-
complete proteins." If they are
eaten with another food, such
as a grain, whose amino acids
"complement" those of the
legumes, the two foods together
contain the essential amino
acids in the right proportions
for our bodies to utilize. It is
not necessary to eat the combination at the very same time,
however, many complementary
foods, such as rice and beans or
grains and corn, often fit easily
into individual recipes and
menus. If the complementary
amino acids are not eaten in the
same day, the protein cannot be
converted to a usable form and
is wasted.

SPANISH BULGUR

▼ ▼ ▼

One 8-ounce can tomatoes with juice
¼ cup uncooked bulgur wheat
1 teaspoon olive oil
½ cup coarsely shredded carrot
3 medium-size mushrooms, sliced
1 tablespoon seeded and chopped green bell pepper
1 tablespoon minced onion
¼ teaspoon minced garlic
½ cup frozen corn
¼ cup water
½ teaspoon chili powder, or to taste
¼ teaspoon dried thyme or 1 teaspoon fresh leaves
¼ teaspoon freshly ground black pepper, or to taste

GARNISH: *sprig fresh parsley*

Pour the tomatoes with their juice into a medium-size saucepan; quarter the tomatoes. Stir in the bulgur. Over high heat, bring the mixture to a boil. Cover the pan, reduce the heat to medium-low, and cook for 5 minutes.

Meanwhile, heat the olive oil in a small skillet over medium heat. Add the carrot, mushrooms, bell pepper, and onion; cook, stirring, until the vegetables are nearly softened, about 4 minutes. Add the garlic; cook 30 seconds longer. Add the sautéed vegetables to the bulgur and tomatoes in the saucepan. Stir in the remaining ingredients. Cover and continue cooking over medium-low heat for about 5 minutes, stirring occasionally. Taste; adjust seasonings. Spoon onto a serving plate; garnish.

Calories 344 (16% from fat)/Protein 10.1g/Carb 62.4g/Fat 6g/Chol 0/Sodium 413mg/Calcium 101mg/Food Exchanges: Veg 3.3/Bread 2.8/Fat 0.9

▼ add beans such as kidney, garbanzo, or black beans during the last 5 minutes of cooking

▼ add raw cashews during the last 5 minutes of cooking

▼ for a spicier flavor, add a dash of ground cumin and/or crushed red pepper

EGGS

Eggs or packaged egg products usually seem to be present in even the most barren refrigerator (or freezer), and they provide endless possibilities for cooking for one in addition to being an excellent protein alternative to fish or chicken. In fact, eggs—noncholesterol or reduced-cholesterol egg products, or even just whites—contain all the amino acids for complete protein.

Just a few small touches can transform eggs from simple, ordinary food to something special. Omelets and frittatas are not only quickly prepared, but nourishing, inexpensive, delicious, and ideal to make in individual servings. Innumerable foods can be added to enhance them, and they are also an ideal way to eat leftovers in a different form. Enjoy my recipes and allow them to spark creations of your own, using the ingredients you like best.

There is some disagreement on the effects of egg consumption on our cholesterol levels. The American Heart Association suggests a limit of 4 egg yolks per week; and we must take into account the eggs hidden in baked goods and other cooked dishes. Egg whites can be used as often as desired, since all of the cholesterol is found in the yolk. I think it is wise to take your heredity and cholesterol count into consideration when including eggs in your menus. I suggest the use of noncholesterol egg product in most of my recipes calling for eggs. These egg products are made from real egg whites; the flavor is enhanced by the addition of a small amount of corn oil; some yellow coloring is added to give the appearance of whole eggs. Preservatives are added so the

TIPS

▼ A basic 2-egg omelet, unfilled and cooked with just 1/2 teaspoon oil, contains 170 calories, 12 grams (or 67%) fat, and 426 milligrams of cholesterol. However, the same omelet prepared with noncholesterol egg product contains 70 calories, 2.3 grams (or 13%) fat, and no cholesterol.

▼ One-fourth cup of noncholesterol egg product, ¼ cup of reduced-cholesterol egg product, or 2 egg whites can be used in place of 1 whole egg in most recipes. (To enhance the color and flavor of plain egg whites, add a dash of turmeric, a yellow-colored seasoning, and a dash of safflower oil or olive oil.)

If you choose to use fresh eggs, here are some tips:

▼ Buy large-size eggs when buying eggs for their whites.

▼ Though eggs will keep for up to 5 weeks in the refrigerator, they do lose their fresh flavor after 1 or 2 weeks. Store them with the large end up, the tapered end down, in the coldest part of your refrigerator. (Actually the molded door rack is not the best place to store eggs. The eggs are exposed to warm air every time the door is opened.) Storing eggs in the carton helps to keep eggs from the aromas of other foods; eggs can absorb odors through their porous shells.

▼ If you have any doubts about freshness, put a raw egg in a bowl of cool water; if it sinks and rests on its side, it is still fresh. If it sinks but stands partially or fully erect on its tapered end, it is over the hill. If it floats, the egg is rotten! Once cracked open, if the white hugs the yolk and yolk is round and plump, the egg is fresh. If the white spreads over the plate and the yolk looks flat, the egg is not fresh.

▼ To separate yolks from whites, the easiest method is to use a kitchen gadget called an "egg separator," or you can use a kitchen funnel. Most experienced cooks break an egg open at the egg's "beltline," empty the white into a bowl, and tip the yolk back and forth between the two halves of the shell to allow any remaining white to flow into the bowl.

product will taste and perform like whole eggs. Purchased frozen, the product keeps well in the freezer for up to 1 year; it can be thawed quickly for cooking. And once thawed, it will keep in the refrigerator for 1 week, so it is possible to keep non-cholesterol egg product on hand for last-minute cooking. Another option, found in the refrigerated section of most supermarkets, are the egg products made from whole eggs from which nearly all of the cholesterol has been removed. Both noncholesterol and reduced-cholesterol products cook more quickly than whole eggs and result in a dish that is lighter and more tender than whole eggs. Further information on the storage and use of these products is provided on the packaging.

In recent years, a new health concern has been raised about eggs—salmonellosis (salmonella-caused food poisoning). Salmonella bacteria, which used to be found in eggs with cracked shells, have now been found in clean, uncracked eggs. To safeguard your health, eggs must be cooked at high enough temperatures to destroy the bacteria. Both yolks and whites should be cooked until firm; undercooked egg dishes like soft-cooked or sunny-side-up fried eggs and recipes which contain raw eggs, like Caesar salad dressing or eggnog, carry the risk of salmonellosis. Both noncholesterol and reduced-cholesterol egg products are pasteurized, eliminating the bacteria, another advantage of using these products.

ITALIAN FRITTATA

▼ ▼ ▼

Frittatas are to Italians what omelets are to the French. The difference is that in a frittata the filling is mixed with the eggs, and the whole mixture is cooked together.

▼ ▼ ▼

ADVANCE PREPARATION
In Italy, frittatas are often served cold cut into thin wedges—so refrigerate the leftovers, if there are any, for tomorrow's lunch!

▼ ▼ ▼

TIPS
▼ Oils can turn rancid at room temperature, but in the refrigerator they will keep for months. When chilled, olive oil will turn partially or totally cloudy and may solidify. Before using, allow it to come to room temperature or briefly place the closed container under warm running water.

1 teaspoon olive oil
1 new potato, cut into slices ⅛-inch thick
4 medium-size mushrooms, sliced
½ cup sliced zucchini (⅛-inch slices)
*¼ medium-size red bell pepper, seeded and cut into 2 by ¼-
    inch strips*
½ scallion (both green and white parts), chopped
¼ teaspoon minced garlic
½ cup noncholesterol egg product
1 tablespoon freshly grated Parmesan cheese
⅛ teaspoon dried basil or ½ teaspoon minced fresh
⅛ teaspoon dried oregano or ½ teaspoon minced fresh
⅛ teaspoon freshly ground black pepper

GARNISH: *freshly ground black pepper, freshly grated
    Parmesan cheese, sprinkling of paprika, sprig fresh pars-
    ley, or fresh basil leaves*

Heat the oil in a medium-size skillet over medium heat. Add the potato slices; cook for 2 minutes, stirring occasionally. Add the mushrooms, zucchini, bell pepper, scallion, and garlic. Cook, stirring occasionally, until the vegetables, especially the potato slices, are tender, about 5 minutes.

Meanwhile pour the egg product into a small bowl. Stir in the Parmesan cheese, basil, oregano, and pepper. Pour this mixture over the cooked vegetables. Set the pan cover askew over the pan, allowing the steam to escape. Cook over medium heat about 3 minutes. Lift up the cooked portion of the egg product, if necessary, to allow the uncooked parts to flow to the bottom of the pan. Be certain the egg product is set and a spatula or knife can be run around the edges.

Using a spatula, slide the frittata from the skillet onto a serving plate. Garnish and serve immediately.

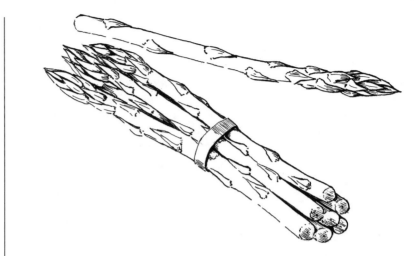

Calories 186 (32% from fat)/Protein 15.2g/Carb 16.2g/Fat 6.7g/Chol 5mg/Sodium 283mg/Calcium 108mg/Food Exchanges: Veg 1.0/Bread 0.5/Meat 1.6/Fat 1.0

VARIATIONS

▼ substitute or add other vegetables such as shredded carrots, corn, peas, tomato cubes, cut asparagus, broccoli florets, small cauliflower florets, diced green bell pepper, chopped artichoke hearts, chopped or sliced onions, or chopped marinated sun-dried tomatoes

▼ as the egg product is added, stir in about ¼ cup cooked rice or pasta or about 1 tablespoon ricotta cheese

▼ substitute ½ cup reduced-cholesterol egg product, 4 egg whites, 2 whole eggs (plus 1 tablespoon water), or 1 whole egg and 2 egg whites. Fresh eggs will require a slightly longer cooking time. (With 2 whole eggs, the frittata contains 272 calories, 16.6 grams or 55% fat, and 431 milligrams of cholesterol.)

▼ top the cooked frittata with Herbed Tomato Sauce (page 34), Chunky Tomato Sauce (page 135), or your favorite store-bought pasta sauce

HUEVOS RANCHEROS

▼ ▼ ▼

TIPS

▼ 1 tablespoon of "lite" sour cream contains 20 calories and 1 gram fat compared to 30 calories in the same amount of regular sour cream. The fat is reduced by one-half; the cholesterol by one-third; the flavor and texture are surprisingly similar.

▼ Spices become bitter if they are cooked over high heat for more than a short period of time. It is best to add seasonings, such as chili powder and pepper, toward the end of the cooking period.

▼ Leftover canned green chili peppers can be frozen in a tightly closed refrigerator container. Chop off the amount needed while still frozen.

▼ Cumin is available in two forms, whole and ground seeds. (The ground form is used in the recipes in this book.) It has a warm, aromatic taste and is widely used in Indian and Mexican cooking. It is also an essential ingredient in curry powder and chili powder.

½ teaspoon olive oil
2 tablespoons seeded and chopped green bell pepper
¼ teaspoon minced garlic
1 medium-size tomato, cut into ½-inch cubes (1 cup)
1 tablespoon canned chopped green chilies
½ scallion, chopped (both green and white parts)
¼ teaspoon chili powder, or to taste
¼ teaspoon dried oregano or ½ teaspoon minced fresh
Dash of ground cumin
Dash of freshly ground black pepper, or to taste
¼ cup noncholesterol egg product
1 tablespoon freshly grated Parmesan cheese
One 6- or 7-inch flour tortilla (white or whole wheat)

GARNISH: *store-bought taco sauce, a dollop of low-fat plain yogurt or reduced-calorie sour cream, sprig cilantro (fresh coriander) or parsley*

In a small skillet over medium heat, heat the olive oil. Add the bell pepper; cook, stirring, about 2 minutes. Add the garlic; cook 30 seconds longer. Stir in the tomato, green chilies, scallion, chili powder, oregano, cumin, and pepper. Cook, uncovered, stirring occasionally, until the vegetables are tender, about 3 minutes. Taste; adjust seasonings.

Meanwhile, pour the egg product into a measuring cup. Using a large spoon, make a shallow well in the cooked tomato-vegetable mixture. Pour the egg product gently into the well. (Some may flow over the sides, but that is not a problem.) Reduce the heat to medium-low, cover, and cook about 2 minutes. Sprinkle with the Parmesan cheese, cover, and cook until the egg product is cooked through and the cheese is melted, 2 more minutes. Remove the pan from the heat. Cover to keep warm.

Put the tortilla between two paper towels and place in the microwave; heat on high until moist and warm, 15 to 20 seconds. Place the heated tortilla on a serving plate. Using a spatula, transfer the tomato-vegetable mixture with the egg topping from the skillet to the top of the tortilla. Garnish; serve immediately.

Calories 240 (25% from fat)/Protein 12.9g/Carb 32.1g/Fat 6.7g/Chol 5mg/Sodium 694mg/Calcium 206mg/Food Exchanges: Veg 2.4/Bread 1.0/Meat 1.0/Fat 0.7

VARIATIONS

▼ add or substitute other vegetables such as broccoli florets, chopped zucchini, coarsely shredded carrot, or coarsely chopped marinated sun-dried tomatoes.

▼ to the tomato-vegetable mixture, add cooked beans such as black, kidney, or garbanzo beans, or shredded cooked chicken breast

▼ for the noncholesterol egg product, substitute 2 egg whites or 1 whole egg; for the whole egg, you may need to increase the egg cooking time to 4 minutes to be certain the yolk is cooked through

▼ for the Parmesan cheese, substitute low-fat shredded Cheddar cheese or Monterey jack cheese

▼ rather than microwaving the tortilla, wrap it in foil and bake at 350° F. for about 10 minutes

▼ rather than layering the tomato mixture on a tortilla, mound it in the center of a bowl surrounded by Baked Tortilla Chips (page 219)

▼ use the tomato-vegetable mixture as a topping for a baked potato or as a filling for a Basic Omelet (page 67)

BASIC OMELET WITH
ASPARAGUS GUACAMOLE

▼ ▼ ▼

Omelets are among my favorite
quick meals. They can be stuffed
with a wide variety of fillings and
topped with many different
sauces. Remember the omelet as a
destination for leftovers!
Regarding methods, there are
many omelet techniques; this
basic omelet is the one that works
the best for me.

▼ ▼ ▼

ADVANCE PREPARATION
**The Asparagus Guacamole may
be made several hours in advance. Make the omelet just
before serving.**

▼ ▼ ▼

TIPS
▼ Omelets are best made in a
well-seasoned stainless steel or
nonstick skillet with sloping
sides; gourmet shops sell special
"omelet pans."

FOR THE ASPARAGUS QUACAMOLE
MAKES ½ CUP
1 cup cut asparagus (1-inch lengths), 6 to 8 spears
2 teaspoons low-fat plain yogurt
¼ teaspoon fresh lemon juice
Dash of hot pepper sauce, or to taste
Dash of freshly ground black pepper, or to taste
Few drops of olive oil

FOR THE BASIC OMELET
½ cup noncholesterol egg product
Olive oil spray

TO COMPLETE THE RECIPE
*2 tablespoons store-bought taco sauce, preferably at room
    temperature*

GARNISH: *dollop low-fat plain yogurt or reduced-calorie sour
    cream, thin tomato slices, thin orange slices, alfalfa
    sprouts*

To prepare the guacamole, place the cut asparagus in a small
microwave-proof dish; add a small amount of water. Microwave
on high until softened, about 4 minutes (or steam the asparagus
in a vegetable steamer). Drain well.

Place the asparagus and the remaining guacamole ingredients
in a food processor or blender. Process until smooth, pushing
down the sides occasionally. Set aside.

Spray a small skillet or omelet pan with olive oil spray and
place over medium heat. Pour in the egg product. As the edges
become firm, push them toward the center without cutting

- ▼ The best asparagus is available in the early spring. Choose the greenest ones with straight, firm stalks; the tips should be firm and tightly closed with a lavender hue. Slender stalks will be more tender; uniformity in size and shape is important for even cooking. If you can't find thin asparagus, you can halve the thicker stalks.
- ▼ For storage, wrap asparagus in a plastic bag and store in the vegetable crisper; use within 2 to 3 days. Do not clean the asparagus until you are ready to cook it. If wilted, stand the stalks in a jar filled with 2 inches of very cold water. Cover with a plastic bag, fasten with a rubber band, and set in the refrigerator for 1 to 2 hours before cooking.

through the omelet so the uncooked portions can reach the hot pan surface. Tilt the pan and move the cooked portions as necessary. (This entire process should take only about 1 minute.)

While the egg product is still moist, spread the center third with the filling perpendicular to the handle of the pan. Using a spatula, turn the third closest to the handle to cover the filling. Reduce the heat to low, cover the pan, and heat for about 2 minutes, just to warm the filling and finish cooking the egg product.

Turn the omelet onto the serving plate by sliding the outermost third onto the plate. Roll the remainder over so the omelet rests, seam side down, on the plate. Spoon the taco sauce over the omelet; garnish.

Basic Omelet: Calories 48 (0% from fat)/Protein 10g/Carb 2g/Fat 0g/Chol 0/Sodium 160mg/Calcium 1mg/Food Exchanges: Meat 1.3

Asparagus Guacamole (entire recipe): Calories 54 (14% from fat)/Protein 5.2g/Carb 8.8g/Fat 1g/Chol 1mg/Sodium 14mg/Calcium 61mg/Food Exchanges: Veg 1.5

VARIATIONS

▼ in the Asparagus Guacamole, for the lemon juice, substitute lime juice and add 1 tablespoon coarsely chopped cilantro (fresh coriander)

▼ to the Asparagus Guacamole, add ½ cup cooked garbanzo beans; purée with the mixture

▼ serve the guacamole as a dip with Baked Tortilla Chips (page 219)

▼ substitute ½ cup reduced-cholesterol egg product, 4 egg whites (plus 1 teaspoon olive oil or safflower oil and a dash of turmeric), or 1 whole egg plus 2 whites, or 2 whole eggs

▼ for an *Italian Omelet*, fill the Basic Omelet with a mixture of ⅓ cup lite ricotta cheese, 1 teaspoon minced fresh parsley, ¼ teaspoon dried basil or oregano, and a dash of freshly ground black pepper; top with Chunky Tomato Sauce (page 135)

▼ for an *Oriental Omelet*, fill the omelet with steamed asparagus spears; top with Ginger Sauce (page 47)

FISH AND SHELLFISH

▾ ▾ ▾

▼ To freshen fish and remove "fishiness," soak it in milk for 10 minutes before cooking.

▼ Low-fat fish (lower than 2.5 percent) include cod, flounder, grouper, haddock, Pacific halibut, red snapper, sole, and whiting. Medium-fat fish (2.5- to 5-percent fat) include Atlantic halibut, swordfish, and yellow fin tuna. Higher fat fish (over 5-percent fat) include anchovies, Pacific herring, Atlantic mackerel, pompano, salmon, sardines, and tuna (albacore, bluefin, and white).

During the years that I happily existed on a lacto-ovo vegetarian diet, restaurant chefs loaded their vegetarian entrées with cheese—their way to compensate for the absence of meat. So, when I ate out, my choices often were limited to those high-fat entrées, omelets, or salads. Though I had always felt morally virtuous for going "meatless," my real motivation was the pursuit of good health. But as I became increasingly aware of the benefits of a low-fat diet, I realized that the more healthful menu choices often were broiled, baked, or grilled fish and shellfish. I could easily request that they be cooked without added butter or salt, and the sauces could be served on the side. Best of all, I discovered that I really enjoyed these foods!

Lean fish and shellfish are relatively low in calories, and most of the fat is polyunsaturated. All types of fish and seafood are excellent sources of protein and good sources of thiamin, riboflavin, and niacin.

Studies show that the anticlogging action of the polyunsaturated omega-3 fatty acids found in fish (and also in leafy vegetables and some seeds and oils) can protect against heart disease and arterial problems. Though dietary supplements containing omega-3 are available, their safety has not been adequately established through research. The best way to get your quota is by eating fish two to four, or even more times per week. All fish contain some amount of omega-3's, but darker fleshed fish generally contain more oil and omega-3 fatty acids than those with lighter flesh.

Of the lower fat fish, those which have higher than average amounts of omega-3's include, whitefish, sablefish, and yellow fin tuna (both fresh and canned).

I usually purchase about 4 ounces of fish for a single serving. And fresh, as always, is best. Since fresh fish is quite perishable,

▼ A general rule for cooking fish
is to allow 10 minutes per inch
of thickness at the thickest
part. As fish cooks, its translucent flesh turns opaque. When
it is opaque at the thickest part,
it is done. Perfectly cooked fish
flakes with a fork, another test
of doneness.

▼ Sockeye is the most expensive
canned salmon because of its
rich red flesh and outstanding
flavor. Most plentiful and least
expensive, therefore most often
canned, is pink salmon.

▼ In some areas of the country,
the very large shrimp may be
called "prawns," a term used in
many cities to refer to shrimp
of any size.

▼ Shrimp are low enough in saturated fat that people on low-
cholesterol diets can eat them
in moderation (once a week)
without worry, providing they
are prepared without extra fat.

when you purchase fish be certain that the odor is delicate and mild. Fish steaks and fillets, the cuts I suggest for most of my recipes, should be firm and moist with no dry edges, and the skin should be shiny. If packaged, avoid those in which liquid has accumulated in the package.

Store the fish in the coldest part of your refrigerator and, if possible, prepare it within 24 hours of purchasing, since the flavors deteriorate rapidly. If you do not plan to cook the fish immediately, it should be frozen, ideally for no more than 1 month.

Many supermarkets carry a wide variety of frozen fish. If you do buy frozen fish, be certain it is simply fish, without coatings or stuffings. Check to see that the package is tightly sealed, solid, and free of brown spots, ice crystals, and freezer burn (indicated by white, dry patches around the edges of the fish). When you plan to use frozen fish, allow time for it to thaw in the refrigerator (about 24 hours) or thaw it under cold running water. Room temperature defrosting is unsafe and can result in a mushy texture. Use the fish promptly after thawing because the flavor will deteriorate if it stands long in the liquid. Never refreeze fish.

When you are ready to use fresh or thawed fish, rinse it with cool water and pat dry. Then proceed with your recipe.

There are almost endless ways to cook fish healthfully—grilled, broiled, sautéed, poached, baked, or steamed. Because fish is fragile and cooks quickly, the secret of moist and succulent fish is to watch it closely, no matter which method of preparation you choose.

Canned fish such as salmon and tuna can be used in several of my recipes. Purchase the types packed in water rather than in oil and look for 3½-ounce single-serving cans. Since this fish is already cooked, simply drain and add to the recipe.

The shellfish I have used in this chapter include shrimp, scallops, and clams. Like fish, shellfish are rich in protein and numerous minerals including phosphorus, iron, iodine, and magnesium. Shellfish vary in cholesterol and fat content.

I prefer using fresh shrimp or, if necessary, those which have been frozen only for shipping. (I avoid the packaged frozen shrimp which have been frozen for months.) Cleaning, deveining, and cooking shrimp take only a short time in quantities for 1 serving. Allow about 4 ounces of shrimp per serving.

When buying either fresh shrimp or scallops, be certain they have been well refrigerated and that they are mild-smelling and firm in texture. Store the package in the coldest part of your refrigerator and use within a day of purchase. If they are frozen, make sure the package is tightly sealed and free of ice crystals. Thaw in your refrigerator or under cold running water rather than at room temperature. Once thawed, use the shellfish promptly and do not refreeze. Before cooking, rinse your shellfish under cool water and pat dry; then add to your recipe.

Overcooking shellfish results in a tough, rubbery texture with little flavor, so follow the directions carefully. To test for doneness, shrimp should be firm and pink, usually 3 to 4 minutes of total cooking time. Scallops should be firm with the centers opaque and white.

For ease and speed of preparation, buy canned clams. They need only to be drained and rinsed before being added to recipes.

Start your meal preparation by making your salad and organizing all of the ingredients for the entrée. Because fish and shellfish cook so quickly, begin to steam your vegetables and to heat your rice or cook your pasta to accompany these dishes before you start cooking the seafood. By following this plan, your entire meal can be ready to eat at the same time.

SAUTÉED FISH AND SHELLFISH

Sautéing fish takes just a few minutes and is one of my favorite methods for preparing thin fillets like sole and snapper. This technique will also allow you to watch closely to avoid overcooking scallops and shrimp. My recipes call for a thin film of oil to cover the surface of your pan; however, if you are intent on cooking with even less fat, the procedure can be accomplished using spray oil. Either method will work best if a nonstick skillet is used. Follow the suggested times, turning the fish only once and promptly removing it from the pan when it is done. The flavorings and sauces will make these fish and shellfish entrées the focal point of your meal.

CARIBBEAN SOLE

▼ ▼ ▼

1 teaspoon olive oil
1 tablespoon sliced almonds
1 small banana (at room temperature), cut into ¼-inch slices
1 tablespoon lemon juice
1 sole fillet (about 4 ounces)

GARNISH: *minced fresh parsley or sprig cilantro (fresh coriander)*

In a medium-size skillet heat the olive oil over medium heat. Add the almonds and cook, stirring, for 2 to 3 minutes to brown lightly. Add the banana slices; cook, stirring gently, until the bananas are softened and lightly browned, about 1 minute. Stir in the lemon juice. Remove this mixture from the skillet, transfer to a bowl, and cover to keep warm.

Place the sole in the skillet; cook over medium heat for about 2 minutes, to brown lightly; turn and cook until the fish flakes with a fork, about 2 minutes.

To serve, using a spatula, carefully remove the fish from the skillet and place on a serving plate. Top with the banana-almond mixture. Garnish with parsley or cilantro.

Sole is a mild-flavored fish which I particularly enjoy sautéed with tropical fruit. I first had a dish similar to this in Jamaica; the flavors still bring back fond memories of dining alfresco with those warm ocean breezes.

TIPS

▼ Bananas should ripen at room temperature; use them within 2 to 3 days after the green disappears. For baking, broiling, and sautéing, bananas which are still slightly green will retain the best texture.

Sole, a fish in the flounder family, has a mild flavor and light texture. Winter flounder from New England is sometimes called "lemon sole"; other flounders are offered as "gray sole," "petrole sole" (a Pacific flounder), or "rex sole." Dover sole is the name for either a type of Pacific flounder or for a type of sole imported from England.

Here, fresh strawberries are combined with some unlikely ingredients to create a unique fish topping. Serve this salsa with other sautéed, poached, or broiled fish. It pairs well with chicken, too.

Calories 339 (29% from fat)/Protein 30.2g/Carb 29.7g/Fat 11g/Chol 77mg/Sodium 121mg/Calcium 50mg/Food Exchanges: Fruit 1.8/Meat 3.8/Fat 1.7

VARIATIONS
▼ in place of the banana slices, substitute slices of fresh mango or sauté a peach or nectarine, peeled and cut into ¼-inch slices
▼ for the sole, substitute other white fish such as perch, cod, halibut, or walleye fillets; some may be thicker than sole and require a longer cooking time

SOLE ALMANDINE WITH STRAWBERRY SALSA
▼ ▼ ▼

FOR THE STRAWBERRY SALSA
⅓ cup cubed strawberries (about 6), preferably at room temperature (¼-inch to ½-inch cubes)
½ scallion (green parts), chopped
½ teaspoon currants
1 teaspoon white rice vinegar
¼ teaspoon Dijon mustard
¼ teaspoon grated lime rind

FOR THE SOLE ALMANDINE
½ teaspoon olive oil
2 teaspoons sliced almonds
2 teaspoons fresh lime juice
½ teaspoon grated lime rind
1 sole fillet (about 4 ounces)

GARNISH: *sprig cilantro (fresh coriander) or parsley; lime wedges*

ADVANCE PREPARATION

The Strawberry Salsa may be made a few hours in advance. Refrigerate, covered; bring to room temperature to serve. Prepare the fish just before serving.

▼ ▼ ▼

TIPS

▼ Cilantro, often sold as fresh coriander or Chinese parsley, is an ancient herb indigenous to the Mediterranean. Its fresh leafy form, found in oriental, Vietnamese, and Thai markets, as well as in supermarkets, has a pungent flavor. The leaves are often used uncooked; if added to a cooked recipe, do so near the end of the cooking period. The dried form is unacceptable. If fresh is unavailable, substitute fresh Italian flat-leaf parsley, or even curly parsley.

To prepare the salsa, in a small bowl, toss together the strawberries, scallion, and currants. In a measuring cup, whisk together the vinegar, mustard, and lime rind. Pour over the strawberry mixture and toss. Set aside at room temperature.

In a small skillet, heat the olive oil over medium heat. Add the almonds; cook, stirring constantly, until lightly browned. Remove the pan from the heat, stir in the lime juice and rind. Spoon the contents of the pan into a small bowl, leaving some of the moisture on the pan surface. Cover the almond mixture and set aside.

Place the skillet over medium heat. Add the sole fillet; cook until the fish is cooked through and flakes with a fork, about 2 minutes on each side. To serve, using a spatula, place the fish on a serving plate. Top with the sautéed almond mixture. Spoon the salsa next to the fish. Garnish with cilantro or parsley and wedges of lime.

Calories 208 (30% from fat)/Protein 29gm/Carb 7.3gm/Fat 7gm/Chol 77mg/Sodium 123mg/Calcium 47mg/Food Exchanges: Fruit 0.3/Meat 3.8/Fat 1.0

Salsa (entire recipe): Calories 24 (8% from fat)/Protein 0.4g/Carb 5.1g/Fat 0.2g/Chol 0/Sodium 4mg/Calcium 10mg/Food Exchanges: Fruit 0.3

VARIATIONS

▼ in the Strawberry Salsa, for the strawberries, substitute cubed grapefruit, cubed papaya, or cubed mango, or 1 kiwi, cubed, or use a combination of strawberries and kiwi

▼ for the rice vinegar, substitute white wine vinegar, red wine vinegar, or raspberry vinegar, or lime, lemon, or orange juice

▼ to the Strawberry Salsa, add 1 teaspoon coarsely chopped cilantro (fresh coriander)

▼ for the sole, substitute a fillet of other mild-flavored white fish such as perch, cod, halibut, or walleye

▼ the fish may be broiled rather than sautéed

▼ for the lime juice, substitute lemon juice or orange juice

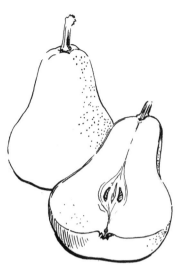

SEA SCALLOPS IN CHUTNEY, APPLE, AND PEAR SAUCE

▼ ▼ ▼

2 tablespoons store-bought chutney
¼ cup skim milk
1 teaspoon olive oil
¼ apple (preferably at room temperature), peeled, cored, and
*   cut into ¼-inch slices*
5 sea scallops (4 to 5 ounces)
½ pear (preferably at room temperature), peeled, cored, and
*   cut into ¼-inch slices*

GARNISH: *sprig fresh parsley*

In a measuring cup or small bowl, stir together the chutney and milk. Set aside.

Heat the olive oil in a medium-size skillet over medium heat. Add the apple slices and cook, stirring, for 1 minute. Add the scallops and pear slices; cook, stirring occasionally, 2 minutes more. Reduce the heat to low; stir in the chutney mixture. Cook, stirring constantly, until the sauce is smooth, evenly distributed, and heated through, 2 minutes. (Do not allow the sauce to simmer or boil.) Check the scallops for doneness. Serve immediately with your choice of garnish.

Calories 302 (18% from fat)/Protein 21.5g/Carb 40.7g/Fat 5.9g/Chol 38mg/Sodium 222mg/Calcium 115mg/Food Exchanges: Milk 0.2/Fruit 2.3/Meat 2.6/Fat 0.9

VARIATIONS
▼ use either apples or pears rather than a combination

TIPS

▼ Chutney is a mixture of fruit and/or vegetables cooked with vinegar, sugar, and spices. It can be served alone or used as an ingredient in sauces. Most often made with mango, it is found in most supermarkets.

▼ Bay scallops are small, cream-colored, and tender. They are sweeter, have a more delicate flavor, and are more expensive than sea scallops, which are larger, very slightly tougher, more plentiful, and readily available. Sea scallops can be cut into ½-inch pieces to use in recipes calling for bay scallops.

CURRIED SHRIMP WITH BANANA

▼ ▼ ▼

This is the ultimate in simple elegance and superb taste, yet it is easy and exceptionally quick to make. For the banana, substitute papaya or mango for a tropical dining experience.

TIPS

▼ When you heat oil in a pan for sautéing, the test for hotness is to splash a drop of water on the oil. When the oil is hot enough, the water will make a sizzling sound.

▼ It is not necessary to devein a shrimp for health's sake; however, the shrimp will be more attractive if you do. To do so, remove the shell, then, using a sharp knife, make a shallow cut lengthwise down the outermost curve of each shrimp. Remove the sand vein with the point of a knife, then rinse under cold running water.

FOR THE CURRY SAUCE
¼ teaspoon lime zest
2 tablespoons fresh lime juice
½ teaspoon sugar
½ teaspoon curry powder
Dash of ground cloves

FOR THE SHRIMP
½ teaspoon olive oil
4 to 5 large shrimp (4 to 5 ounces), shelled and deveined
1 tablespoon chopped scallion (green parts)
¼ teaspoon minced garlic
½ medium-size banana (at room temperature), cut into 8 strips 1½ inches by ½ inch

GARNISH: *sprig cilantro (fresh coriander) or parsley*

In a measuring cup or small bowl, stir together the sauce ingredients. Set aside.

In a small skillet, heat the olive oil over medium-high heat. Add the shrimp, scallion, and garlic; cook, stirring, for 2 minutes, making certain the shrimp are cooked on both sides. Reduce the heat to low, add the banana strips, and continue to cook, stirring gently, for 1 minute.

Pour the sauce over the ingredients in the skillet. Heat for about 30 seconds; the sauce will be absorbed and reduced. Spoon onto a serving plate; garnish.

Calories 218 (19% from fat)/Protein 24g/Carb 20.2g/Fat 4.6g/Chol 175mg/Sodium 172mg/Calcium 75mg/Food Exchanges: Fruit 1.0/Meat 3.2/Fat 0.4

VARIATIONS

▼ for the banana, substitute strips of papaya or mango

BROILED FISH AND SHELLFISH

Broiling is an excellent method for preparing moist, higher fat, and flavorful fish which are at least ¾ inch thick, such as salmon steaks. Begin by adjusting your oven rack to 4 to 5 inches from the heating element and preheat your oven broiler before organizing the recipe ingredients. Brush both sides of the fish lightly with oil to add and seal in moisture; then place the fish on a lightly oiled broiler pan or baking sheet. Sprinkle with pepper and your favorite dried herb or seasoning mixture. Broil the fish until it is cooked through, about 10 minutes, or slightly less, per inch of thickness measured at the thickest part of the fish. Turn the fish once about halfway through the cooking period.

Simple broiled fish may be accompanied by a sauce such as Orange Curry Sauce (page 95), Lemon-Sesame Sauce (page 97), Sesame-Ginger Sauce (page 121), Chunky Tomato Sauce

TIPS

▼ A typical marinade has three components: acid, oil, and aromatics. The acid helps break down the fibers, acting as a tenderizer. The oil coats the exterior of the meat, fish, or seafood, preventing it from drying out during cooking. The aromatics add flavor.

▼ Use a glass, ceramic, or stainless steel dish for marinating.

- Always marinate your food in the refrigerator rather than at room temperature to avoid spoilage.
- A simple method is to marinate food in a sealed plastic bag set in a bowl, turning the bag occasionally to coat the entire surface of the food. When finished, simply discard the bag.
- The longer a food is left in a marinade, the more flavor it absorbs. Thirty minutes is a minimum; six to twenty-four hours is usually best for the flavor to be absorbed into thicker pieces of fish, like salmon steaks, and for chicken. Thin delicate pieces of fish will become mushy if marinated for too long.
- Be sure to drain the marinated food well before broiling or grilling; use the reserved marinade for basting during cooking. Then discard the remaining marinade; it is not recommended to reuse a marinade nor to use it as a sauce for the cooked fish or chicken.

(page 135), Herbed Tomato Sauce (page 34), or Strawberry Salsa (page 77).

For additional moistness, seafood (and chicken) is often marinated before broiling and then basted during the broiling period. Marinating is also one of the best ways to give food flavor without adding excess fat. My nutritional analyses include only the amount of marinade actually consumed.

In addition to the marinades in this chapter, any of the five marinades in the chicken chapter can be used for seafood. And within this chapter, feel free to use the marinades for fish or shellfish other than those specified in the recipe.

As for accompaniments, a green salad, crusty bread, perhaps some steamed vegetables, and rice or pasta will make your meal complete. Be sure to consider many of the pasta or grain entrées in those chapters as side dishes when planning your meals centered around broiled fish or shellfish. Because broiling requires so little time, start your accompaniments before placing your entrée under the broiler.

And don't overlook using broiled fish, warm or chilled, as a salad ingredient. Arrange it on top or toss it with greens. Or break up the broiled seafood, toss it with low-fat mayonnaise and/or yogurt, add flavoring such as chutney, and stuff the mixture into pita bread or a tomato half.

BROILED SALMON WITH LIME-GINGER MARINADE

▼ ▼ ▼

Sometimes, in the summer, I broil this flavorful salmon in advance and serve it later chilled on a bed of shredded salad spinach tossed with Ginger-Soy Vinaigrette (page 196).

▼ ▼ ▼

ADVANCE PREPARATION
The salmon can be broiled in advance, refrigerated, and served chilled later the same day.

▼ ▼ ▼

TIPS
▼ Zesting removes long thin strips of citrus rind; it is done with a kitchen gadget called a zester, which has a short, flat blade with a beveled end and 5 small holes. When drawn over the skin of a lemon, lime, or orange, the tool removes long thin strips of the colored zest. Ideally, zest before cutting the fruit and work over the dish you are preparing to make use of the oils, too.

FOR THE LIME-GINGER MARINADE
¼ teaspoon lime zest
1 tablespoon fresh lime juice
½ teaspoon olive oil
1 teaspoon low-sodium soy sauce
¼ teaspoon dark sesame oil
¼ teaspoon grated fresh ginger
Dash of freshly ground black pepper
1 scallion (green parts), julienned

FOR THE SALMON
1 salmon steak (4 to 5 ounces)
Vegetable oil spray

In a measuring cup or small bowl, stir together the marinade ingredients. Pour half of the marinade into the bottom of a glass baking dish or flat refrigerator container. Place the salmon on top; pour on the remaining marinade. Refrigerate, covered, for at least 30 minutes or up to 24 hours, turning the salmon occasionally.

When ready to cook, place the oven rack 4 to 5 inches from the heating element and preheat the oven broiler. Coat a baking sheet or broiler pan lightly with vegetable oil spray.

Remove the salmon steak from the marinade and place on the prepared pan, reserving the excess marinade and julienned scallion. Broil the salmon for 5 minutes, turn, and brush with marinade. Broil the second side for about 5 minutes; check to be certain salmon is cooked through. Discard the remaining marinade. To serve, place the salmon on serving plate, topped with the reserved scallion.

Calories 180 (42% from fat)/Protein 24.8g/Carb 1.2g/Fat 8.5g/Chol 44mg/Sodium 152mg/Calcium 3mg/Food Exchanges: Meat 3.4/Fat 0.3

Lime-Ginger Marinade (1/2 recipe); Calories 21 (73% from fat)/Protein 0.2g/Carb 1.2g/Fat 1.7g/Chol 0/Sodium 100mg/Calcium 3mg/Food Exchanges: Fat 0.3

VARIATIONS

▼ for the Lime-Ginger Marinade, substitute Teriyaki Marinade (page 130)
▼ use the Lime-Ginger Marinade on other fish or seafood such as fresh tuna, halibut, shrimp, or scallops

TUNA-VEGETABLE KABOBS WITH MAPLE-SOY MARINADE

▼ ▼ ▼

FOR THE MAPLE-SOY MARINADE
1 tablespoon low-sodium soy sauce
1 tablespoon mirin
1 teaspoon pure maple syrup
1 teaspoon dark sesame oil
½ teaspoon grated fresh ginger
¼ teaspoon minced garlic

FOR THE TUNA-VEGETABLE KABOBS
1 tuna steak (4 to 6 ounces), cut into 5 chunks about 1½ inches by 1 inch
Vegetable oil spray
Three 1½ by 1-inch strips yellow bell pepper
Three 1½ by 1-inch strips red bell pepper
Three 1½ by ½-inch strips onion
3 medium-size mushrooms

▼ When it comes to tuna, yellowfin tuna contains 8% fat; bluefin 32%!
▼ Mirin, a sweet rice wine for cooking, is used as a seasoning and sweetener. During cooking, the alcohol evaporates, leaving a flavor and glaze that is distinctly Japanese. Mirin is available at Asian markets and in the gourmet or oriental section of many supermarkets.

▼ For the best flavor and quality, buy "pure," not "maple-flavored" syrup, which is stretched with corn syrup. Even less desirable is "pancake syrup" which rarely contains any maple syrup. Once open, maple syrup should be refrigerated. If crystals develop, immerse the container in a pan of hot water until they disappear.

SPECIAL EQUIPMENT: *two 8-inch bamboo skewers (or one 14-inch metal skewer)*

In a medium-size bowl, stir together the marinade ingredients. Place the tuna chunks in a flat glass pan or refrigerator container; stir in the marinade. Cover and refrigerate for a minimum of 30 minutes or up to 24 hours, stirring at least once.

Prior to cooking, place the oven broiler rack 4 to 5 inches from the heating element. Preheat the broiler. Spray a baking sheet or broiler pan with vegetable oil spray.

Thread the tuna onto the skewers, alternating with bell peppers, onion, and mushrooms. Reserve the remaining marinade. Place the skewers on the prepared pan. Baste the vegetables with the marinade. Broil for 3 minutes, turn, and baste the tuna and vegetables with the marinade. Broil for about 2 minutes on the second side. Check to be certain the tuna is cooked through. Discard the remaining marinade and serve.

(using yellowfin tuna): Calories 187 (17% from fat)/Protein 28.2g/Carb 10.5g/Fat 3.6g/Chol 51mg/Sodium 348mg/Calcium 33mg/Food Exchanges: Veg 1.1/Meat 3.7/Fat 0.4

(using bluefin tuna): Calories 227 (32% from fat)/Protein 28.1g/Carb 10.5g/Fat 8g/Chol 43mg/Sodium 350mg/Calcium 15mg/Food Exchanges: same

Maple-Soy Marinade (½ recipe): Calories 38 (54% from fat)/Protein 0.5g/Carb 3.8g/Fat 2.3g/Chol 0/Sodium 304mg/Calcium 3mg/Food Exchanges: Fat 0.4

VARIATIONS

▼ for the Maple-Soy Marinade, substitute 3 tablespoons store-bought lite teriyaki sauce or Lime-Ginger Marinade (page 83)

▼ in place of the tuna steaks, substitute other firm-fleshed fish such as halibut or 4 sea scallops; the vegetables can be omitted, if desired

▼ as you thread the skewers, substitute or add cherry tomatoes, partially cooked new potatoes, chunks of zucchini, or other vegetables

POACHED FISH

Poaching fish is accomplished by cooking the fish while it is immersed in a simmering liquid; since poaching adds moisture, it is a good choice for cooking the drier, lower fat types of fish. The flavored liquids will transfer flavor and moisture to your fish as it cooks without adding any fat.

Select a skillet which is large enough to accommodate the fish in a single layer. In general, add enough liquid to barely cover the fish. Heat the poaching liquid over medium-high heat until it comes to a boil. Reduce the heat to medium and add the fish. Cook, either covered or uncovered, keeping the liquid at a simmer rather than at a rapid boil; cook for 10 minutes per inch of thickness. The fish is done when it is cooked through and flakes when tested with a fork at its thickest point.

Poached fish can be served warm or chilled and served with a sauce such as Orange Curry Sauce (page 95). And, for variety and protein, add warm or chilled poached fish to pasta recipes and green salads.

ORANGE POACHED WALLEYE

▼ ▼ ▼

½ cup orange juice
½ teaspoon dried tarragon or 2 teaspoons minced fresh
Dash of freshly ground black pepper
Zest of 1 orange
1 walleye fillet (about 4 ounces)

GARNISH: *minced fresh parsley, orange slice*

When life is busy, simplicity is the key. Ready to eat in minutes, this is my standby for preparing fish in a hurry.

TIPS

▼ One way to check fish for freshness is to press it with your finger. If the flesh springs back, the fish is fresh. If a dent remains, it isn't.

In a small skillet, stir together the orange juice, tarragon, pepper, and orange zest. Bring to a boil over high heat. Reduce the heat to medium; add the fillet. Cook, uncovered, as the liquid simmers, for about 2 minutes. Turn and cook the other side until the fish is cooked through and flakes with a fork, about 2 minutes. Using a spatula, remove the fish and place on a serving plate; cover to keep warm.

Reduce the heat to low; continue cooking the orange juice, stirring constantly, until the mixture darkens and is reduced, 1 to 2 minutes. Pour over the fillet, garnish, and serve.

Calories 164 (9% from fat)/Protein 22.8g/Carb 14.6g/Fat 1.6g/Chol 97mg/Sodium 59mg/Calcium 152mg/Food Exchanges: Fruit 0.8/Meat 3.0

VARIATIONS

▼ for the tarragon, substitute dillweed
▼ for the walleye, substitute a fillet of another mild-flavored white fish such as orange roughy, cod, or sole
▼ rather than reducing the orange juice mixture, serve the fillet with Orange Curry Sauce (page 95)

SOLE WITH
ALMOND-CURRANT SAUCE

▼ ▼ ▼

TIPS

▼ Parsley is a good herb to blend with others because it has a less dominant sweet flavor. Italian parsley, with its broad flat leaves, has the more interesting flavor; curly parsley may also be used for cooking and is an attractive garnish. Dried parsley doesn't compare in flavor; fresh parsley is inexpensive and keeps well in the refrigerator.

▼ To mince parsley very finely, place it under running water to clean; then dry it with a dish towel so the pieces will not stick together as you use an electric mincer, a food processor, or a French chef's knife. If you have excess minced parsley, it can be frozen and spooned out as needed for recipes.

FOR THE ALMOND-CURRANT SAUCE
¼ cup water
¼ teaspoon vegetable stock powder
2 teaspoons sliced or slivered almonds
1 tablespoon minced fresh parsley
½ teaspoon olive oil
½ teaspoon minced garlic
¼ teaspoon dried oregano or 1 teaspoon minced fresh
⅛ teaspoon freshly ground black pepper
1 tablespoon currants

TO COMPLETE THE DISH
1 sole fillet (about 4 ounces)

GARNISH: *sprig fresh parsley*

To prepare the sauce, in a measuring cup dissolve the stock powder in the water. Pour into a food processor or blender. Add the almonds, parsley, olive oil, garlic, oregano, and pepper; purée. Stir in the currants.

Pour the sauce into a small skillet; bring it to a boil over medium-high heat. Reduce the heat to medium-low; add the fish. Cover and cook until the fish is cooked through and flakes with a fork, about 2 minutes on each side. Using a slotted spatula, remove the fish from the skillet; place on a serving plate and cover to keep warm.

Reduce the heat to low; cook the sauce, uncovered, stirring constantly until the sauce is reduced to about 2 tablespoons, 1 to 2 minutes. Spoon the sauce and currants over the fish. Garnish and serve.

Calories 216 (29% from fat)/Protein 29.2g/Carb 9.3g/Fat 6.9g/Chol 77mg/Sodium 123mg/Calcium 55mg/Food Exchanges: Veg 0.2/Fruit 0.4/Meat 3.8/Fat 1.0

VARIATIONS

▼ for the oregano, substitute other herbs such as basil, dill, marjoram, or tarragon
▼ for the sole, substitute other fish such as a walleye fillet or orange roughy

BAKED FISH AND SHELLFISH

Basic fish baking is uncomplicated. The method works best with oily fish, but leaner fish can also be baked, if moisture is added. Preheat the oven to 350° to 400° F. Place the fish in a shallow baking dish, brush with oil, sprinkle with lemon juice, pepper, parsley, or herbs—or cover with a sauce, which can be as simple as your favorite store-bought pasta sauce—and bake, uncovered, until the fish flakes easily. As usual, this will require about 10 minutes per inch of thickness. This method requires little supervision and frees your time for preparing other components of your meal.

The magic of this recipe is the blending of flavors when the goat cheese melts into the tomato sauce. My friend Nancy multiplies this recipe to use for special occasion entertaining.

▼ ▼ ▼

ADVANCE PREPARATION
This may be assembled in the baking dish several hours in advance; refrigerate. If chilled, add about 2 minutes to the baking time.

▼ ▼ ▼

TIPS
▼ Crushed red pepper, or red pepper flakes, are the seeds and flakes of fiery hot peppers; a small amount will go a long way!
▼ Dried rosemary tends to be a splintery herb. To enhance the flavor and improve the texture, crush the leaves between your fingers before adding to your recipe. Especially in dried form, rosemary has a bold taste; use it sparingly.

BAKED SALMON WITH GOAT CHEESE

▼ ▼ ▼

¼ teaspoon olive oil
1 teaspoon minced shallot
One 8-ounce can tomatoes, with ½ cup of the juice
¼ teaspoon dried rosemary, crushed, or 1 teaspoon minced fresh
Pinch of crushed red pepper, or to taste
Dash of freshly ground black pepper, or to taste
Olive oil spray
1 salmon fillet (4 to 5 ounces)
1 tablespoon goat cheese (chevre)

GARNISH: sprig cilantro (fresh coriander) or parsley

Preheat the oven to 375° F. Heat the olive oil in a small saucepan over medium heat. Add the shallot and cook, stirring, until tender but not brown, about 1 minute. Stir in the tomatoes with juice, rosemary, and red and black pepper. Cut the tomatoes into quarters. Cook, uncovered, stirring occasionally, until the sauce is reduced, 4 minutes. Taste; adjust seasoning.

Meanwhile, spray a 1-quart baking dish with olive oil. Place the salmon fillet in the baking dish, skin side down. Pour the tomato sauce over and around the fish; place the dollop of goat cheese on top of the fish. Cover and bake 10 to 12 minutes, checking to be sure the salmon is cooked through.

Using a spatula, place the fish on a serving plate; spoon the tomatoes and sauce around and over the fish. Garnish and serve.

Calories 264 (40% from fat)/Protein 28.8g/Carb 10.9g/Fat 11.6g/Chol 54mg/Sodium 473mg/Calcium 60mg/Food Exchanges: Veg 1.9/Meat 3.4/Fat 0.2

- To remove fresh rosemary leaves, run 2 fingers along the length of the stem.
- The skin of salmon will help to hold it together as it bakes. It is edible, but most people prefer to eat around it.

▼ ▼ ▼

ADVANCE PREPARATION
The fish and cooked sauce with feta cheese topping may be assembled in the baking dish several hours in advance; refrigerate. If chilled, add about 2 minutes to the baking time.

▼ ▼ ▼

TIPS
- Use a serrated knife to cut tomatoes.
- To peel a tomato, immerse it in a pot of boiling water for 15 to 60 seconds, depending on the size and the ripeness, just long enough to loosen the skin with-

VARIATIONS
- for the rosemary, substitute other herbs such as basil or oregano
- for the salmon fillet, substitute other fish such as a rainbow trout fillet or a salmon steak
- for the goat cheese, substitute mild feta cheese
- omit the goat cheese; add a dollop of Chevre Cream (page 159) after the fish has baked

GREEK SNAPPER WITH FETA CHEESE

▼ ▼ ▼

¼ teaspoon olive oil
1 tablespoon minced shallot
1 medium-size tomato, peeled and cut into ½-inch cubes (1 cup)
¼ teaspoon dried oregano or 1 teaspoon minced fresh
⅛ teaspoon freshly ground black pepper, or to taste
Olive oil spray
1 red snapper fillet (about 4 ounces)
1 tablespoon crumbled mild feta cheese
1 teaspoon capers, drained and rinsed
1 teaspoon minced fresh parsley

GARNISH: *sprig fresh Italian flat-leaf parsley*

Preheat the oven to 375° F. In a small skillet over medium heat, heat the olive oil. Add the shallot; cook, stirring, until tender but not brown, about 1 minute. Add the tomato, oregano, and pepper; cook, uncovered, stirring occasionally, until the tomato is softened, about 4 minutes. Taste; adjust seasonings.

out cooking the tomato. Remove with a slotted spoon and plunge immediately into a bowl of cold water. Cut the stem with a sharp knife and peel the skin down in strips; they should come off easily.

▼ Do not refrigerate tomatoes until they are fully ripe—they are most flavorful at room temperature. (If you do store them in your refrigerator, take them out an hour or so before serving.) To ripen, put tomatoes in a closed paper bag with a few holes in it. Once ripe, they will usually keep about 1 week.

This is my favorite way to prepare shrimp! The technique of cooking *en papillote* can be used for many other types of shellfish and fish, too.

▼ ▼ ▼

ADVANCE PREPARATION

The packet may be assembled and refrigerated up to 1 hour before baking. Baking time will be slightly longer if the contents are chilled.

▼ ▼ ▼

Meanwhile, spray a small shallow baking dish with olive oil. Place the fish in center of the dish; top with the cooked tomato mixture. Bake, uncovered, until the fish flakes easily with a fork, about 10 minutes.

While the fish is cooking, in a small bowl, toss together the feta cheese, capers, and minced parsley. Set aside. When the fish is done, using a spatula, carefully remove it from the baking dish; transfer it to a serving plate. Spoon on the tomato mixture; top with the cheese mixture. Garnish and serve.

Calories 179 (25% from fat)/Protein 25.8g/Carb 8g/Fat 4.9g/Chol 50mg/Sodium 180mg/Calcium 92mg/Food Exchanges: Veg 1.1/Meat 3.4/Fat 0.4

VARIATION

▼ for the oregano, substitute thyme

SHRIMP IN PARCHMENT

▼ ▼ ▼

1 teaspoon olive oil
½ medium-size carrot, cut into 2 by ⅛-inch strips
½ rib celery, cut into 2 by ⅛-inch strips
¼ leek, white part only, cut into 2 by ⅛-inch strips
4 to 5 large shrimp (4 to 5 ounces), shelled and deveined
Dash of ground white pepper
Two ¼-inch-thick slices plum tomato
1 teaspoon minced fresh parsley

SPECIAL EQUIPMENT: *1 sheet parchment paper, about 16 inches in length*

Preheat the oven to 425° F. (1) Fold the sheet of parchment in half and cut into the shape of a half circle. Set aside.

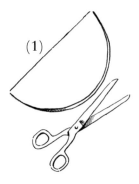

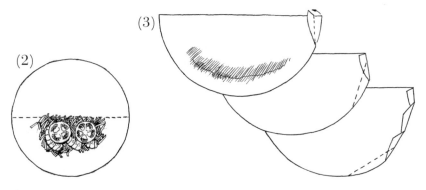

TIPS

▼ In some cookbooks you will see instructions for creating baking packets from aluminum foil. Since the aluminum may seep into the food, I don't like that method and prefer using natural paper packets.

▼ Parchment for cooking is available in the plastic and aluminum wrap aisle in most supermarkets. When foods such as fish, chicken, vegetables, or fruits are cooked in parchment pockets, *en papillote*, no added fat is necessary and nutrients are retained. Parchment can also be used to line baking pans and baking sheets as an oil-free method to prevent cakes, cookies, or broiled foods from sticking.

Heat ½ teaspoon of the olive oil in a small skillet over medium heat. Add the carrot, celery, and leek; cook, stirring, until softened, 4 to 5 minutes. Remove the pan from the heat. (2) Open the parchment circle. Place the sautéed vegetables in the center of one half of the paper. Top with the shrimp, arranging them side by side in a single layer. Drizzle with the remaining olive oil; sprinkle with pepper. Place the tomato slices on top; sprinkle with the parsley.

(3) Close the parchment flap. Seal the parchment by starting at one end; fold the cut edges toward the packet contents, creating many small overlapping folds. Be sure to fold the edges tightly to keep the juices in. Place the parchment packet on a baking sheet; bake for about 6 minutes. Open the packet and check the shrimp for doneness. To serve, place the parchment packet on a serving plate.

Calories 203 (30% from fat)/Protein 24.3g/Carb 11.3g/Fat 6.7g/Chol 175mg/Sodium 210mg/Calcium 100mg/Food Exchanges: Veg 1.7/Meat 3.2/Fat 0.9

VARIATIONS

▼ for the leek, substitute scallion whites
▼ for the shrimp, substitute sea scallops (bake for about 8 minutes) or a fish steak or fillet (increase baking time to 10 to 15 minutes)

STEAMED FISH

The secret of steaming is simply that the food cooks above—not in—water. Vegetables retain their vitamins and color; fish retains its moisture. Any fish that can be poached is also appropriate to steam.

For minimal expense, you can purchase a steamer. I think the most aesthetically pleasing are Chinese bamboo steaming baskets. Other steamers are made from aluminum, stainless steel, or pottery. You can also improvise by placing a colander into a pot with a tight-fitting lid.

Whichever type of steamer you choose, the procedure is the same. Pour an inch or so of water into a pot, and place your steamer inside. Make sure the water level is below the floor of the steamer. Remove the steamer, and arrange the food in it. Bring the water in the pot to a boil; then add the steamer containing the food, covering the pot or the steaming basket with a tight lid. Check the water level occasionally; it may be necessary to add hot water during cooking. Steaming time will depend on the size and density of the ingredients.

You can line your steamer with cheesecloth to make it easier to remove the fish and vegetables; or wrap the fish in cheesecloth to prevent thin, tender pieces of fish from falling apart in the steamer. I usually pair thick pieces of fish with dense, slower-cooking vegetables and thin fish fillets with more tender, quick-cooking vegetables so they can all be placed in the steamer together and will be done at the same time. But if you prefer, with some practice you can pair any foods; just plan to steam the denser foods longer.

Ingredients, such as ginger, can add some flavor while the foods steam, but because steaming imparts mild tastes, I usually prepare an interesting sauce to accompany the steamed foods.

With the addition of a green salad and rice, you'll have a complete meal.

STEAMED HALIBUT AND VEGETABLES WITH ORANGE CURRY SAUCE

▼ ▼ ▼

This flavorful sauce is a great complement to mild steamed halibut. Add more curry powder for a zestier flavor.

▼ ▼ ▼

ADVANCE PREPARATION
The Orange Curry Sauce can be made several hours in advance and refrigerated; steam the fish and vegetables just before serving

▼ ▼ ▼

1 halibut steak, ¾ to 1 inch thick (about 4 ounces)
¼ teaspoon olive oil
½ medium-size carrot, cut into ¼-inch slices (¼ cup)
½ cup cauliflower florets
½ cup broccoli florets

FOR THE ORANGE CURRY SAUCE
¼ cup low-fat plain yogurt
2 teaspoons orange juice
1 tablespoon minced fresh parsley
1 teaspoon minced scallion (green parts)
½ teaspoon curry powder, or to taste
¼ teaspoon honey
Dash of freshly ground black pepper, or to taste

GARNISH: *toasted sesame seeds (pages 30–31), sprig cilantro (fresh coriander), orange zest*

If you like, line the steamer with a doubled layer of cheesecloth.

Brush one side of the halibut steak lightly with the olive oil. Place the fish in the steamer, oiled side down. Surround the fish with the carrot slices, cauliflower, and broccoli.

Bring ½ to 1 inch of water to a boil in a skillet over medium-high heat. (The amount depends on the steamer design.) Cover the steamer and place in the skillet. (Or if you are using a saucepan with a steamer insert, cover the saucepan.) Steam until the fish flakes easily with a fork and the vegetables are crisp-tender, 8 to 10 minutes. (Be sure to check the water level and add more hot water, if necessary.)

▼ Rubbing fish with lemon juice before steaming, baking, broiling, or poaching will lend flavor and help to preserve color.

▼ When you buy cauliflower, pick one that is white (or near white), hard, and tightly packed. Store in a sealed plastic bag stem side up to keep moisture from collecting on top in the vegetable crisper drawer; use it within a day or two. Many supermarkets sell separated cauliflower florets, the best choice when only a small amount is needed.

While the fish and vegetables are steaming, combine the sauce ingredients in a small saucepan. Heat, over low heat, stirring constantly for about 3 minutes just to warm. (Do not allow the sauce to boil.) Taste; adjust seasonings. Remove from heat; cover to keep warm.

To serve, with a spatula (or with the cheesecloth) remove the fish and vegetables from the steamer; arrange on a serving plate. Drizzle the sauce over them; garnish.

Calories 227 (20% from fat)/Protein 29.6g/Carb 15.7g/Fat 5.1g/Chol 39mg/Sodium 135mg/Calcium 214mg/Food Exchanges: Milk 0.3/Veg 1.6/Meat 3.3/Fat 0.4

Orange Curry Sauce (entire recipe): Calories 52 (18% from fat)/Protein 3.3g/Carb 7.3g/Fat 1.1g/Chol 3mg/Sodium 42mg/Calcium 115mg/Food Exchanges: Milk 0.3/Fat 0.1

VARIATIONS

▼ for the halibut, substitute other fish such as a salmon steak

▼ substitute or add other vegetables such as cut asparagus, cut green beans, or snap peas (If you add softer vegetables, steam the fish for a few minutes first, then add the vegetables.)

▼ substitute other sauces such as Lemon-Sesame Sauce (page 97), Sesame-Pepper Dressing (page 30), or Ginger Sauce (page 47)

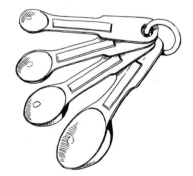

ADVANCE PREPARATION

The Lemon-Sesame Sauce can be made several hours in advance and refrigerated; steam the fish and vegetables just before serving.

▼ ▼ ▼

TIPS

▼ After each use, bamboo steamers must be washed carefully using a brush to remove any trapped food particles; do not wash in the dishwasher.

▼ Be sure to scrub lemons and other citrus fruits well to remove insecticides; dry them thoroughly before grating the rind. Before cutting the fruit, grate diagonally rather than up and down and grate only the outer yellow part with its aromatic oils—the white portion tends to be bitter. Lemons yield about 1 tablespoon grated rind; the thinner peels of limes yield only about ½ teaspoon.

GINGER STEAMED RED SNAPPER WITH LEMON-SESAME SAUCE

▼ ▼ ▼

1 red snapper fillet (about 4 ounces)
¼ teaspoon safflower oil
4 medium-size mushrooms, halved
5 asparagus spears
½ scallion (green parts), cut into thin strips
3 ⅛-inch-thick slices fresh ginger
Three ⅛-inch-thick slices lemon

FOR THE LEMON-SESAME SAUCE

1 tablespoon low-sodium soy sauce
½ teaspoon grated lemon rind
1 tablespoon lemon juice
½ teaspoon dark sesame oil
¼ teaspoon minced garlic
¼ teaspoon sugar

If you like, line the steamer with a double layer of cheesecloth.

Brush one side of the red snapper with the safflower oil. Place the fish in the steamer, oiled side down. Surround the fish with the mushrooms and asparagus; arrange in an even layer not more than 1½ inches deep. Top the fish with the scallion, ginger, and 2 of the lemon slices, in that order.

Bring ½ to 1 inch of water to a boil in a skillet over medium-high heat. (The amount depends on the steamer design.) Cover the steamer and place in the skillet. (Or if you are using a saucepan with a steamer insert, cover the saucepan.) Steam until the fish flakes easily with a fork and the asparagus is crisp-tender, about 4 minutes. (Check the water level and add more water, if necessary.)

While the fish and vegetables are steaming, in a small bowl or measuring cup combine the sauce ingredients, stirring to dissolve the sugar.

To serve, with a spatula (or with the cheesecloth), remove the fish and vegetables from the steamer. Arrange on a serving plate, surrounding the fish with the vegetables. Remove and discard the ginger and lemon slices. Drizzle the sauce over the fish and vegetables. Garnish with the remaining lemon slice.

Calories 208 (15% from fat)/Protein 29.4g/Carb 14.9g/Fat 3.4g/Chol 42mg/Sodium 382mg/Calcium 104mg/Food Exchanges: Veg 2.1/Fruit 0.2/Meat 3.3/Fat 0.2

Lemon-Sesame Sauce (½ recipe): Calories 21 (49% from fat)/Protein 0.5g/Carb 2.1g/Fat 1.1g/Chol 0/Sodium 300mg/Calcium 3mg/Food Exchanges: Fat 0.2

VARIATIONS

▼ for the red snapper, substitute 4 ounces bay scallops; reduce cooking time to about 2 minutes
▼ for the asparagus, substitute other vegetables such as cut green beans, snap peas, or snow peas (for the snow peas, steam only for 2 minutes)
▼ substitute Orange Curry Sauce (page 95), Sesame-Pepper Dressing (page 30), or Ginger Sauce (page 47)

FUSILLI WITH CREAMY CLAM SAUCE

▼ ▼ ▼

3 ounces long fusilli

FOR THE CREAMY CLAM SAUCE
½ teaspoon olive oil
¼ teaspoon minced garlic
One 6½-ounce can chopped or minced clams, drained, re-
*   serving ¼ cup juice*
¼ cup skim milk
2 tablespoons lite ricotta cheese
1 tablespoon minced fresh parsley
2 teaspoons minced fresh basil or ½ teaspoon dried
⅛ teaspoon freshly ground black pepper, or to taste

TO COMPLETE THE DISH
1 teaspoon fresh lemon juice

GARNISH: *freshly ground black pepper, freshly grated*
*   Parmesan cheese, minced fresh parsley, tomato slices*

Bring a medium-size saucepan of water to a boil over high heat. Reduce the heat to medium-high; add the fusilli and cook until *al dente*, 10 to 12 minutes.

While the pasta is cooking, heat the olive oil in a medium-size skillet over medium heat. Add the garlic and cook for 30 seconds, stirring to prevent browning. Add the clams; continue cooking for 1 minute, stirring occasionally.

In a measuring cup or small bowl, stir together the reserved clam juice, the milk, ricotta cheese, parsley, dried basil (if used),

TIPS

▼ Long fusilli are long curly strands of pasta.

▼ Clams are especially rich in calcium, phosphorus, iron, and potassium.

▼ Fragile fresh herbs such as parsley, chervil, tarragon, mint, basil, and cilantro are at their pungent best when not overcooked. It is best to add them during the last few minutes of the cooking. In dried form they can be cooked longer since the moisture will hydrate them and bring out the flavor.

and pepper; stir into the skillet. Reduce the heat to medium-low; cook, uncovered, for 3 minutes, stirring occasionally. Add the parsley and fresh basil (if using) during the last minute.

When the pasta is done, drain well. Pour into the skillet and combine with the clam sauce, tossing over low heat. Remove from the heat; stir in the lemon juice. Taste; adjust seasonings. Spoon into a shallow bowl; top with your choice of garnishes and serve.

Calories 496 (15% from fat)/Protein 31.8g/Carb 73.4g/Fat 8.4g/Chol 125mg/Sodium 174mg/Calcium 286mg/Food Exchanges: Milk 0.2/Veg 0.1/Bread 4.2/Meat 1.8/Fat 0.6

VARIATIONS

▼ for the clams, substitute a 3½-ounce can of salmon or solid white tuna packed in water. Add the liquid from the can plus an extra 3 tablespoons skim milk. (Check the salmon when it is drained to remove any small bones.)

CIOPPINO

½ teaspoon olive oil
2 tablespoons seeded and chopped green bell pepper
1 tablespoon finely chopped onion
¼ teaspoon minced garlic
2 ounces linguine
½ cup water
1 tablespoon tomato paste
One 8-ounce can tomatoes with juice
1 teaspoon lemon juice
⅛ teaspoon dried basil or ½ teaspoon minced fresh
⅛ teaspoon dried thyme or ½ teaspoon fresh leaves

ADVANCE PREPARATION
May be made early the day it is
to be served; refrigerate. Take
care not to overcook the
shrimp or break the fish when
reheating. (Or make only the
sauce in advance; add the cod
and shrimp and cook them as
the sauce reheats.) Pour the
warmed sauce over freshly
cooked pasta.

▼ ▼ ▼

TIPS

▼ Cod is one of the five most popular fish eaten in the United
States; it is caught on both the
East and West coasts. The flesh
is firm, white, and mild in flavor; this very lean fish can be
cooked by almost any method.
Small cod, under 3 pounds, are
sometimes marketed as
"scrod"; they are sweeter and
more tender than full-grown
cod.

▼ A sweetener such as sugar or
honey is often added to tomato-
based soups and sauces to cut
the acidity of the tomatoes, especially canned tomatoes.

⅛ teaspoon freshly ground black pepper, or to taste
Pinch of sugar
2 drops hot pepper sauce, or to taste
1 piece cod fillet (about 3 ounces), cut into 1-inch squares
*3 to 4 medium-size shrimp (about 2 ounces), shelled and de-
veined*
1 tablespoon minced fresh Italian flat-leaf parsley

GARNISH: *freshly ground black pepper, freshly grated
Parmesan cheese*

Bring a medium-size saucepan of water to a boil over high
heat.

Meanwhile, heat the olive oil in a medium-size skillet over
medium heat. Add the bell pepper and onion; cook, stirring occasionally, until the vegetables are tender, about 3 minutes. Add
the garlic; cook 30 seconds longer.

Reduce the heat under the boiling water to medium-high.
Add the linguine; cook until *al dente*, about 8 minutes.

Meanwhile, in a measuring cup, stir together the water and
tomato paste. Add to the skillet along with the tomatoes with
juice, lemon juice, dried basil and dried thyme (if used), pepper,
sugar, and hot pepper sauce. Quarter the tomatoes. Cook, uncovered, for 5 minutes.

While the pasta and sauce are cooking, prepare the cod and
shrimp. Add to the tomato mixture, stirring to immerse in the
liquid. Stir in the parsley. (Add the fresh basil and thyme, if
used, at this time, too.) Cook, uncovered, until the shrimp and
cod are opaque all the way through, about 3 minutes. Stir occasionally, gently, so the fish will not be broken into pieces. Taste;
adjust seasonings.

When the pasta is done, drain well. To serve, place the pasta
in a shallow bowl. Top with the stew, garnish, and serve.

Calories 434 (11% from fat)/Protein 37.1g/Carb 59g/Fat 5.5g/Chol
124mg/Sodium 518mg/Calcium 131mg/Food Exchanges: Veg 2.9/Bread
2.8/Meat 3.7/Fat 0.4

VARIATIONS

- ▾ add sliced mushrooms; sauté with the bell pepper and onion
- ▾ add coarsely chopped marinated sun-dried tomatoes; stir in with the tomatoes
- ▾ for the cod, substitute flounder, grouper, or other firm white fish, or a 3½-ounce can of solid white tuna packed in water, drained.

FISH SOUPS

SHRIMP AND RICE SOUP
▾ ▾ ▾

MAKES 2 SERVINGS
1 teaspoon olive oil
¼ cup minced onion
2 tablespoons seeded and minced red bell pepper
½ teaspoon minced garlic
One 14½-ounce can unsalted tomatoes with juice
1 cup water
2 tablespoons tomato paste
2 tablespoons uncooked basmati rice
1 teaspoon vegetable stock powder
½ teaspoon dried rosemary, crushed, or 1½ teaspoons minced fresh
6 to 8 medium-size shrimp (about 4 ounces), shelled and deveined
1 tablespoon minced fresh Italian flat-leaf parsley
⅛ teaspoon freshly ground black pepper, or to taste
Pinch of sugar

GARNISH: sprigs fresh Italian flat-leaf parsley

This is a thick, robust soup that can be varied using orzo or bulgur wheat in place of the rice—and beans in place of the shrimp.

▾ ▾ ▾

ADVANCE PREPARATION
Will keep for 2 days in the refrigerator. It thickens as it sets so it may be necessary to add extra water when reheating. Take care not to overcook the shrimp when reheating. (They can be removed with a slotted spoon and added just briefly when reheating; or make the remainder of the soup in advance and cook the shrimp as the soup reheats.)

▾ ▾ ▾

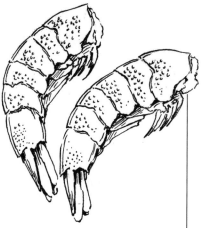

In a medium-size saucepan over medium heat, heat the olive oil. Add the onion and bell pepper; cook, stirring, until the vegetables are nearly tender, 3 minutes. Add the garlic; cook 30 seconds longer. Add the tomatoes with juice; quarter the tomatoes. Stir in the water, tomato paste, basmati rice, stock powder, and rosemary. Increase the heat to high; bring the mixture to a boil. Reduce the temperature to medium-low; cover and cook for 10 minutes. Add the shrimp; cook 2 to 3 minutes. Check to be certain the rice is tender and the shrimp cooked through.

Stir in the parsley, pepper, and sugar. Add more water if you prefer a thinner consistency. Taste; adjust seasonings. Ladle into a serving bowl, 3 or 4 shrimp per serving, and garnish.

Calories 198 (18% from fat)/Protein 15.3g/Carb 25.1g/Fat 4g/Chol 87mg/Sodium 433mg/Calcium 105mg/Food Exchanges: Veg 2.7/Bread 0.6/Meat 1.6/Fat 0.4

VARIATIONS

▼ for the garlic and onion, substitute 2 tablespoons minced shallot
▼ for the rosemary, substitute ¼ teaspoon dried thyme and ¼ teaspoon dried basil
▼ in addition to the shrimp, or instead, add ½ cup cooked beans such as black, garbanzo, or kidney beans; add while the soup is simmering
▼ add ½ cup shredded spinach during the last 2 minutes of the simmering period

TIPS

▼ Canned tomatoes are available with or without salt; read the small print. In addition to tomatoes and tomato juice, stewed tomatoes contain garlic, onion, green bell pepper, celery, and salt.
▼ Simmer, never boil, shrimp; boiling and overcooking will toughen them. Shrimp are cooked when they start to turn pink.

TIPS

▼ When buying canned tuna,
read the labels!

  ▼ Oil-packed is usually packed
  in low-grade vegetable oil, so
  tuna packed in spring water
  is not only lower in calories
  but has a better flavor.

  ▼ Solid-pack tuna is a continu-
  ous piece of tuna, more expensive than flaked or
  chunk, but better in flavor
  and texture.

  ▼ Solid-pack tuna comes in
  three grades: white, light,
  and dark meat. The white is
  more expensive but preferable for its flavor and appearance.

▼ The salt in canned tuna (as
well as other canned foods) can
be reduced by rinsing the fish
under cool running tap water
for 1 minute.

TUNA CHOWDER

▼ ▼ ▼

MAKES 2 SERVINGS

1 cup water
2 teaspoons vegetable stock powder
1 teaspoon olive oil
½ cup coarsely shredded carrot
1 scallion (both green and white parts), chopped
1 medium-size potato, peeled and cut into ½-inch cubes
  (1 cup)
1 cup skim milk
One 6-ounce can solid white tuna packed in water, drained
  and broken into ½-inch chunks
½ cup frozen peas
1 teaspoon low-sodium soy sauce
½ teaspoon dried basil or 2 teaspoons minced fresh
¼ teaspoon dried oregano or 1 teaspoon minced fresh
⅛ teaspoon freshly ground black pepper, or to taste

GARNISH: *minced fresh parsley or finely shredded carrot*

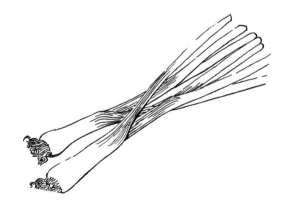

▼ Dill, a sharply aromatic herb with a mild lemony taste, is commonly used to complement the flavors of fish and cucumbers. When using fresh dill, use scissors to cut the feathery dill tips. Dried dill, called dillweed, is acceptable, if necessary, but use it in moderation.

In a measuring cup, dissolve the stock powder in the water. Set aside.

Over medium heat, heat the olive oil in a medium-size saucepan. Add the carrot and scallion; cook, stirring, about 2 minutes to soften. Add the vegetable stock and potato, increase the heat to high, and allow the mixture to come to a boil. Reduce the heat to medium-low, cover, and cook until the potato cubes are softened, about 5 minutes.

Pour the mixture into a blender or food processor. Add the skim milk; purée. Pour the puréed mixture back into the saucepan. Add the remaining ingredients. Place the pan over medium heat to warm, stirring occasionally. (Do not allow the mixture to boil.) Taste; adjust seasonings. Ladle into a soup bowl, garnish, and serve.

1 serving: Calories 280 (15% from fat)/Protein 30.6g/Carb 28.5g/Fat 4.8g/Chol 38mg/Sodium 544mg/Calcium 180mg/Food Exchanges: Milk 0.4/Veg 0.5/Bread 1.2/Meat 3.1/Fat 0.4

VARIATIONS

▼ for the scallion, substitute 1 minced shallot
▼ for the basil and oregano, substitute other herbs such as herbes de Provence, thyme, summer savory, or dill

FISH IN WRAPPERS

Part of the fun of going out to eat is ordering and enjoying unusual ethnic creations, but sometimes I crave those flavors at home, too. I have pared down the number of ingredients and some of the intricate preparations for three of my favorites. All are composed of fish, vegetables, and other ingredients encased in some sort of "wrapper"—for flavor, and of course, for visual interest. Buying some of the ingredients may require a trip to an oriental market; but once these items are on your pantry shelf, you will be prepared to feast on short notice.

RICE PAPER SPRING ROLLS WITH SPICY PEANUT SAUCE

▼ ▼ ▼

Every since my diet-conscious, friend, Sandra, taught me to make fresh spring rolls, they have become one of my favorite lunches. The procedure may sound difficult, but after one try, you'll have the technique mastered.

▼ ▼ ▼

ADVANCE PREPARATION
The rice can be made several hours in advance; cover with a damp towel and refrigerate. Ideally, bring to room temperature to make the rolls. The spring rolls can be made up to 2 hours in advance. Wrap in plastic wrap and refrigerate. Ideally, bring to room temperature to serve. The sauce will keep for several days refrigerated.

▼ ▼ ▼

MAKES 3 ROLLS
½ cup uncooked short-grain white rice (sushi rice)
1½ cups water

FOR THE SPICY PEANUT SAUCE (MAKES ¼ CUP)
1 tablespoon hoisin sauce
1 teaspoon peanut butter
¼ teaspoon chili paste with garlic, or to taste
1 tablespoon low-fat plain yogurt
1 tablespoon water
¼ teaspoon dark sesame oil

FOR THE ROLLS
Three 8-inch sheets rice paper
3 leaves tender, soft lettuce, ribs removed
Six ¼-inch-thick slices cucumber, cut into ⅛-inch strips
2 imitation crab strips (artificial crab), cut into ⅛-inch strips
6 to 9 fresh mint leaves

GARNISH: *finely chopped peanuts on the peanut sauce; sprig fresh mint on the serving plate*

To prepare the short-grain white rice, place the rice and water in a small saucepan. Bring to a boil over high heat. Reduce the heat to low; cover and simmer about 10 minutes, until the water is absorbed. Remove the covered pan from the heat and allow to stand for 3 to 5 minutes to continue steaming the rice.

To prepare the sauce, while the rice is cooking, whisk together the hoisin sauce, peanut butter, and chili paste in a small bowl. Whisk in the yogurt, water, and sesame oil. Set aside.

- Hoisin sauce is a thick, sweet, reddish brown sauce made from soybeans, vinegar, chilies, spices, and garlic. Refrigerated, it will keep almost indefinitely. There is no substitute.

- Rice papers, or rice sheets, are flat, thin, opaque, brittle round sheets made from white rice, flour, salt, and water. They will keep indefinitely if stored flat and away from moisture.

- Imitation crab strips, or seafood sticks, are made from a firm bland fish such as pollock; using natural and artificial flavorings, the fish is made to taste like crab legs. Most supermarket seafood departments stock it in either fresh or frozen form.

Also while the rice is cooking, prepare the spring roll ingredients. To soften the rice paper, begin by holding a heavy-duty paper towel (or a thin kitchen towel) under warm running water. Squeeze out the excess moisture; lay flat on the kitchen counter. Hold a sheet of rice paper under warm running water, being certain to wet both sides. Lay the rice paper flat on top of the towel. Top with another layer of moist toweling, taking care to cover the edges of the rice paper. Repeat layers with the second and third sheets of rice paper and more moist toweling. Allow to set for 5 minutes to soften. (If allowed to set too long, the paper will become too moist and too fragile to handle.)

To assemble the rolls, remove the top layer of wet toweling and discard. (1) The ingredients should be arranged in the center of the rice paper allowing about 1½ inches of rice paper on each side to remain uncovered. Place 1 lettuce leaf at the end of the rice paper closest to you, touching the edge of the rice paper. Top with rice, starting at the end closest to you and spreading about 3 tablespoons of rice to a ½-inch thickness. Above the rice, moving toward the top of the rice paper, horizontally arrange one third of the cucumber strips and seafood strips. Near the top of the rice paper, horizontally arrange 2 or 3 of the mint leaves.

(2) Fold the two sides of the rice paper circle to the center

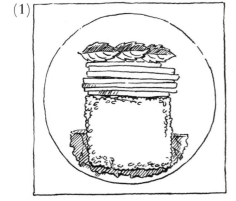

(1)

(2)

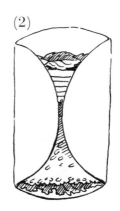

(3)

until the edges touch. (3) Starting at the end closest to you, gently, roll the paper and ingredients firmly, squeezing as you roll. Place the completed roll, edge down, on the serving plate. Remove the next layer of toweling and repeat the procedure with the second and third sheets of rice paper. (If, during the rolling process, the rice paper splits, simply moisten another sheet and roll it over the broken one.)

To serve, pour the sauce into a small serving bowl accompanied by a small spoon. Add garnishes to the sauce bowl and the serving plate. Eat the rolls with your fingers, drizzling sauce over the end of the roll to season each bite. (Be warned, spring rolls tend to fall apart if they are dipped!)

Note: When cooking less than 1 cup of rice, the proportions of rice to water differ from the usual quantities; the cooking time also is reduced. If using the quantities on page 106, the yield is $1\frac{1}{2}$ cups cooked rice; only $\frac{3}{4}$ cup is needed to prepare the Spring Rolls, but it is difficult to cook rice in a smaller quantity. If you have short-grain rice already cooked, this recipe requires about $\frac{3}{4}$ cup cooked rice.

Rice Paper Spring Rolls with Spicy Peanut Sauce: Calories 299 (16% from fat)/Protein 13.3g/Carb 49.7g/Fat 5.2g/Chol 12mg/Sodium 611mg/Calcium 74mg/Food Exchanges: Veg 0.2/Bread 2.4/Meat 1.1/Fat 0.6

Spicy Peanut Sauce (entire recipe): Calories 62 (59% from fat)/Protein 2.3g/Carb 4.1g/Fat 4g/Chol 1mg/Sodium 125mg/Calcium 35mg/Food Exchanges: Meat 0.1/Fat 0.6

VARIATIONS

▼ for the rice, substitute Chinese wheat noodles, rice noodles, bean threads, or couscous

▼ to the Spicy Peanut Sauce, add 1 tablespoon finely shredded carrots and/or 1 tablespoon mashed beans such as black beans

▼ to the Spicy Peanut Sauce, add $\frac{1}{4}$ teaspoon peeled and minced fresh ginger

- in place of the Spicy Peanut Sauce, use Ginger Sauce (page 47), store-bought plum sauce thinned with a little water, or lite teriyaki sauce
- in place of the crab strips, substitute cooked shrimp, strips of cooked fish, drained canned tuna, shredded cooked chicken, chopped peanuts, scrambled eggs (or noncholesterol egg product)
- for the mint, substitute cilantro (fresh coriander) or watercress
- to the rolls, add or substitute other raw vegetables such as sliced mushrooms, bok choy, shredded carrots, strips of avocado, sprouts, julienned scallion, zucchini, snow peas, or red bell pepper

CALIFORNIA ROLLS
▼ ▼ ▼

Authentic sushi chef expertise requires years of apprenticeship. And today there is some well-deserved skepticism regarding eating raw fish. But California Rolls, which contain neither raw fish nor require elaborate assembly techniques, are another story. Anne, who became my friend during one of my pasta classes, has become my "sushi mentor" and has taught me a trick or two for making these.

MAKES 8 PIECES
½ cup uncooked short-grain white rice (sushi rice)
1½ cups water
1 teaspoon wasabi powder
1 teaspoon water
Three 5 by ¼-inch cucumber strips, peeled and seeded
Six 2 by ¼-inch avocado strips
Two 5 by ¼-inch imitation crab strips (artificial crab)
1 tablespoon seasoned white rice vinegar
One 7 by 8-inch sheet dried seaweed (hoshi nori)
1 tablespoon toasted sesame seeds (pages 30–31)

ACCOMPANIMENTS: *low-sodium soy sauce, pickled ginger*
SPECIAL EQUIPMENT: *plastic wrap, bamboo rolling mat (sudare)*

The rice can be made several hours in advance; cover with a damp towel and refrigerate. Bring to room temperature to make the rolls. Serve the rolls immediately after preparing.

▼ ▼ ▼

TIPS

▼ Seasoned white rice vinegar contains rice vinegar, sugar, and salt. It is available in the gourmet section of many supermarkets and in oriental markets.

▼ Authentic wasabi, or Japanese horseradish, is very expensive and difficult to find. The powdered, canned type commonly found in U.S. markets is actually horseradish with mustard powder added. When combined with water to form a thick paste, an intense and pungent flavor will develop. Use sparingly!

▼ Sheets of seaweed, called nori, are available in oriental markets and in the gourmet section of many supermarkets. Store at room temperature away from moisture.

Place the rice and water in a small saucepan. Bring the water to a boil over high heat. Reduce the heat to low, cover, and simmer until the water is absorbed, about 10 minutes. Remove the covered pan from the heat and allow to stand for 3 to 5 minutes to continue steaming the rice.

While the rice is cooking, stir together the wasabi powder and water in a small bowl to form a paste. Cover, or turn the container upside down, and allow to set for about 10 minutes to allow the flavor to mature.

Also, while the rice is cooking, prepare the cucumber, avocado, and crab strips for the filling. When the rice is done, transfer to a small bowl. Add the vinegar; fold it into rice using a rubber spatula. Set aside, uncovered, to allow the rice to come to room temperature.

Toast the sheet of seaweed over a stove burner. If using a gas stove, wave the sheet of seaweed back and forth, about 7 to 8 inches over a medium flame, for about 15 seconds. Flip the sheet, and repeat with the other side. If using an electric stove, set a burner on high. As the burner heats, wave the nori back and forth about 4 to 5 inches above the burner, 15 seconds on each side.

To assemble the rolls (1), place the sheet of seaweed, rough side up, on a cutting board, the longer edge facing you. Using a rubber spatula, spread the rice over the seaweed in an even layer. (Take care not to crush the rice grains.) Sprinkle the surface of the rice with the sesame seeds. Cover with a sheet of plastic wrap and press lightly (2). Flip, placing the seaweed up, rice down. Spread a small amount, about ⅛ teaspoon, of wasabi paste across the center horizontally. Then arrange the strips of cucumber, avocado, and crab horizontally from edge to edge.

Keeping the plastic wrap attached (3), roll up by hand, squeezing firmly as you roll. Press down on the cutting board on each of the four sides, forming a square. (This can be done more simply by placing a bamboo rolling mat, or sudare, around the roll.) Flatten and firm the ends by pressing inward with your hands.

▼ Pickled ginger is a cool, sharp condiment made from fresh ginger that has been marinated in seasoned vinegar. Serve chilled, eating small bites to cleanse the palate.

▼ For shaping rolled sushi, sushi chefs use a sudare, a bamboo rolling mat which is made from skewer-type bamboo sticks woven together with string. This inexpensive accessory is available in most oriental markets.

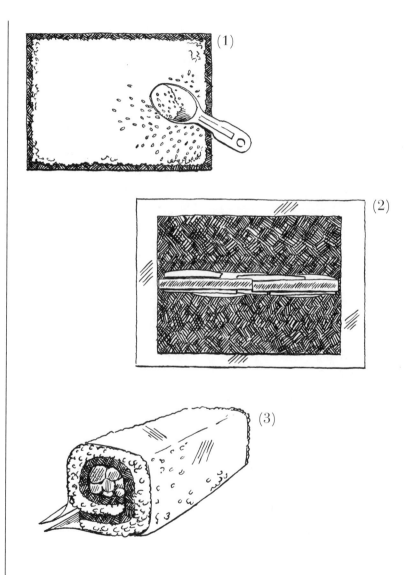

(1)

(2)

(3)

Remove the bamboo mat and/or the plastic wrap. Place the roll on a cutting board, seam side down. Moisten a sharp knife (serrated works best) with water or vinegar between cuts and use a sawing motion to cut the roll in half; then cut each half into 4 equal slices.

Arrange the rolls on a serving plate. Accompany with a small mound of pickled ginger and the remaining wasabi paste. Serve immediately.

Eat by hand, dipping in soy sauce or soy sauce mixed with a small amount of the wasabi paste. Eating the pickled ginger along with the rolls will enhance the flavors and cleanse your palate!

Calories 493 (23% from fat)/Protein 11.3g/Carb 84g/Fat 12.4g/Chol 4mg/Sodium 180mg/Calcium 97mg/Food Exchanges: Veg 0.1/Fruit 0.2/Bread 4.9/Meat 0.3/Fat 2.2

VARIATIONS

▼ if the short-grain rice is cooked in advance, use 1½ cups
▼ for the filling, add or substitute thin strips of well-cooked carrot, thin radish strips, slivers of scallion, plum paste, or seasoned gourd strips
▼ for the imitation crab strips, substitute well-drained canned or frozen crab or strips of cooked shrimp

ROMAINE SPRING ROLLS

▼ ▼ ▼

▼ ▼ ▼

ADVANCE PREPARATION
The filling may be made in advance and served later the same day, chilled or at room temperature.

▼ ▼ ▼

TIPS

▼ Bok choy, sometimes called mustard cabbage, pak choy, or pak choi, should have unwilted bright dark green leaves attached to crisp lighter green unblemished ribs. Store in a plastic bag in the refrigerator for 3 days. If unavailable, substitute celery.

▼ Five-spice powder, sometimes called five-fragrance powder, is a sweet and pungent mixture of ground fennel, anise, ginger, licorice root, cinnamon, and cloves. A licorice flavor predominates. It is available in the ethnic section of supermarkets and in oriental markets.

2 tablespoons Chinese plum sauce
1 tablespoon water
3 large romaine leaves
½ teaspoon safflower oil
1 rib bok choy, cut into ¼-inch slices (also coarsely chop the green tops)
1 scallion (both green and white parts), chopped
1 tablespoon seeded and diced red bell pepper
½ teaspoon minced garlic
6 to 8 medium-size shrimp (about 4 ounces), shelled, deveined, and halved lengthwise
¼ teaspoon five-spice powder

In a small serving bowl, stir together the plum sauce and water. (You may need a little more or less water to bring the sauce to maple syrup consistency, depending upon the brand of plum sauce you buy.) Arrange the romaine leaves on a serving plate.

In a small skillet, heat the oil over medium-high heat. Add the bok choy, scallion, and red bell pepper; cook, stirring, until crisp-tender, about 2 minutes. Add the garlic; cook 30 seconds longer. Add the shrimp and 5-spice powder; continue to cook, stirring constantly, until the shrimp are cooked through, 2 to 3 minutes. Spoon the shrimp mixture into a serving bowl.

To assemble the rolls, at the table, place a spoonful of the warm shrimp mixture in a romaine leaf; drizzle with plum sauce. Roll up the sides of the leaf and enjoy!

Calories 166 (24% from fat)/Protein 24.3g/Carb 7.3g/Fat 4.4g/Chol 175mg/Sodium 297mg/Calcium 105mg/Food Exchanges: Veg 0.5/Meat 3.2/Fat 0.4

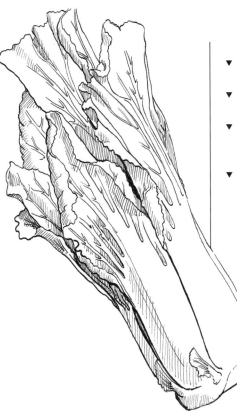

VARIATIONS

▼ for the plum sauce, substitute Ginger Sauce (page 47) or Spicy Peanut Sauce (page 106)

▼ for the shrimp, substitute ½ chicken breast (about 4 ounces), cut into ½-inch cubes

▼ along with the bok choy, scallion, and garlic, sauté other vegetables such as shredded carrot, sliced mushrooms, chopped bamboo shoots, or bean sprouts

▼ serve the shrimp or chicken mixture as a salad mounded on a lettuce leaf; drizzle with the plum sauce—or stuff the mixture into pita bread

CHICKEN

▾ ▾ ▾

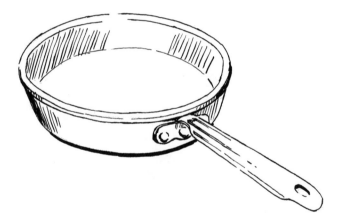

▼ A 3-ounce serving of skinless
boneless cooked chicken has
about one-third fewer grams of
fat than the same amount of
ground beef.

▼ Using a low-fat cooking
method, a 4-ounce serving has
170 calories and 3 grams of fat
(19 percent). If that same portion is battered and fried with
skin intact, the calories soar to
295 and fat measures 15
grams (47 percent).

Chicken is the perfect singles' food—easy to prepare and inexpensive. It pairs well with many other foods and is remarkably compatible with most herbs and spices, so it lends itself to a wide variety of cuisines.

Free-range, or organic, chickens are tastier than mass-produced ones, but they are more expensive and can be difficult to find. Supermarkets carrying mass-produced chickens have a large variety of cuts available. Split, or halved, chicken breasts of about 4 ounces are used in my recipes. Since almost one-half of the fat in chicken is found in the skin, I prefer to purchase the chicken breasts skinned and boned. (To use, simply cut off the tendon and any remaining visible yellow fat.)

When buying fresh chicken, look for firm, moist-looking flesh. Keep the chicken in the coldest part of your refrigerator for no longer than 2 days; or for longer storage freeze it in individual portions, tightly sealed to avoid freezer burn and ice crystals. Gradual refrigerator thawing is recommended to preserve quality and for reasons of food safety. If you prefer, you can follow the manufacturer's directions for thawing chicken in your microwave oven. Cook the chicken soon after defrosting and do not refreeze it.

When you are ready to cook the chicken, wash it with cool water and pat it dry with paper towels. I usually cut my chicken with poultry shears, avoiding the use of a cutting board. Using warm soapy water, wash all work surfaces, plates that held the raw chicken, knives, shears, and your hands. Also for reasons of food safety, cook the chicken thoroughly, making certain no pink remains; thorough cooking will destroy any bacteria.

Chicken cooks quickly, especially if it is cut up. For the most tender texture, cut chicken with the grain. Cook it completely until fork-tender using moderate heat; overcooking will toughen chicken. The low-fat methods used in this chapter include sautéing, stir-frying, broiling, and baking. Full-bodied flavors are achieved by including herbs, fruits, vegetables, marinades, and interesting sauces.

Remember, too, that chicken may be added to many of the pasta dishes, soups, salads, as well as many of the ethnic and vegetarian entrées; suggestions are provided with these recipes.

SAUTÉED AND STIR-FRIED CHICKEN

CHICKEN WITH CURRIED FRUIT

▼ ▼ ▼

½ teaspoon olive oil
1 tablespoon water
1 teaspoon curry powder, or to taste
½ boneless, skinless chicken breast (about 4 ounces), cut into
    1-inch squares
¼ cup orange juice
1 teaspoon light brown sugar
1 peach (preferably at room temperature), peeled, pitted,
    and cut into ¼-inch wedges

GARNISH: *chopped walnuts*

Heat the olive oil in a small skillet over medium heat. Add the water, stir in the curry powder, and heat until bubbly.

Add the chicken and cook, covered, stirring occasionally, until the chicken is lightly browned and cooked through, 4 to 5 minutes.

▼ Curry powder, a combination of many herbs and spices, has literally thousands of versions which vary according to the country or village of origin. Typically included are cardamom, cayenne, chili pepper, coriander, cumin, fennel, fenugreek, ginger, and turmeric. Domestic curry powders are usually quite mild; imported brands are much more intense in flavor. If you do not plan to serve your curry dish right away, be aware that the curry flavor becomes stronger in a dish that is allowed to stand or is kept refrigerated and then reheated.

Meanwhile, in a measuring cup, combine the orange juice and brown sugar, stirring until the sugar is dissolved.

Remove the chicken from the pan; place in a bowl and cover to keep warm. Reduce the heat to low. Add the peach wedges and orange juice mixture to the skillet; stir until the fruit is lightly cooked and the sauce bubbly, about 2 minutes. Stir in the chicken and heat for 30 seconds. Taste; adjust the seasonings. Spoon the mixture onto a serving plate; garnish with chopped walnuts.

Calories 319 (18% from fat)/Protein 34.7 g/Carb 30.9g/Fat 6.2g/Chol 87mg/Sodium 73mg/Calcium 44mg/Food Exchanges: Fruit 1.6/Meat 4.7/Fat 0.4

VARIATIONS

▼ for the fresh peach, ½ to ¾ cup frozen peach wedges may be substituted; thaw in advance and follow the same procedure, taking care not to overcook the fruit
▼ substitute ½ to ¾ cup "lite" canned peach wedges, pear slices, pineapple chunks, or apricots (or a mixture of fruits); drain, reserving ¼ cup juice which may be used in place of the orange juice
▼ for the peach, substitute a fresh pear

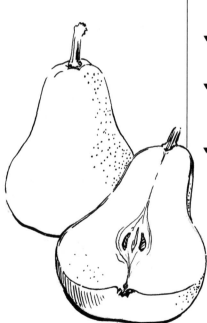

CHUTNEY-YOGURT CHICKEN

▼ ▼ ▼

TIPS

▼ Yogurts vary in the amount of fat they contain, based upon the type of milk used. Those made from whole milk contain 3.5 percent milk fat and 150 calories per cup. Low-fat yogurt has .5 to 3.25 percent fat. Nonfat yogurt has less than .05 percent fat; 1 cup contains 100 calories. Check the fine print on the label. Some yogurts contain artificial sweeteners and colorings; others contain gelatin, creating a firmer texture which is less creamy. Check the expiration date when buying yogurt; if refrigerated, it will keep for 1 week beyond that date.

▼ If possible, bring yogurt to room temperature before adding it to hot foods; blend a little of the hot food into the yogurt first to prevent curdling and separation. Keep temperatures low and add yogurt to already warm dishes at the end of the cooking period to allow a shorter heating time.

1 tablespoon store-bought chutney
2 tablespoons low-fat peach yogurt (if fruit layer is separate, stir in)
Dash of freshly ground black pepper, or to taste
½ teaspoon olive oil
⅛ teaspoon minced garlic
¼ teaspoon grated fresh ginger
½ boneless, skinless chicken breast (about 4 ounces), cut into 1-inch squares

GARNISH: *sprig fresh parsley or cilantro (fresh coriander)*

In a measuring cup or small bowl, stir together the chutney, yogurt, and pepper. Set aside.

Heat the olive oil in a small skillet over medium heat. Add the garlic and ginger; cook, stirring, about 30 seconds. Add the chicken. Cook, turning occasionally, until lightly browned and cooked through, 4 to 5 minutes.

Reduce the heat to low. Gently stir the chutney-yogurt mixture into the chicken. Heat, stirring constantly, for about 30 seconds. (Do not allow the yogurt to boil.) Taste; adjust the seasonings. Spoon onto a serving plate, garnish, and serve immediately.

Calories 248 (21% from fat)/Protein 35.6g/Carb 13.6g/Fat 5.7g/Chol 89mg/Sodium 106mg/Calcium 153mg/Food Exchanges: Fruit 0.6/Bread 0.2/Meat 4.7/Fat 0.4

VARIATIONS

▼ for the peach yogurt, substitute apricot, orange, pear, or your choice of other fruit yogurt

CHICKEN-ASPARAGUS STIR-FRY

▼ ▼ ▼

TIPS

▼ Cashews are always sold shelled because their shells contain a caustic oil; the nuts must be carefully extracted to avoid contamination with this oil. Forty-five percent of the cashew is fat. This is less than in many nuts but still enough to discourage using them in large quantities, especially since they are relatively high in saturated fat. Even in small quantities, though, they will provide protein and interesting flavor. For cooking, raw cashews are preferable as they do not contain salt and the added fat of roasted cashews. They will absorb the other flavors in your recipe and soften and plump up slightly to a pleasing consistency.

▼ Sautéing and stir-frying are similar cooking procedures. In sautéing, the heat is medium to high, and the food is stirred frequently. Stir-frying is done in a hotter pan so the food needs to be moved around constantly; the result is food with a more crisp-tender texture than those

FOR THE SESAME-GINGER SAUCE

⅓ cup water
1 teaspoon cornstarch
2 teaspoons low-sodium soy sauce
1 teaspoon grated fresh ginger
½ teaspoon dark sesame oil
½ teaspoon vegetable stock powder
Pinch of crushed red pepper, or to taste

FOR THE STIR-FRY

1 teaspoon safflower oil
½ boneless, skinless chicken breast (about 4 ounces), cut into
*   1 by ½-inch strips*
½ teaspoon minced garlic
1 cup cut asparagus (1-inch lengths)

GARNISH: *raw cashews, sliced or slivered almonds, strips of red bell pepper*

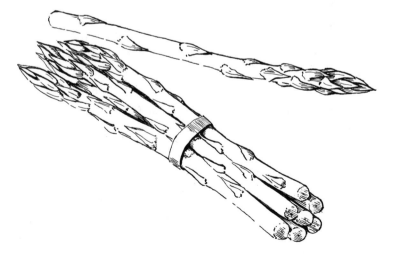

sautéed. For low-fat cooking, both can be done with a small amount of oil, or even stock.
▼ You don't need a wok to stir-fry; a skillet will do. Always begin with the firmest vegetables (broccoli, carrots, and cauliflower), adding the softest vegetables (zucchini and mushrooms) last. Do not cover the pan or the vegetables will lose their crispness.

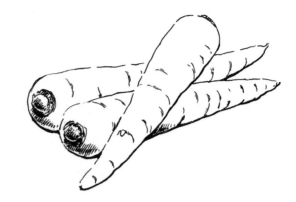

To prepare the sauce, in a small bowl add the water to the cornstarch, stirring until dissolved. Add the remaining sauce ingredients; stir until the stock powder is dissolved. Set aside.

In a medium-size skillet, heat ½ teaspoon of the oil over medium heat. Add the chicken and garlic and stir-fry until the chicken is lightly browned and cooked through, 4 to 5 minutes. Remove from the pan; set aside in a covered bowl to keep warm.

Increase the heat to medium-high; heat the remaining oil. Add the asparagus; stir-fry until crisp-tender, about 4 minutes. Reduce the heat to medium-low. Stir the sauce. Add to the skillet and stir until it is thickened and bubbly. Stir in the cooked chicken; heat for about 30 seconds. Taste; adjust the seasonings. Spoon onto a serving plate and garnish.

Calories 299 (33% from fat)/Protein 38.2g/Carb 12.2g/Fat 10.8g/Chol 87mg/Sodium 479mg/Calcium 63mg/Food Exchanges: Veg 1.6/Bread 0.1/Meat 4.7/Fat 1.3

VARIATIONS

▼ add or substitute other vegetables such as broccoli florets, thinly sliced carrots, sliced mushrooms, snow peas, snap peas, or red bell pepper strips
▼ omit the chicken; add more vegetables

CHICKEN FAJITAS

▼ ▼ ▼

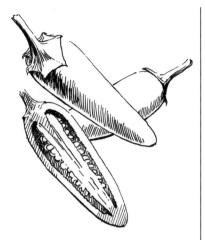

1 tablespoon fresh lime juice
½ teaspoon chili powder, or to taste
¼ teaspoon minced garlic
⅛ teaspoon freshly ground black pepper, or to taste
Dash of ground cumin
½ boneless, skinless chicken breast (about 4 ounces), cut into
    2 by ¼-inch strips
½ teaspoon olive oil
½ small onion, sliced (about ¼ cup)
½ medium-size red bell pepper, seeded and cut into 2 by
    ¼-inch strips
1 jalapeño pepper, seeded and finely chopped
Three 6- or 7-inch flour tortillas (white or whole wheat)

In a small bowl, combine the lime juice, chili powder, garlic, pepper, and cumin. Add the chicken strips and toss; set aside for 5 to 10 minutes, stirring occasionally.

Heat the olive oil in a small skillet over medium heat. Add the onion and peppers; cook, stirring, for 3 minutes. Add the chicken mixture with juice; cook, stirring, until the chicken is tender and light brown and the vegetables are softened, 4 to 5 minutes. Taste; adjust seasonings.

Meanwhile, place the tortillas between two paper towels. Microwave on high until moist and warm, 15 to 20 seconds. (Or, wrap them in aluminum foil and heat in a preheated 350° F. oven for about 10 minutes while the vegetables and chicken are cooking.)

To serve, place the warm tortillas on a plate; cover to keep warm. Spoon the chicken mixture into a bowl. Assemble the fajitas as you eat by spooning some of the chicken mixture into the center third of the tortilla and rolling.

TIPS

▼ Limes change from dark green to pale green to yellow as they age; select the very green ones for the tartest and tangiest flavor. Occasionally the skin is marked with a "scald," a brownish dry patch; if these spots are small they do not affect the quality of the lime.

▼ Always use fresh rather than bottled, reconstituted lime juice.

▼ In many gourmet shops, you can buy tortilla heating baskets which can be used for heating the tortillas as well as keeping them warm at the table.

Calories 526 (20% from fat)/Protein 42.1g/Carb 62.9g/Fat 11.8g/Chol 87mg/Sodium 502mg/Calcium 195mg/Food Exchanges: Veg 1.3/Bread 3.0/Meat 4.7/Fat 1.0

VARIATIONS

▼ spread Asparagus Guacamole (page 67) on each tortilla before adding the chicken mixture
▼ to the chicken mixture, add coarsely chopped cilantro (fresh coriander)
▼ add chopped tomatoes, shredded lettuce, chopped avocado, plain yogurt, lite sour cream, and/or shredded cheese when rolling the tortillas
▼ for a nontraditional version, spread a layer of chevre (goat cheese) or crumble feta cheese on the tortilla before adding the chicken

LEMON-BASIL CHICKEN IN PITA BREAD

½ boneless, skinless chicken breast (about 4 ounces)
½ teaspoon olive oil
1 tablespoon low-fat plain yogurt
1 teaspoon store-bought chutney
½ teaspoon lemon juice
¼ teaspoon grated lemon rind
3 large fresh basil leaves (do not use dried)
Half of a 6-inch pita bread (whole wheat or white), sliced vertically
2 leaves soft leaf lettuce (such as bibb, Boston, green leaf, or red leaf)

▼ ▼ ▼

ADVANCE PREPARATION
The chicken may be prepared in advance and served chilled. Assemble in the pita just before serving.

▼ ▼ ▼

▼ To squeeze more juice from citrus fruits, bring them to room temperature; roll the fruit around on a hard surface, pressing hard with the palm of your hand. Or microwave chilled fruit for 30 seconds (pierce the fruit with a fork or knife first) on high before cutting or squeezing. If you need only a small amount of juice, save the fruit for future use by making a deep X-shaped incision into the fruit with a paring knife. Squeeze out the juice you need; then store the fruit in a sealed plastic bag in the refrigerator.

▼ Freshly squeezed lemon juice is always the most flavorful. Next best is the frozen lemon juice found near the juice concentrates in the freezer section of supermarkets. Thawed, it will keep for about two months in your refrigerator. Or keep it in the freezer, removing it just long enough to thaw the amount you need, then refreeze. Avoid using the chemical-laden and artificial-tasting reconstituted lemon juice.

Place the chicken breast between two sheets of plastic wrap or place in a baggie; using a rolling pin, flatten the chicken to a ¼-inch thickness.

In a small skillet, heat the oil over medium-high heat. Add the chicken; cook until cooked through, about 2 minutes on each side. Remove from the heat; cover to keep warm and set aside.

In a small bowl or measuring cup, stir together the yogurt, chutney, and lemon juice and rind. Spread the mixture on one side of the chicken breast; arrange the basil leaves on top.

Open the pita pocket half; line with the lettuce leaves. Slip in the chicken breast. Serve immediately.

Calories 262 (22% from fat)/Protein 36g/Carb 15.5g/Fat 6.3g/Chol 88mg/Sodium 191mg/Calcium 68mg/Food Exchanges: Fruit 0.2/Bread 0.7/Meat 4.7/Fat 0.4

VARIATIONS

▼ for the yogurt, substitute reduced-fat, cholesterol-free mayonnaise
▼ for the basil, substitute fresh spinach leaves
▼ cut the cooked chicken into cubes, toss with the chutney-yogurt mixture, and stuff into pitas or serve on a bed of greens as a chicken salad, warm or chilled

BROILED CHICKEN

With a little advance planning, broiled chicken can be on the table in 10 minutes. For the recipes in this section, begin by preparing the marinade. It usually is recommended that chicken marinates 30 minutes at a minimum, ideally for 6 to 24 hours. The chicken will become flavorful as it sits in the marinade and will retain its moistness as it broils. For variety, either of the two marinades in the Fish chapter can be used for marinating chicken.

Always marinate your chicken in the refrigerator rather than at room temperature. The marinade can be used for basting as the chicken cooks, but do not reuse it or use it in uncooked form as a sauce or for dipping. Note that the nutritional analyses include only the portion of the marinade actually consumed. (See additional tips on marinades, pages 81–82.)

Actually, I like chicken prepared with any of these marinades equally as well served warm or chilled. The chilled chicken can be served in pita bread, as a chicken sandwich, or sliced on a bed of greens. (In fact, warm chicken breasts are also enjoyable served on a bed of greens.)

If you want to broil a chicken breast without advance planning, brush both sides of the chicken lightly with olive oil to seal in the moisture and sprinkle it with herbs and pepper, if you like. Broil 4 to 5 inches from the heating element until the chicken is cooked through, about 5 minutes on each side.

Accompany your broiled chicken (with or without marinating) with a green salad, crusty bread, steamed or marinated vegetables, and rice or pasta. Many of the recipes in the Pasta chapter and the Grains section of Ethnic and Vegetarian Entrées make appealing accompaniments, too.

APRICOT-GLAZED CHICKEN

▼ ▼ ▼

This marinade, made from apricot jam, is fat-free, incredibly simple to prepare, and exceptionally flavorful. Since nearly all fruits are compatible with chicken, improvise and try other fruit jams—orange marmalade is great!

▼ ▼ ▼

ADVANCE PREPARATION
The chicken may be broiled in advance, refrigerated, and served later, chilled.

▼ ▼ ▼

TIPS
▼ Many jams and jellies are now available with "no sugar added." Sweetened with concentrated fruit juices, most contain no preservatives, artificial colors, or artificial flavors.

FOR THE APRICOT MARINADE
2 tablespoons apricot jam
1 tablespoon red wine vinegar
1 teaspoon grated fresh ginger
Dash of freshly ground black pepper

TO COMPLETE THE DISH
½ boneless, skinless chicken breast (about 4 ounces)
Vegetable oil spray

GARNISH: *sprig fresh mint, cilantro (fresh coriander), or parsley*

In a small bowl or measuring cup, stir together the marinade ingredients. Pour half of the marinade into the bottom of a shallow glass baking dish or flat refrigerator container. Place the chicken on top; pour on the remaining marinade. Refrigerate, covered, for at least 30 minutes or as long as 24 hours, turning the chicken occasionally.

When ready to cook, set the oven broiler rack 4 to 5 inches from the heating element; preheat the broiler.

Lightly spray vegetable oil on a broiler pan or baking sheet. Place the chicken on the prepared pan, reserving the excess marinade. Broil the chicken for 5 minutes, turn, and brush with marinade. Broil the second side until the chicken is cooked through, about 5 minutes. Discard the remaining marinade. Place the chicken on a serving plate, garnish, and serve.

Calories 241 (13% from fat)/Protein 32.9g/Carb 19.5g/Fat 3.4g/Chol 87mg/Sodium 73mg/Calcium 21mg/Food Exchanges: Meat 4.7

Apricot Marinade (2 tablespoons): Calories 78 (0% from fat)/Protein .02g/Carb 19.5g/Fat 0/Chol 0/Sodium 3mg/Calcium 6mg/Food Exchanges: 0

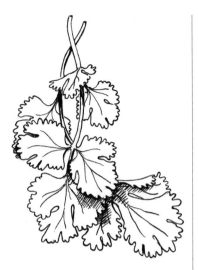

- in the Apricot Marinade, for the red wine vinegar, substitute raspberry vinegar
- using the same method, prepare *Orange-Glazed Chicken:* for the marinade combine 2 tablespoons orange marmalade, 1 tablespoon red wine vinegar (or raspberry vinegar), ½ teaspoon dried rosemary, and a dash of pepper
- for the chicken, substitute 4 to 5 ounces shrimp (shelled and deveined); broil 2 to 3 minutes, depending on the size
- for the chicken, substitute fish such as salmon, broil for 10 minutes per inch of thickness, turning halfway through the broiling period
- serve the broiled chicken, fish, or shrimp, warm or chilled, on a bed of greens tossed with a light dressing such as Ginger-Soy Vinaigrette (page 196) or Sesame-Ginger Dressing (page 186)

PLUM-GLAZED CHICKEN

▼ ▼ ▼

ADVANCE PREPARATION

The chicken may be broiled in advance, refrigerated, and served later, chilled.

▼ ▼ ▼

FOR THE PLUM MARINADE
2 tablespoons Chinese plum sauce
1 tablespoon white rice vinegar
½ teaspoon Dijon mustard
½ teaspoon minced garlic
Dash of crushed red pepper

TO COMPLETE THE DISH
½ boneless, skinless chicken breast (about 4 ounces)
Vegetable oil spray

GARNISH: *sprig fresh parsley, mint, or cilantro (fresh coriander)*

▼ Chinese plum sauce is a thick
sauce made from plums, apricots, chilies, vinegar, and
spices. It is used as a table
condiment or as an ingredient
in sauces. Look for it in the oriental section of most supermarkets. Store it in the refrigerator
after opening.

In a small bowl or measuring cup, stir together the marinade ingredients. Pour half of the marinade into the bottom of a shallow glass baking dish or flat refrigerator container. Place the chicken on top; pour on the remaining marinade. Refrigerate, covered, for at least 30 minutes or as long as 24 hours, turning the chicken occasionally.

Prior to cooking, place the oven broiler rack 4 to 5 inches from the heating element; preheat the broiler.

Lightly spray a baking sheet or a broiler pan with vegetable oil spray. Place the chicken on the prepared pan, reserving the excess marinade. Broil the chicken for 5 minutes, turn, and baste with remaining marinade. Broil until the chicken is cooked through, 5 more minutes. Discard the remaining marinade. Place the chicken on a serving plate, garnish, and serve.

Calories 236 (13% from fat)/Protein 32.9g/Carb 18.3g/Fat 3.5g/Chol 87mg/Sodium 79mg/Calcium 22mg/Food Exchanges: Meat 4.7

Plum Marinade (2 tablespoons): Calories 74 (0% from fat)/Protein .1g/Carb 18g/Fat 0/Chol 0/Sodium 8mg/Calcium 8mg/Food Exchanges: 0

VARIATIONS

▼ for the chicken, see the shrimp and fish substitutes suggested for Apricot-Glazed Chicken (page 128)

▼ see salad suggestion for Apricot-Glazed Chicken (page 128)

TERIYAKI CHICKEN

▼ ▼ ▼

FOR THE TERIYAKI MARINADE
1 tablespoon mirin
1 teaspoon low-sodium soy sauce
1 teaspoon pure maple syrup
½ teaspoon grated fresh ginger
½ teaspoon dark sesame oil
¼ teaspoon minced garlic

TO COMPLETE THE DISH
Vegetable oil spray
½ boneless, skinless chicken breast (about 4 ounces)

GARNISH: *toasted sesame seeds (pages 30–31), sprig cilantro (fresh coriander)*

Combine the marinade ingredients. Pour half the marinade into the bottom of a shallow glass baking dish or flat refrigerator container. Place the chicken on top; pour on the remaining marinade. Refrigerate, covered, for 30 minutes or up to 24 hours, turning the chicken occasionally.

When ready to cook, set the oven broiler rack to 4 to 5 inches from the heating element; preheat the broiler.

Lightly spray vegetable oil on a broiler pan or baking sheet. Place the chicken on the prepared pan, reserving the excess marinade. Broil the chicken for 5 minutes, turn, and brush with the marinade. Broil the second side until the chicken is cooked through, about 5 minutes. Discard the remaining marinade. Place the chicken on a serving plate, garnish, and serve.

Calories 174 (21% from fat)/Protein 32.9g/Carb 1.6g/Fat 4g/Chol 87mg/Sodium 122mg/Calcium 15mg/Food Exchanges: Meat 4.7/Fat 0.1

Teriyaki Marinade (1/2 of total recipe): Calories 24 (42% from

▼ ▼ ▼

ADVANCE PREPARATION
The chicken may be broiled in advance, refrigerated, and served later, chilled.

▼ ▼ ▼

TIPS
▼ Low-sodium or "lite" soy sauce contains about 40 percent less sodium than traditional soy sauce or tamari, but it provides nearly the same flavor. It is still a sodium product to be avoided if you follow a strict sodium-reduced diet.

▼ Basting means to pour small quantities of liquid over food that is cooking to keep the food moist, juicy, and to add flavor. A spoon, bulb baster, or basting brush can be used. (The basting brush works best with single-serving quantities.)

fat)/Protein 0.2g/Carb 3.3g/Fat 1.1g/Chol 0/Sodium 104mg/Calcium 2mg/Food Exchanges: Fat 0.2

VARIATIONS

▼ in the marinade, for the maple syrup, substitute ½ teaspoon sugar
▼ for the chicken, see the shrimp and fish suggestions for Apricot-Glazed Chicken (page 128)
▼ see salad suggestion for Apricot-Glazed Chicken (page 128)

TANDOORI CHICKEN

▼ ▼ ▼

Here is an adaptation of a traditional Indian flavoring for chicken. I like to serve it with Chutney-Yogurt Cucumber Slices (page 132)

▼ ▼ ▼

ADVANCE PREPARATION
The chicken may be broiled in advance, refrigerated, and served later, chilled.

▼ ▼ ▼

FOR THE TANDOORI MARINADE
¼ cup low-fat plain yogurt
1 tablespoon fresh lime juice
½ teaspoon grated fresh ginger
¼ teaspoon minced garlic
⅛ teaspoon ground cinnamon
⅛ teaspoon paprika
⅛ teaspoon freshly ground black pepper
Dash of ground cumin

TO COMPLETE THE DISH
½ boneless, skinless chicken breast (about 4 ounces)
Vegetable oil spray

GARNISH: *sprig cilantro (fresh coriander), parsley, mint, or chopped scallion greens*

In a measuring cup or small mixing bowl, whisk together the marinade ingredients.
Pour half the marinade into the bottom of a shallow glass

baking dish or a flat refrigerator container. Place the chicken on top; pour on the remaining marinade. Refrigerate, covered, for at least 1 hour or up to 24 hours, turning the chicken at least once.

When ready to cook, set the oven broiler rack 4 to 5 inches from the heating element; preheat the broiler.

Lightly spray vegetable oil on a broiler pan or baking sheet. Place the chicken on the prepared pan, reserving the marinade. Broil for 5 minutes, turn, and brush with the marinade. Broil the second side until the chicken is cooked through, about 5 minutes. Discard the remaining marinade.

Place the chicken on a serving plate, garnish, and serve.

Calories 186 (19% from fat)/Protein 34.4g/Carb 3.2g/Fat 3.9g/Chol 89mg/Sodium 91mg/Calcium 70mg/Food Exchanges: Milk 0.1/Meat 4.7

Tandoori Marinade (2 tablespoons): Calories 23 (18% from fat)/ Protein 1.6g/Carb 3.2g/Fat 0.5g/Chol 2mg/Sodium 20mg/Calcium 56mg/ Food Exchanges: Milk 0.1

VARIATIONS

▼ for the chicken, substitute 4 to 5 ounces shrimp (shelled and deveined); broil 2 to 3 minutes, depending on the size of the shrimp

▼ cook the chicken in advance and chill. Cut the cooked chicken into strips; toss with shredded cabbage, spinach, or lettuce and cucumber slices. Stuff the mixture into pita bread; top with a dollop of nonfat plain yogurt mixed with a spoonful of chutney or Chutney-Yogurt Cucumber Slices (see below).

▼ *Chutney-Yogurt Cucumber Slices:* Cut ½ cucumber in half lengthwise, remove the seeds, and cut into ¼-inch slices. Mix with a combination of 1 tablespoon nonfat plain yogurt, 2 teaspoons chutney, and a dash of pepper.

TIPS

▼ Of the many varieties of mint, spearmint is the most commonly used in cooking. As a flavoring, mint goes well with chicken and most vegetables; use it to flavor peas, carrots, cauliflower, or zucchini.

CHICKEN KABOBS WITH TOMATO-SOY MARINADE

▼ ▼ ▼

My favorite accompaniment for this is Sesame Rice (see page 212).

FOR THE TOMATO-SOY MARINADE
1 tablespoon low-sodium soy sauce
1 teaspoon honey
1 teaspoon tomato paste
¼ teaspoon minced garlic
Dash of freshly ground black pepper

FOR THE KABOBS
½ boneless, skinless chicken breast (about 4 ounces), cut into
  1-inch squares
Vegetable oil spray
¼ cup fresh pineapple chunks
Six ¼-inch slices zucchini

SPECIAL EQUIPMENT: *three 8-inch bamboo skewers or one 14-inch metal skewer*

TIPS
▼ *En brochette* is a term often used in recipes and on menus to describe foods cooked on a skewer.
▼ Soak bamboo skewers in water before threading on the ingredients to prevent them from burning and darkening under the broiler.

In a small bowl or measuring cup whisk together the marinade ingredients. Pour half the marinade into the bottom of a shallow glass baking dish or a flat refrigerator container. Place the chicken on top; pour on the remaining marinade. Stir gently and cover. Refrigerate for at least 30 minutes or for as long as 24 hours, stirring occasionally.

Prior to cooking, place the oven broiler rack 4 to 5 inches from the heating element; preheat the boiler.

Lightly spray a baking sheet or broiler pan with vegetable oil spray. Thread the chicken onto three bamboo skewers (reserving the remaining marinade), alternating with the pineapple and zucchini. Place the skewers on the prepared pan. Broil for 4 minutes, turn, and baste with the marinade. Broil until the chicken is cooked through, about 2 more minutes. Discard the marinade. Place the skewers on a serving plate.

Calories 236 (14% from fat)/Protein 34.6g/Carb 15.8g/Fat 3.8g/Chol 87mg/Sodium 676mg/Calcium 29mg/Food Exchanges: Veg 0.4/Fruit 0.4/Meat 4.7

Tomato-Soy Marinade (entire recipe): Calories 39 (1% from fat)/Protein 1.2g/Carb 8.5g/Fat 0.1g/Chol 0/Sodium 604mg/Calcium 7mg/Food Exchanges: Veg 0.2

VARIATIONS

▼ for the chicken, substitute about 4 ounces of a firm fish, such as swordfish
▼ as you thread the skewers, substitute or add mandarin orange segments, canned pineapple chunks, mushrooms, chunks of green or red bell pepper, onion slices, and/or cherry tomatoes
▼ sprinkle the kabobs with sesame seeds before broiling

BAKED CHICKEN

PARMESAN CHICKEN WITH CHUNKY TOMATO SAUCE

▼ ▼ ▼

Reminiscent of crispy fried chicken, this version has much less fat and far more flavor. Accompanied by rice or pasta and a crispy green salad, the menu is satisfying and complete. For quick preparation, eliminate the sauce; the chicken is tasty on its own, too.

Olive oil spray
½ boneless, skinless chicken breast (about 4 ounces)
1 tablespoon noncholesterol egg product
2 teaspoons toasted wheat germ
1 teaspoon freshly grated Parmesan cheese
⅛ teaspoon dried basil

⅛ teaspoon dried thyme
⅛ teaspoon freshly ground black pepper

FOR THE CHUNKY TOMATO SAUCE (MAKES 1/2 CUP)
½ teaspoon olive oil
1 tablespoon seeded and diced red bell pepper
¼ teaspoon minced garlic
1 medium-size tomato, cut into ½-inch cubes (1 cup)
1 tablespoon coarsely chopped marinated sun-dried toma-
    toes
1 tablespoon water
1 teaspoon tomato paste
1 tablespoon minced fresh parsley
¼ teaspoon dried basil or 1 teaspoon minced fresh
Dash of freshly ground black pepper, or to taste

GARNISH: *freshly ground black pepper, sprig fresh parsley*

Preheat the oven to 400° F. Spray a baking sheet or flat pan with olive oil spray. Set aside.

Place the chicken breast between two sheets of plastic wrap or in a baggie; using a rolling pin, flatten the chicken to a ½-inch uniform thickness.

Pour the egg product into a small bowl. In a separate flat bowl, stir together the wheat germ, Parmesan, basil, thyme, and pepper. Dip the chicken into the egg product, turning to moisten both sides. Lay the chicken in the wheat germ-Parmesan mixture and press gently; turn to coat the other side, again pressing gently.

Place the chicken on the prepared baking pan. Bake for 5 minutes; turn and bake until the chicken is cooked through and crispy, 4 minutes longer.

To prepare the sauce, while the chicken is baking, heat the olive oil in a small skillet over medium heat. Add the red bell pepper; cook, stirring, until nearly tender, about 3 minutes. Add the garlic; cook 30 seconds longer. Stir in the remaining sauce

▼ ▼ ▼

ADVANCE PREPARATION
The Parmesan Chicken must be made just before serving. The sauce can be made up to a day in advance, refrigerated, and reheated.

▼ ▼ ▼

TIPS
▼ Crushing dried herbs with your fingers just before adding them to your recipes helps to release their full flavor and aroma.

ingredients. Reduce the heat to low, cover, and cook for 5 minutes, stirring occasionally. Taste; adjust seasonings.

When the chicken is done, place it on a serving plate. Top with the sauce and garnish.

Calories 301 (20% from fat)/Protein 38.2g/Carb 22.4g/Fat 6.4g/Chol 87mg/Sodium 484mg/Calcium 111mg/Food Exchanges: Veg 2.4/ /Meat 4.7/Fat 0.4

Chunky Tomato Sauce (entire recipe): Calories 133 (20% from fat)/ Protein 4.4g/Carb 22.2g/Fat 3g/Chol 0/Sodium 413mg/Calcium 95mg/ Food Exchanges: Veg 2.4/Fat 0.4

VARIATIONS

▼ for the egg product, substitute reduced-cholesterol egg product, 1 large egg, lightly beaten, or 1 large egg white
▼ to the Chunky Tomato Sauce, add oregano and/or a pinch of crushed red pepper
▼ use the Chunky Tomato Sauce on a baked potato, steamed vegetables (such as green beans), pasta, or over a vegetable-filled omelet or crepes. For variety, add orange zest and top it with milk goat cheese (chevre).
▼ the Chunky Tomato Sauce can be puréed

CURRIED CHICKEN IN PARCHMENT

▼ ▼ ▼

Serve this over pasta or couscous cooked while the packet bakes.

▼ ▼ ▼

ADVANCE PREPARATION
The parchment packet may be assembled 1 hour in advance. (Any longer causes the parchment to become soggy.) Refrigerate; the chilled food will require about 2 minutes longer to bake.

▼ ▼ ▼

TIPS
▼ Currants are the dried fruit of a small, dark, seedless grape from Corinth, Greece, from which they take their name. "Zante" currants refer to the Greek island where this type of grape first grew. In the supermarket, they are found with the raisins and dried fruits. About one quarter the size of raisins, currants are less sweet but have a stronger flavor than raisins.

½ boneless, skinless chicken breast (about 4 ounces), cut into 1-inch squares
¼ apple, cut into ¼-inch cubes
1 tablespoon currants
2 tablespoons skim milk
1 tablespoon tomato paste
1 teaspoon low-sodium soy sauce
1 teaspoon curry powder
½ teaspoon grated fresh ginger
Dash of freshly ground black pepper

SPECIAL EQUIPMENT: *1 sheet baking parchment, about 16 inches in length*

Preheat the oven to 425° F.

In a medium-size bowl, toss together the chicken, apple, and currants. In a measuring cup or small bowl, stir together the remaining ingredients. Pour this mixture over the chicken and stir to combine.

See page 93 for an illustration of the following procedure. Fold the parchment in half and cut into the shape of a half circle. Open the parchment circle. Spoon the chicken mixture onto one half of the parchment. Close the parchment flap. Seal the parchment by starting at one end; fold the cut edges toward the packet contents, creating many small overlapping folds.

Place the parchment packet on a baking sheet; bake for 12 minutes. To serve, open the packet and spoon the chicken onto a serving plate.

Calories 248 (15% from fat)/Protein 35.5g/Carb 17.3g/Fat 4g/Chol 88mg/Sodium 299mg/Calcium 79mg/Food Exchanges: Milk 0.1/Veg 0.6/Fruit 0.6/ Meat 4.7

- ▼ for the currants, substitute raisins
- ▼ add sliced or slivered almonds
- ▼ add 1 tablespoon coarsely chopped cilantro (fresh coriander)

CHICKEN SALADS

CURRIED CHICKEN SALAD WITH MANGO

▼ ▼ ▼

½ teaspoon olive oil
½ boneless, skinless chicken breast (about 4 ounces), cut into
  1-inch squares

FOR THE CHUTNEY-YOGURT DRESSING
2 tablespoons low-fat plain yogurt
1 teaspoon store-bought chutney
½ teaspoon curry powder, or to taste
⅛ teaspoon ground cumin
Dash of freshly ground black pepper, or to taste

TO COMPLETE THE DISH
1 medium-size mango (preferably at room temperature),
  peeled, pitted, cut into 1-inch cubes (about 1 cup)
2 tablespoons chopped celery
½ scallion, chopped (green parts)
1 teaspoon fresh lime juice
1 large leaf of lettuce

GARNISH: sprig cilantro (fresh coriander), raw cashews,
  toasted sliced almonds (page 232), or unsalted dry-
  roasted peanuts

▼ ▼ ▼

ADVANCE PREPARATION
To serve chilled, cover and
refrigerate for about an hour
before serving.

▼ ▼

TIPS
▼ Select a mango which is mostly
yellow tinged with red or orange;
it should yield slightly to pressure when squeezed. (A green-
skinned, hard mango will never
ripen properly.) To ripen, place
in a paper bag at room temperature for 1 or 2 days; it should
turn yellow-orange to red and

have a pleasant aroma. Check the fruit daily; black spots indicate overripe fruit. Once ripened, a mango will keep 2 to 3 days in the refrigerator. (However, the flavor is at its best served at room temperature.)

▼ The mango is one of the most difficult fruits to cut neatly because the pulpy flesh is very juicy and clings to the flat pit. The simplest way is to hold it horizontally; cut in two lengthwise, slightly off-center, so the knife just misses the pit. Repeat the cut on the other side so a thin layer of flesh remains around the pit. Holding a half in the palm of your hand, slash the flesh into a lattice, cutting down, but not through, the peel. Holding the flesh upward, carefully push the center of the peel with your thumbs to turn it inside out, opening the cuts of the flesh. Then cut the mango cubes from the peel.

In a small skillet, heat the olive oil over medium heat. Add the chicken; cook, stirring, until cooked through, 4 or 5 minutes. Remove from the skillet and place in a medium-size bowl to cool.

In a small bowl or measuring cup, whisk together the dressing ingredients. Taste; adjust the seasonings. Set aside.

When the chicken has cooled, add the mango, celery, scallion, and lime juice; toss. Add the dressing and toss again. Place the lettuce leaf on a serving plate; top with the chicken salad mixture. Serve immediately at room temperature or cover and refrigerate to serve later, chilled. Garnish before serving.

Calories 373 (17% from fat)/Protein 35.7g/Carb 42.2g/Fat 6.9g/Chol 89mg/Sodium 109mg/Calcium 100mg/Food Exchanges: Milk 0.1/Fruit 2.5/Meat 4.7/Fat 0.5

Chutney-Yogurt Dressing (entire recipe): Calories 35 (15% from fat)/Protein 1.6g/Carb 5.9g/Fat 0.6g/Chol 2mg/Sodium 22mg/Calcium 57mg/Food Exchanges: Milk 0.1/Fruit 0.2

VARIATIONS

▼ substitute canned mango, well drained
▼ for the lime juice, substitute lemon juice
▼ rather than serving as a salad, stuff the chicken mixture into pita bread

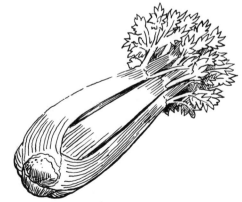

Chicken salad can be far more interesting than simply chicken tossed with mayonnaise!

▼ ▼ ▼

ADVANCE PREPARATION
The dressing and salad may be made in advance and refrigerated separately. Combine just before serving.

▼ ▼ ▼

TIPS
▼ Chinese cabbage, sometimes called Napa cabbage or celery cabbage, can be recognized by its solid oblong heads of long smooth stalks with pale green leaves.

▼ Bean sprouts are the tender shoots of the soya or mung bean. They are a good source of vitamins A and C and some B vitamins. They also contain potassium, phosphorus, calcium, and iron. Sprouted mung beans will keep in the refrigerator for a week, though the nutrition lessens with time. Chill bean sprouts briefly in ice

CHINESE CHICKEN SALAD WITH SESAME-GINGER DRESSING
▼ ▼ ▼

3 tablespoons Sesame-Ginger Dressing (page 186)
½ teaspoon safflower oil
½ boneless, skinless chicken breast (about 4 ounces), cut into 2 by ½-inch strips
8 snow peas, stems and strings removed
2 cups shredded Chinese cabbage
1 rib bok choy, chopped (include green tops)
1 scallion (green parts), chopped
⅓ cup drained mandarin oranges

GARNISH: *toasted pine nuts (page 36), toasted sesame seeds (pages 30–31), or toasted sliced or slivered almonds (page 232)*

Bring a small saucepan of water to a boil.
Prepare the dressing; set aside.
Heat the oil in a small skillet over medium heat. Add the chicken; cook, stirring occasionally, until cooked through and lightly browned, 4 to 5 minutes. Remove from the pan; place on a plate and set aside to cool.

Place the peas in a small mesh strainer; blanch by immersing them for about 30 seconds in the saucepan of boiling water. Immediately place under cold running water; drain well.

In a large mixing bowl, toss together the Chinese cabbage, peas, bok choy, and scallion. Spread the salad mixture on a serving plate. Arrange the cooked chicken strips and oranges on top. Drizzle with the dressing; garnish. Serve immediately.

water to add crispness for eating raw. Avoid using canned bean sprouts—they lack texture, flavor, and nutrition.

▼ Blanching means to cook very lightly. Food may be blanched by being submerged in simmering water, by having boiling water poured over it, or by being steamed briefly over boiling water. Always follow blanching by running the food under cold water to stop the cooking process. This method brightens the color of many vegetables and enhances their flavor by adding sweetness.

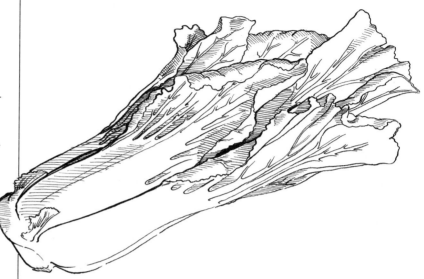

Calories 312 (25% from fat)/Protein 37.7g/Carb 20.5g/Fat 8.8g/Chol 87mg/Sodium 318mg/Calcium 231mg/Food Exchanges: Veg 1.2/Fruit 0.4/Bread 0.1/Meat 4.7/Fat 0.9

VARIATIONS

▼ for the Sesame-Ginger Dressing, substitute Chinese plum sauce (page 113) thinned with water
▼ for the chicken, substitute sautéed, boiled, or broiled shrimp
▼ for the Chinese cabbage, substitute shredded romaine lettuce or fresh spinach
▼ for the bok choy, substitute celery, water chestnuts, or strips of jicama
▼ add or substitute other vegetables such as bean sprouts, chopped cucumber, steamed cut asparagus, julienned carrots, sliced mushrooms, peas, or red or green bell pepper strips
▼ for the oranges, substitute grapes or pineapple
▼ add raisins or currants
▼ add chopped cilantro (fresh coriander)

HOT CHICKEN SALAD WITH WALNUT VINAIGRETTE

▼ ▼ ▼

1 recipe Walnut Vinaigrette (page 203)
2 cups bite-size pieces romaine lettuce
1 plum tomato, cut into 6 wedges
½ teaspoon olive oil
½ boneless, skinless chicken breast (about 4 ounces), cut
    into 1 by ½-inch strips
1 teaspoon red wine vinegar
1 teaspoon minced fresh parsley
¼ teaspoon dried tarragon or 1 teaspoon minced fresh

GARNISH: *toasted pine nuts (page 36), roasted hazelnuts
(see Tips, left), or chopped walnuts*

▼ ▼ ▼

ADVANCE PREPARATION
The vinaigrette may be made
in advance and refrigerated for
2 days. The salad may be
assembled, refrigerated for
several hours, and served
chilled. Add the vinaigrette just
before serving.

▼ ▼ ▼

TIPS
▼ A new product called "lettich"
is available in some specialty
produce markets. A cross
between lettuce and spinach, it
is excellent in salads.
▼ Tarragon has a sweet aromatic
scent and aniselike flavor.
▼ To enhance the flavor of hazelnuts, roast them by spreading
them in a single layer in a pan
and putting them in a preheated 375° F. oven for 5 to 10
minutes. Hazelnuts are high in
fat (over 60 percent); most of
the fat is unsaturated. Since
they are very flavorful, just a

few will add their unique character. Like other nuts, store them in the refrigerator or freezer; they will be become rancid at room temperature in 2 months.

▼ Blanch snow peas, or Chinese pea pods, to bring out the color and flavor while preserving the crisp texture. Some varieties are stringless but often strings must be removed; start at the bottom tip and pull the string up the front, then snap off the stem and pull the string down the back.

Prepare the vinaigrette. Set aside.

Mound the lettuce onto a serving plate. Arrange the tomato wedges around the edges. Set aside.

Heat the olive oil in a small skillet over medium heat; add the chicken strips. Cook, stirring occasionally, until cooked through, 4 to 5 minutes. Remove the skillet from the heat; stir in the vinegar, parsley, and tarragon.

Arrange the hot chicken strips on the lettuce. Drizzle the vinaigrette over the salad; garnish. Serve immediately.

Calories 279 (35% from fat)/Protein 35.1g/Carb 10.3g/Fat 10.8g/Chol 87mg/Sodium 282mg/Calcium 71mg/Food Exchanges: Veg 1.4/Meat 4.7/Fat 1.3

VARIATIONS

▼ for the Walnut Vinaigrette substitute Raspberry Vinaigrette (page 204) or Balsamic Vinaigrette (page 184)
▼ substitute other greens such as fresh spinach, bibb, Boston, leaf, or iceberg lettuce
▼ add other vegetables such as blanched snow peas, chopped scallion, or chopped red bell pepper

SOUPS

There is nothing like homemade soup. But great soup once meant enormous pots of ingredients that required hours of simmering and resulted in days of eating leftovers. Then came fast soup, the kind you made by opening a can and adding some milk or water. Now you can even just drop a bag into boiling water—but these soups either seem to be tasteless or too salty.

This chapter brings you the best of both. These soups are flavorful and satisfying. And they get that way in very little time. The quantities are just right. The soups are healthful. And even though they are quick to prepare, your kitchen will be filled with the fragrant aromas of homemade soup.

A tasty stock base is the essence of many of these soups. Making stock from scratch is not practical for the 15-minute cook, but there are other alternatives. When it comes to vegetable stock, my choice is to use a high-quality, unsalted vegetable stock powder which I buy in bulk at a food co-op. It is made from ground dehydrated vegetables—no preservatives, no salt. It keeps forever on the shelf in my spice cabinet. In this product, no single flavor predominates; and since it is unseasoned, the mild flavor blends well with the herbs in my recipes. I usually dissolve about 1 teaspoon per cup of water. Some health food stores sell acceptable products in cube form. In most grocery store varieties, the first ingredient is salt; and often flavor enhancers and preservatives are added. So, read the small print. Once you have found a stock powder that pleases you, keep a supply in your pantry at all times. For chicken stock, I prefer canned to powdered or cubed, although I usually keep all three on hand. I look for a low-sodium and defatted product with no added flavorings.

My soup recipes provide two generous servings, one to eat right away and an extra serving to enjoy later, or to share with a friend. No need for freezing, because soups keep well for a day or two and often seem to improve with age.

Except for the light chilled fruit soups, most of the soups in this chapter are hearty and nourishing enough to stand on their own as a main course; add a salad on the side and bread or an accompaniment such as Bruschetta (page 217), Pita Crisps (page 218), or Baked Tortilla Chips (page 219). Or serve a smaller portion to begin a meal.

CHILLED SOUPS

The soups in this section are uncooked, requiring just minutes to assemble the ingredients and purée them. Though my food processor is my first choice for many tasks, a smooth consistency for puréed soups is best achieved by using a blender.

If chilled ingredients are used, these soups can be served cold as soon as they are prepared. However, they all seem to taste best after they have been thoroughly chilled and the flavors have had an opportunity to mellow. If you begin with fresh ingredients, these soups will keep at least 2 days in the refrigerator.

CHUNKY GARDEN GAZPACHO

▼ ▼ ▼

A little oil seems to round out the flavor of this soup, but follow the variation to make it fat free, if you prefer.

MAKES 2 SERVINGS
One 8-ounce can tomato sauce, preferably unsalted
1 tablespoon extra-virgin olive oil
1 tablespoon red wine vinegar
1 teaspoon honey

ADVANCE PREPARATION
Will keep in the refrigerator
for several days. If it thickens,
you may need to thin by adding
water or tomato juice.

▼ ▼ ▼

TIPS

▼ Store garlic in a cool, dark,
well-ventilated place such as a
garlic cellar (a ceramic pot with
holes and a lid); or refrigerated
in a plastic bag to keep it dry.
It will keep from a few weeks to
a few months.

▼ To peel garlic, place the flat
end of a chef's knife on a clove;
using your fist, pound the
knife. The skin will separate
from the clove inside and the
clove also automatically will be
minced.

1 plum tomato, cut into ½-inch cubes (½ cup)
1 scallion, chopped (green parts)
½ cup chopped cucumber
¼ cup seeded and chopped green bell pepper
¼ cup seeded and chopped red bell pepper
½ teaspoon minced garlic
¼ teaspoon freshly ground black pepper, or to taste
2 drops hot pepper sauce, or to taste

GARNISH: Herbed Croutons (page 220), sprigs fresh parsley,
minced fresh chives, chiffonade of lettuce (page 152), dollop of plain yogurt

In a medium-size bowl, combine the tomato sauce, olive oil,
vinegar, and honey. Stir in the remaining ingredients.
Serve chilled, topped with the garnish of your choice.

1 serving: Calories 124 (51% from fat)/Protein 2.3g/Carb 13g/Fat
7g/Chol 0/Sodium 147mg/Calcium 39mg/Food Exchanges: Veg 1.1/Bread
0.2/Fat 1.3

VARIATIONS

▼ omit the olive oil to reduce calories to 56 per serving (4%
from fat)

▼ add or substitute other raw vegetables such as chopped celery
or cubed zucchini

▼ add ½ cup frozen cooked baby shrimp (thawed)

▼ add herbs such as basil or cilantro, preferably fresh

CHILLED
STRAWBERRY-MINT SOUP

▼ ▼ ▼

MAKES 2 SERVINGS

1½ cups sliced fresh strawberries
1½ cups low-fat plain yogurt
2 tablespoons orange juice
1 tablespoon honey, or to taste
1 tablespoon minced fresh mint leaves

GARNISH: fresh strawberry slices or a strawberry fan (page 239), kiwi slices, sprigs fresh mint

Place the strawberries, yogurt, orange juice, and honey in a blender or food processor; purée. Stir in the minced mint. Taste for sweetness; if necessary, add more honey. Refrigerate. Serve chilled, topped with your choice of garnish.

1 serving: Calories 187 (15% from fat)/Protein 9.7g/Carb 30g/Fat 3.1g/Chol 10mg/Sodium 121mg/Calcium 329mg/Food Exchanges: Milk 1.0/Fruit 0.6/Fat 0.5

VARIATIONS

▼ for the yogurt, substitute buttermilk
▼ for the orange juice, substitute other juices such as apple, lemon, lime, white or red grape juice
▼ add ½ teaspoon grated orange rind

TIPS

▼ When buying strawberries, look for solid-colored, dark red berries with fresh-looking leaves. If packed in baskets, check the bottom to be sure the berries are dry and free of mold. Small and medium-size berries tend to have more flavor than larger ones; save the large ones for garnishing.

▼ Buttermilk is made from low-fat or skim milk to which a bacterial culture has been added to ferment the milk sugar. It has a tart flavor and thick texture. When made from skim milk, 1 cup contains 88 calories and 0.2% fat. Store in the refrigerator where it will keep 1 to 2 weeks.

CHILLED MELON-LIME SOUP

▼ ▼ ▼

MAKES 2 SERVINGS
3 cups 1-inch cubes cantaloupe
½ cup low-fat plain yogurt
1 tablespoon honey, or to taste
1 tablespoon fresh lime juice
Dash of ground nutmeg, or to taste
2 tablespoons minced fresh mint (do not use dried)

GARNISH: *dollop low-fat plain yogurt, melon balls, thin lime slice, a strawberry fan (page 230), sprigs fresh mint*

Place the cantaloupe, yogurt, honey, lime juice, and nutmeg in a blender or a food processor; purée until smooth. Stir in the mint. Taste; adjust the honey and nutmeg. Serve chilled, topped with the garnish of your choice.

1 serving: Calories 168 (8% from fat)/Protein 5.1g/Carb 33.3g/Fat 1.6g/Chol 3mg/Sodium 62mg/Calcium 131mg/Food Exchanges: Milk 0.3/Fruit 1.3/Fat 0.1

VARIATIONS

▼ substitute all or part honeydew melon or 1 cup cantaloupe plus 2 cups halved strawberries
▼ add some sliced bananas
▼ for the yogurt, substitute buttermilk
▼ for the honey, substitute maple syrup
▼ for the lime juice, substitute lemon juice
▼ for the nutmeg, substitute ½ teaspoon peeled and grated fresh ginger; omit the mint. Top with a dollop of *Wasabi Cream* made by stirring together 1 tablespoon low-fat plain yogurt, ¼ teaspoon wasabi powder, and ¼ teaspoon honey.

TIPS

▼ When selecting melons at the market, look for:
   ▼ hollow rounded scars, slight softness, and a sweet smell at the stem end
   ▼ heavy weight
   ▼ uniform raised webbing on the skin of cantaloupes
   ▼ smooth, cream-colored skin on honeydew melons
▼ If unripe, ripen melons at room temperature for 1 to 3 days. Ripened melons should be wrapped in a plastic bag and stored in the refrigerator. Use ripe melons within 3 days after ripening.
▼ If you plan to store a cut melon for several days, don't remove the seeds; their moisture will help to prevent the flesh from drying out.

CHILLED CUCUMBER-SPINACH SOUP

▼ ▼ ▼

MAKES 2 SERVINGS

1½ cups peeled, seeded, and cubed cucumber (½-inch cubes)
1 cup coarsely chopped fresh spinach (stems removed)
1 cup low-fat plain yogurt
¼ cup watercress leaves
1 teaspoon olive oil
1 teaspoon sugar
⅛ teaspoon freshly ground black pepper, or to taste

GARNISH: *dollop low-fat plain yogurt topped with watercress leaves, minced fresh chives, small tender spinach leaf or a chiffonade of spinach (page 152), finely chopped hard-cooked egg, sprigs fresh dill*

Place all the ingredients in a blender or food processor; process until smooth. Taste; adjust the seasonings. Serve chilled, topped with a garnish or two.

1 serving: Calories 121 (31% from fat)/Protein 7.3g/Carb 13.4g/Fat 4.2g/Chol 7mg/Sodium 105mg/Calcium 252mg/Food Exchanges: Milk 0.7/Veg 0.5/Fat 0.8

VARIATIONS

▼ for the spinach, substitute lettuce, any type
▼ for the yogurt, substitute buttermilk
▼ for the watercress, substitute cilantro (fresh coriander) leaves
▼ add 1 tablespoon minced fresh chives, parsley, or dill
▼ 1 chopped scallion or 1 teaspoon curry powder, or to taste

TIPS

▼ Many cucumbers are sold with a waxy coating to prolong their shelf life; unfortunately, the substance also seals in pesticides. The only way to remove the wax is by peeling; or, better yet, buy unwaxed cucumbers. The elongated European cucumbers (sometimes called Japanese or English cucumbers) are usually the best bet. They are grown hydroponically (in water) without pesticides. They cost more but have an excellent mild flavor, more tender texture, and fewer seeds.

▼ Vegetable leaves such as spinach, cabbage, and lettuce, may be cut into coarse shreds, known as a "chiffonade." Herbs with large leaves, such as basil, may also be cut in this manner. Stack the leaves and roll the pile tightly. Slice across the roll to make fine or coarse strips, depending on the leaf you are using and the use intended.

PURÉED SOUPS

There are various ways a soup can be thickened. Most common in traditional recipes is the use of cream; but puréeing cooked ingredients such as potatoes, beans, or peas reduces the mixture to a smooth consistency with the starch acting as the thickener. The result is a soup with body, flavor, plenty of nutrients, and fewer calories.

When potatoes are the thickening agent, it is best to use brown-skinned baking potatoes, Russets or Idahos (which have been peeled). They are higher in starch than red-skinned potatoes, which remain firmer after being cooked. Potatoes, as well as beans and peas, need to be well cooked, rather than firm, to perform well in their role as a thickener.

Another trick I use in this chapter is to chop and sauté some of the vegetables in a small amount of oil before they are simmered in the stock. This method adds flavor and eliminates the need for lengthy cooking.

Once the soup mixture is cooked, a blender is the most effective for achieving a totally smooth soup. Food processors purée unevenly; and if overprocessed, potatoes become gummy. But a food processor can be used, if necessary—just don't overdo it. Since the quantities are small, the entire batch can be puréed all at once using any of these appliances.

Most of the recipes in this section call for vegetable stock; however, chicken stock can be substituted (I recommend low-sodium and defatted). And there are innumerable possibilities for using different vegetables and seasonings, too.

Like the other recipes in this chapter, these recipes provide 2 servings. They will keep for 2 days in the refrigerator. After they have set, many of these soups thicken, so it may be necessary to add milk, vegetable stock, or water to thin them to the proper consistency. When reheating, do not allow those containing milk to boil.

▼ Store either new or mature potatoes in a cool, dry, well-ventilated dark place where they will remain at their best for 1 to 2 weeks. Do not store in the refrigerator; their starch will begin to convert to sugar, and they may turn brown when you cook them. If stored in bright light, potatoes will turn green and develop a bitter flavor.

CREAMY POTATO- CARROT SOUP

▼ ▼ ▼

With all the possible variations, and your own too, this can serve as your basic warm puréed soup recipe.

MAKES 2 SERVINGS

1 cup water
1 teaspoon vegetable stock powder
2 teaspoons olive oil
1 cup chopped carrot
¼ cup chopped celery
1 tablespoon minced shallot
1 medium-size potato, peeled and cut into ½-inch cubes
  (1 cup)
1 cup skim milk
1 teaspoon low-sodium soy sauce
½ teaspoon dried thyme or 1½ teaspoons fresh leaves
¼ teaspoon ground sage
⅛ teaspoon freshly ground black pepper, or to taste

GARNISH: *dash of paprika, minced fresh parsley, chopped walnuts, Herbed Croutons (page 220)*

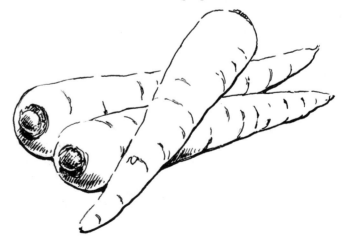

TIPS

▼ Shallots are small bulbous herbs midway between onion and garlic in taste. There is no substitute for fresh shallots; de-hydrated or powdered products will not do justice to your dishes. Fresh shallots will keep for months in the bottom bin of your refrigerator; use them be-fore they begin to sprout.

▼ If you do not have fresh shal-lots, for 1 tablespoon minced shallot, you can substitute 1 ta-blespoon minced onion and ½ teaspoon minced garlic.

- The term "1 shallot" in a recipe means 1 medium-size clove, not the whole bulb. Like garlic, remove the parchmentlike peeling; also, like garlic, when cooking do not allow them to brown or they will give a bitter taste.
- Dissolving ¼ cup milk powder per cup of milk in creamy soups and sauces will provide added calcium and protein without altering the flavor or adding fat.

In a measuring cup, dissolve the stock powder in the water. Set aside.

Heat the olive oil in a medium-size saucepan over medium heat. Add the carrot and celery; cook, stirring, until the vegetables begin to soften, about 4 minutes. Add the shallot and sauté 30 seconds longer. Stir in the vegetable stock and potato. Increase the heat to high; allow the mixture to come to a boil. Reduce the heat to medium-low, cover, and cook until the potato cubes are tender, about 5 minutes.

Transfer the mixture to a blender or food processor. Add the milk; process until smooth. Return the mixture to the saucepan. Stir in the soy sauce, thyme, sage, and pepper. Heat, stirring constantly; do not allow the mixture to boil. Taste; adjust the seasonings. Ladle into a soup bowl and garnish.

1 serving: Calories 177 (25% from fat)/Protein 6.3g/Carb 26.8g/Fat 4.9g/Chol 2mg/Sodium 200mg/Calcium 181mg/Food Exchanges: Milk 0.4/Veg 1.2/Bread 0.9/Fat 0.9

VARIATIONS

- for the carrot, substitute broccoli florets, cut asparagus, sliced zucchini, corn, or your choice of other vegetables
- for the thyme and sage, substitute rosemary, dill, a dash of nutmeg, or about ¼ cup Basil Pesto (page 25)
- when the puréed mixture is returned to the saucepan, add ¼ cup freshly grated Parmesan or Romano cheese, stirring to melt; or, add ½ cup shredded spinach; cover and cook over low heat until it is softened, about 5 minutes

CURRIED SWEET POTATO SOUP

▼ ▼ ▼

MAKES 2 SERVINGS

1 cup water
1 teaspoon vegetable stock powder
1 teaspoon olive oil
1 tablespoon minced shallot
1 teaspoon curry powder, or to taste
1 small potato, peeled and cut into ½-inch cubes (½ cup)
One 8-ounce can sweet potatoes, drained
1 cup skim milk
⅛ teaspoon freshly ground black pepper, or to taste

GARNISH: *dollop low-fat plain yogurt, minced fresh parsley, cilantro (fresh coriander) leaves, unsalted sunflower seeds, chopped walnuts*

In a measuring cup, dissolve the stock powder in the water. Set aside.

Heat the olive oil in a medium-size saucepan over medium heat. Add the shallot; cook, stirring, until tender but not browned, about 30 seconds. Stir in the curry powder. Stir in the vegetable stock and potato. Increase the heat to high and bring the mixture to a boil. Reduce the heat to medium-low, cover, and cook until the potato cubes are tender, about 5 minutes. Pour the cooked potato with liquid into a blender or food processor. Add the sweet potatoes and milk; purée. Pour the puréed mixture into the saucepan; stir in the pepper. Place over medium heat to warm, stirring occasionally. Taste; adjust the seasonings. Garnish and serve.

1 serving: Calories 207 (13% from fat)/Protein 6.9g/Carb 38.3g/Fat 2.9g/Chol 2mg/Sodium 126mg/Calcium 185mg/Food Exchanges: Milk 0.4/Veg 0.1/Bread 1.8/Fat 0.4

TIPS

▼ Sweet potatoes and yams are plump, smooth-skinned tubers of a plant in the morning glory family; they are actually not related to potatoes! They have a light skin, firm texture, and the flesh is yellow in color. The soft-fleshed variety, called yams, is moist, orange, and quite sweet when cooked; this is the type usually used for canning. Read the labels when buying canned sweet potatoes; some are "candied"; the better choice is a can containing simply sweet potatoes.

- ▼ with the shallot, sauté 1 tablespoon chopped Anaheim pepper
- ▼ for the sweet potato, substitute one 12-ounce package frozen cooked winter squash, thawed
- ▼ with the pepper, stir in ½ teaspoon grated fresh ginger or a dash of ground cumin

PEA SOUP
▼ ▼ ▼

MAKES 2 SERVINGS
1 cup water
1 teaspoon vegetable stock powder
1 teaspoon olive oil
¼ cup chopped celery
1 tablespoon minced shallot
1½ cups frozen peas
Dash of ground white pepper, or to taste
½ cup skim milk
Dash of ground nutmeg

GARNISH: *Parmesan Cream (page 157), freshly grated Parmesan cheese, Herbed Croutons (page 220), minced fresh parsley*

In a measuring cup, dissolve the stock powder in the water. Set aside.

Heat the olive oil in a medium-size saucepan over medium heat. Add the celery; cook, stirring, until tender, about 3 minutes. Add the shallot; sauté 30 seconds longer, taking care not to brown the shallot. Stir in the vegetable stock, peas, and white pepper. Increase the heat to high and bring the mixture to a boil. Reduce the heat to medium-low, cover, and cook about 5 min-

TIPS
- ▼ Freshly ground nutmeg is much more aromatic and flavorful than preground nutmeg. Many types of nutmeg graters are available in gourmet shops; when grating, the entire nutmeg is usable. Stored in a jar in your spice cabinet, whole nutmeg will keep its flavor for years.
- ▼ Generally, for flavor, baby peas are preferable to the standard-size ones; petit pois or baby peas, harvested when young, remain especially sweet after picking.
- ▼ For a flavorable soup garnish make *Parmesan Cream*. For 2 servings, stir together until smooth: 2 tablespoons low-fat plain yogurt, 1 tablespoon freshly grated Parmesan cheese, and a dash of freshly ground black pepper. (24 calories—1.2g fat per serving)

utes. Transfer the soup mixture into a blender or food processor. Add the milk; purée. Pour the puréed mixture into the saucepan; stir in the nutmeg. Heat through, about 5 minutes, stirring constantly. Taste; adjust the seasonings. Ladle the soup into a soup bowl; top with the garnish of your choice.

1 serving: Calories 144 (17% from fat)/Protein 8.5/Carb 21.5g/Fat 2.7g/Chol 1mg/Sodium 149mg/Calcium 112mg/Food Exchanges: Milk 0.2/Veg 0.1/Bread 1.1/Fat 0.4

VARIATIONS

▼ vary the texture of the soup by not completely puréeing it
▼ along with the milk and nutmeg, stir in 1 carrot, sliced and steamed until tender, more whole peas, or sautéed sliced mushrooms

SPICY TOMATO-CARROT SOUP WITH CHEVRE CREAM

▼ ▼ ▼

MAKES 2 SERVINGS
1 teaspoon olive oil
½ cup finely chopped carrot
2 tablespoons finely chopped celery
1 tablespoon minced shallot
2 large ripe tomatoes, peeled (pages 91–92) and cut into
   ½-inch cubes (3 cups)
1½ cups tomato juice (10-ounce bottle)
1 bay leaf
1 teaspoon sugar (optional)
1 teaspoon dried basil or 1 tablespoon minced fresh
½ teaspoon dried thyme or 1½ teaspoons fresh leaves

▼ ▼ ▼

ADVANCE PREPARATION
This reheats well or may be served chilled. Refrigerate the Chevre Cream separately.

▼ ▼ ▼

▼ The best tomatoes for cooking
are those which are vine-
ripened. Though more expensive, greenhouse tomatoes are
often the better choice in the
winter.

▼ You can freeze vine-ripened
tomatoes when they are in season. Wash them, cut into quarters, and spread them on
baking sheets. Freeze; then
transfer to plastic bags. When
you're ready to use them, the
peeling will be easy to remove
as the tomatoes begin to de-
frost. The texture will be mushy
but works just fine in recipes
where the tomatoes are to be
cooked.

▼ It is not necessary to remove
the tiny thyme leaves one by
one. Hold the bunch of thyme
in one hand; and with the
other, scrape downward with a
sharp knife or with your fingers, removing most of the
leaves. The tender stems at the
tip can be minced along with
the leaves. Thyme actually
dries with better flavor than
many herbs, so dried thyme is
an acceptable alternative.

½ teaspoon freshly ground black pepper, or to taste

FOR THE CHEVRE CREAM
1 tablespoon goat cheese (chevre)
1 tablespoon low-fat plain yogurt
½ teaspoon balsamic vinegar, or to taste

GARNISH: *minced fresh parsley or chives, or fresh basil leaves*

Heat the olive oil in a medium-size saucepan over medium
heat. Add the carrot and celery; cook, stirring, about four minutes. Add the shallot and sauté about 30 seconds more, until the
vegetables are tender but not browned.

Stir in the remaining ingredients (except for the fresh basil, if
used). Increase the heat to high; bring the mixture to a boil.
Reduce the heat to medium-low, cover, and cook for 10 minutes,
stirring occasionally. (Add fresh basil during the last minute.)

While the soup is cooking, mix the Chevre Cream ingredients
in a small bowl until smooth. Taste; add more balsamic vinegar
if you want a stronger flavor. Set aside.

Remove the bay leaf. Pour the soup mixture into a blender or
food processor; purée. Taste; adjust the seasonings. Spoon into a
soup bowl, top with a dollop of the cream, and garnish.

1 serving: Calories 142 (29% from fat)/Protein 4.4g/Carb 20.8g/Fat
4.6g/Chol 5mg/Sodium 77mg/Calcium 53mg/Food Exchanges: Veg
2.8/Fat 0.4

VARIATIONS

▼ for the fresh tomatoes, substitute one 14½-ounce can tomatoes with juice
▼ after the soup is puréed, add about ½ cup hot cooked rice
▼ for the Chevre Cream, substitute Parmesan Cream (page
157), a dollop of low-fat plain yogurt or chevre, crumbled
mild feta cheese, or Herbed Croutons (page 220)

▼ Buy fresh corn for immediate use because the flavor deteriorates noticeably within days after it has been harvested. Look for:

- ▼ vivid green husks that snugly encase the kernels
- ▼ exposed corn silk that is silky rather than brown and dry
- ▼ a cut stem end that is soft and moist
- ▼ a garden-fresh smell
- ▼ in peeling back part of the husk, find rows that are parallel, not crooked
- ▼ ripe kernels that, when popped with your fingernail, are milky
- ▼ If you must store corn, leave it in its own husks, seal it in a plastic bag, and refrigerate.

▼ Paprika is a bright red powder made from a certain variety of pepper. The most flavorful variety comes from Hungary where it is produced in pungency from mild to very hot. There is also a Spanish version called *pimenton*. In addition to hotness, paprika also provides sweetness. Store your container of paprika in the refrigerator to preserve the color and flavor.

CURRIED CORN AND PEPPER CHOWDER

▼ ▼ ▼

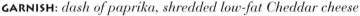

MAKES 2 SERVINGS
3 cobs fresh sweet corn, kernels cut from cob (1½ cups)
1 cup water
1 teaspoon vegetable stock powder
2 teaspoons olive oil
¼ cup seeded and diced green bell pepper
¼ cup seeded and diced red bell pepper
1 tablespoon minced shallot
2 teaspoons curry powder, or to taste
1 small potato, peeled and cut into ½-inch cubes (½ cup)
1 cup skim milk
¼ teaspoon freshly ground black pepper, or to taste

GARNISH: *dash of paprika, shredded low-fat Cheddar cheese*

Place the corn in a microwave-proof dish, add a small amount of water, cover, and cook on high for 7 to 8 minutes (a shorter time if corn is very fresh), until tender.

In a measuring cup, combine the stock powder and water; set aside.

In a medium-size saucepan, over medium heat, heat the olive oil. Add the bell peppers; cook, stirring, until tender, 5 minutes. Add the shallot and curry powder; cook until the shallot is tender but not browned, 30 seconds longer. Remove 2 tablespoons of the vegetables; set aside in a small bowl.

When the corn is cooked, drain and remove ½ cup corn; set aside with the bell peppers.

Stir the remaining corn into the saucepan along with the vegetable stock and the cubed potato. Over high heat, bring the mixture to a boil; reduce the heat to medium-low, cover, and cook until the potato is tender, 5 minutes.

Pour the contents of the saucepan into a blender or food processor. Add the milk and pepper; purée. Return the soup to the saucepan; stir in the reserved corn and peppers. Heat over medium heat. Taste; adjust the seasonings. Ladle the soup into a serving bowl and garnish.

1 serving: Calories 246 (19% from fat)/Protein 9g/Carb 40.9g/Fat 5.2g/Chol 2mg/Sodium 73mg/Calcium 170mg/Food Exchanges: Milk 0.4/Veg 0.2/Bread 2.0/Fat 0.9

VARIATIONS

▼ for the fresh corn, substitute frozen (one 9-ounce package); reduce microwaving time to 4 to 6 minutes

▼ to make the soup hotter, when puréeing the soup, add a pinch of cayenne or crushed red pepper, or 1 tablespoon canned chopped green chilies

▼ to the cooked soup, add chicken cut into 1-inch squares and sautéed

I usually enjoy one serving of this soup hot—and a day or two later, the second serving cold. When cold, it tastes much like Vichyssoise, a French soup made by puréeing leeks and potatoes with heavy cream.

▼ ▼ ▼

ADVANCE PREPARATION
Will keep for 2 days refrigerated. Serve chilled or reheat.

▼ ▼ ▼

TIPS
▼ Leeks look like gigantic green onions but have a milder and sweeter flavor than onions. When buying, check the leaves; they should be bright green and have a texture that is not too fibrous. Also look for a thin white stem which is long for the size of the leek. Small or medium-size leeks, not exceeding 1½ inches in diameter, will be the most tender and delicate tasting. Store in a sealed plastic bag in the vegetable crisper drawer; they will keep for up to a week.

ASPARAGUS-LEEK SOUP
▼ ▼ ▼

MAKES 2 SERVINGS
1 cup water
1 teaspoon vegetable stock powder
2 cups cut asparagus (1-inch lengths)
1 medium-size potato, peeled and cut into ½-inch cubes (about 1 cup)
1 medium-size leek (white part only), cut into ⅛-inch slices (½ cup)
1 teaspoon olive oil
1 cup sliced mushrooms
1 cup skim milk
1 teaspoon low-sodium soy sauce
1 teaspoon curry powder, or to taste
¼ teaspoon freshly ground black pepper, or to taste
½ cup frozen corn, thawed

GARNISH: *dash of paprika and cooked asparagus tips*

In a measuring cup, dissolve the vegetable stock powder in the water. Pour into a medium-size saucepan. Stir in the asparagus, potato, and leek. Place the pan over high heat and bring to a boil. Reduce the heat to medium-low, cover, and cook until the potatoes and asparagus are tender, 5 minutes.

Meanwhile, heat the olive oil in a small skillet over medium heat. Add the mushrooms; cook, stirring, until tender, about 3 minutes. Set aside.

From the saucepan, remove 4 asparagus tips; set aside. Pour the remaining vegetables and the liquid into a blender or food processor. Add the milk; purée. Return the puréed mixture to saucepan. Stir in the soy sauce, curry powder, pepper, corn, and sautéed mushrooms. Heat over medium heat, stirring occasion-

▼ To use leeks, cut off the roots and tough outer leaves, split the remainder in half lengthwise, and wash very well under cold running water to remove the sand which collects between the layers and flat leaves. Chop or slice the white part; in many recipes you can also use up to 2 inches of the green part, if it is tender.

ally. Taste; adjust the seasonings. Ladle into a soup bowl; garnish with paprika and the reserved asparagus tips.

1 serving: Calories 254 (12% from fat)/Protein 12.7g/Carb 42.9g/Fat 3.5g/Chol 2mg/Sodium 184mg/Calcium 227mg/Food Exchanges: Milk 0.4/Veg 2.5/Bread 1.4/Fat 0.4

VARIATIONS
▼ for the asparagus, substitute 2 cups broccoli florets; omit the corn; serve warm
▼ for the leek, substitute 2 tablespoons chopped onion
▼ for the curry powder, substitute ½ teaspoon dried tarragon (delicious with the broccoli variation, too)

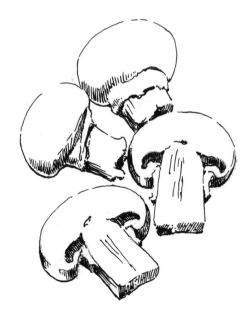

BLACK BEAN SOUP

▼ ▼ ▼

MAKES 2 SERVINGS

1 teaspoon olive oil
¼ cup chopped celery
2 tablespoons minced onion
½ teaspoon minced garlic
1 large tomato, peeled (pages 91–92) and cut into ½-inch
*   cubes (1½ cups)*
½ jalapeño pepper, seeds removed and minced (1 tablespoon)
½ teaspoon ground cumin
½ teaspoon dried oregano or 2 teaspoons minced fresh
1 cup water
1 teaspoon vegetable stock powder
1 cup drained and rinsed canned black beans
¼ teaspoon freshly ground black pepper, or to taste
1½ teaspoons minced cilantro (fresh coriander)—do not use
*   dried*

GARNISH: *dollop low-fat plain yogurt, diced red bell pepper,*
minced hard-cooked egg, sprig cilantro

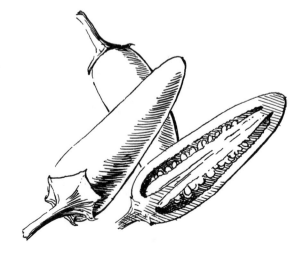

▼ ▼ ▼

ADVANCE PREPARATION

This keeps in the refrigerator for several days; it reheats well. You may need to add extra water since it thickens after setting.

▼ ▼ ▼

TIPS

▼ Buy plump, unshriveled, and unblemished chili peppers with bright-hued skin and no soft spots.

▼ Because they are quite hot, peppers should be minced finely and used sparingly; and since much of the "hotness" comes from the seeds and connecting membranes, remove them for a milder flavor.

▼ Be careful to avoid rubbing

your eyes, nose, or lips after you have handled chilies because burning can result. Wash your hands, knife, and cutting board well in hot soapy water to remove the volatile oil. And, especially if you wear contact lenses, you might want to wear disposable plastic gloves when working with hot peppers.

▼ Keep peppers refrigerated in a plastic bag or wrapped in paper towels; they will keep 1 to 3 weeks. You can freeze them by chopping or slicing them, placing the pieces on a tray, and freezing until firm. Transfer to a plastic bag or freezer container, label, and use as needed.

In a medium-size saucepan over medium heat, heat the olive oil. Add the celery and onion; cook, stirring, until the vegetables are tender, 4 minutes. Add the garlic; sauté 30 seconds longer. Stir in the tomato, jalapeño, cumin, and oregano. Continue to cook over medium heat for 5 minutes.

In a measuring cup, dissolve the stock powder in the water; add to the soup. Stir in the beans and pepper. Heat over medium heat, uncovered, for 5 minutes, adding the cilantro during the last minute. Remove ½ cup of the soup; purée in a blender or food processor. Stir back into the soup. Taste; adjust the seasonings. Ladle into a soup bowl; garnish.

1 serving: Calories 103 (29% from fat)/Protein 3.7g/Carb 14.7g/Fat 3.3g/Chol 0/Sodium 681mg/Calcium 38mg/Food Exchanges: Veg 1.0/Bread 0.5/Meat 0.1/Fat 0.5

VARIATIONS

▼ for a milder flavor, for the jalapeño, substitute 1 tablespoon minced Anaheim pepper or canned chopped green chilies
▼ when sautéing the vegetables, add diced green or red bell pepper or carrot
▼ for the black beans, substitute other beans such as kidney or cannellini beans
▼ for a spicier soup, add a dash of chili powder and/or cayenne pepper
▼ after the soup is puréed, add cooked corn or brown rice

CHUNKY SOUPS

These soups remind me of the kind my grandmother used to make. Her lifestyle allowed her hours at home as the pot simmered; she delighted in creating large quantities and her home was filled with wonderful aromas.

Here, the quantities are reduced. And sautéing the vegetables before adding the stock reduces the cooking time to a minimum to suit today's busy schedules—but the flavor is still distinctly homemade.

MINESTRONE SOUP
▼ ▼ ▼

This hearty Italian soup is a pared-down version of my old minestrone recipe, which simmered all day and made enough to serve a crowd.

▼ ▼ ▼

ADVANCE PREPARATION
Will keep for several days in the refrigerator. You may need to add extra liquid (use water, vegetable stock, or tomato juice) when reheating.

▼ ▼ ▼

MAKES 2 SERVINGS
1 cup water
1 teaspoon vegetable stock powder
1 teaspoon olive oil
½ cup diced carrot
½ cup diced zucchini
1 tablespoon seeded and chopped green bell pepper
1 tablespoon minced onion
½ teaspoon minced garlic
One 14½-ounce can tomatoes with juice
1 tablespoon tomato paste
¾ teaspoon dried basil or 1 tablespoon minced fresh
¾ teaspoon dried oregano or 1 tablespoon minced fresh
½ teaspoon freshly ground black pepper, or to taste
One 8-ounce can kidney beans (about 1 cup), drained and rinsed
¼ cup macaroni
1 tablespoon minced fresh parsley

GARNISH: *freshly grated Parmesan cheese*

▼ Many fresh herbs can be frozen. Wash and mince them; place 1 tablespoon in ice cube tray compartments. Add a small amount of water to cover; freeze. Once frozen, remove the cubes from the tray and store in a labeled container or plastic bag. Fresh herbs frozen in this way are ideal to drop into soups as they cook, though they aren't presentable as a garnish.

In a measuring cup, dissolve the stock powder in the water; set aside.

In a medium-size saucepan over medium heat, heat the olive oil. Add the carrot, zucchini, bell pepper, and onion. Cook, stirring, until the vegetables are tender but not browned, 4 to 5 minutes. Add the garlic; sauté 30 seconds longer. Stir in the vegetable stock and tomatoes; cut the tomatoes into quarters. Increase the heat to high.

In a measuring cup, stir together the tomato paste, dried basil and oregano (if using), and pepper. Thin with 2 tablespoons of the soup, then stir into the saucepan. Also stir in the kidney beans and macaroni. When the mixture comes to a boil, reduce the heat to medium-low. Cook, covered, until the macaroni is tender, 10 minutes. Add the parsley (and the fresh basil and oregano, if used) during the last minute or two. Taste; adjust the seasonings. Ladle into a soup bowl and garnish.

1 serving: Calories 253 (13% from fat)/Protein 11.4g/Carb 43.6g/Fat 3.6g/Chol 0/Sodium 724mg/Calcium 110mg/Food Exchanges: Veg 2.8/Bread 1.8/Fat 0.4

VARIATIONS

▼ for the kidney beans, substitute other beans such as garbanzo, black, navy, great northern, or cannellini beans

▼ for the macaroni, substitute other pasta such as small shells, orzo, or spaghetti broken into 1-inch lengths, or bulgur wheat or basmati rice

▼ with the tomatoes, add other vegetables such as steamed broccoli or cauliflower florets, or green beans; or sauté sliced mushrooms and chopped red bell pepper strips along with the other vegetables

▼ reduce the water to ¼ cup to make a thick "goulash-type" mixture which can be served as an entrée; raw cashews or cooked chicken can be added

VEGETABLE-BARLEY SOUP

▼ ▼ ▼

A good basic vegetable soup, I love this for a winter lunch; it is also light enough to serve as a first course any time of the year.

TIPS

▼ Barley contains five times more fiber than rice and twice as much as pasta. It is cholesterol- and sodium-free, low in fat, and a good source of protein. The nutrient-laden outer covering is removed when "pearl" barley is husked and polished, but many valuable nutrients remain. Although it is a grain, barley is usually found alongside the dried beans in supermarkets. Store it in an airtight and bug-proof container in a cool, dry place.

MAKES 2 SERVINGS

2½ cups water
2 teaspoons vegetable stock powder
2 teaspoons olive oil
½ cup thinly sliced carrot
½ cup sliced zucchini (halved lengthwise and cut into ¼-inch slices)
¼ cup thinly sliced celery
1 small onion, chopped (about ¼ cup)
1 medium-size tomato, cut into ½-inch cubes (1 cup)
2 tablespoons quick-cooking barley
1 bay leaf
¼ teaspoon dried oregano or 1 teaspoon minced fresh
¼ teaspoon ground sage or 1½ teaspoons minced fresh
1 tablespoon tomato paste
1 tablespoon minced fresh parsley
¼ teaspoon freshly ground black pepper, or to taste

GARNISH: *freshly grated Parmesan cheese, Herbed Croutons (page 220)*

In a measuring cup, dissolve the stock powder in the water. Set aside.

In a medium-size saucepan over medium heat, heat the olive oil. Add the carrot, zucchini, celery, and onion. Cook, stirring, until the vegetables are tender but not brown, 4 to 5 minutes. Stir in the vegetable stock; increase the heat to high. Stir in the tomato, barley, bay leaf, oregano, and sage. When the mixture comes to a boil, reduce the heat to medium-low. Cook, covered, until the barley is tender, 10 minutes.

Remove the bay leaf from the saucepan. Stir in the tomato paste, parsley, and pepper. Heat for a minute or so. Taste; adjust the seasonings. Ladle into a soup bowl and garnish.

1 serving: Calories 137 (34% from fat)/Protein 3.4g/Carb 19.2g/Fat 5.2g/Chol 0/Sodium 37mg/Calcium 36mg/Food Exchanges: Veg 1.7/Bread 0.5/Fat 0.9

VARIATIONS

▼ when sautéing, add or substitute other vegetables such as red bell pepper strips, sliced mushrooms, or sliced yellow squash

▼ for the fresh tomato, substitute one 7½-ounce can tomatoes with juice; quarter the tomatoes; reduce the amount of water added to 1¾ cups

▼ with the tomato, stir in steamed vegetables such as broccoli florets or cut green beans; or add frozen vegetables such as peas or corn; or 3 chopped marinated sun-dried tomatoes; or canned beans that have been drained and rinsed such as black, great northern, garbanzo, or cannellini beans

▼ for the barley, substitute bulgur wheat or basmati rice

MEXICAN TACO SOUP

▼ ▼ ▼

Corn and beans combine to form a complete protein in this hearty main-course soup.

▼ ▼ ▼

ADVANCE PREPARATION
Will keep, refrigerated, for several days. The flavors will blend, and it reheats well.

▼ ▼ ▼

TIPS
▼ Garbanzo beans are sometimes called chick peas, ceci beans, or Spanish beans. They are nutlike in flavor and nutlike in appearance, too, for they are a shape and size similar to a hazelnut. One of the most nutritious of the legumes, they contain high amounts of calcium, phosphorus, and potassium. They are higher in fat than most beans, but most of that is unsaturated.

MAKES 2 SERVINGS
¼ cup water
1 teaspoon vegetable stock powder
1 teaspoon olive oil
2 tablespoons minced celery
2 tablespoons minced onion
2 tablespoons seeded and minced red bell pepper
½ teaspoon minced garlic
One 14½-ounce can tomatoes with juice
½ cup drained and rinsed canned garbanzo beans
¼ cup frozen corn
1 tablespoon canned chopped green chilies
¼ teaspoon ground cumin
¼ teaspoon freshly ground black pepper, or to taste
1 tablespoon minced fresh parsley
1 teaspoon minced cilantro (fresh coriander)—do not use dried

GARNISH: *Baked Tortilla Chips (page 219), sprig cilantro, shredded reduced-fat Cheddar or Monterey jack cheese*

Preheat the oven to 400° F. if Baked Tortilla Chips are your choice of garnish.

In a measuring cup, dissolve the stock powder in the water; set aside.

In a medium-size saucepan over medium heat, heat the olive oil. Add the celery, onion, and red bell pepper and cook, stirring, until tender, 4 to 5 minutes. Add the garlic; sauté 30 seconds longer. Stir in the tomatoes, vegetable stock, beans, corn, chilies, cumin, and pepper. Quarter the tomatoes. Increase the heat to high. When the mixture comes to a boil, reduce the heat to medium-low. Cook, covered, for 10 minutes. Add the parsley and cilantro during the last minute or two.

While the soup is cooking, prepare the tortilla chips if you plan to use them as a garnish.

Taste the soup; adjust the seasonings. Ladle into a soup bowl and top with the tortilla chips and/or other garnishes.

1 serving: Calories 141 (23% from fat)/Protein 4.9g/Carb 22.3g/Fat 3.6g/Chol 0/Sodium 563mg/Calcium 82mg/Food Exchanges: Veg 2.0/Bread 0.8/Fat 0.4

VARIATIONS

▼ when adding the canned tomatoes, stir in 1 drained 5-ounce can white chicken packed in water or add freshly cooked and shredded chicken breast

▼ for the garbanzo beans, substitute other beans such as kidney, pinto, or black beans

▼ rather than topping the soup with the Baked Tortilla Chips, line the soup bowl with ½ by 1½-inch strips of corn tortillas; then add the soup; cover and allow to set for a few minutes to allow the strips to soften

VEGETARIAN CHILI

▼ ▼ ▼

MAKES 2 SERVINGS

2 teaspoons olive oil
½ cup coarsely shredded carrot
½ cup seeded and chopped green bell pepper
2 tablespoons chopped celery
2 tablespoons chopped onion
½ teaspoon minced garlic
One 8-ounce can tomatoes with juice
One 8-ounce can kidney beans (about 1 cup), drained and
  rinsed
1 cup water
3 tablespoons tomato paste
1 teaspoon sugar
¾ teaspoon chili powder, or to taste
½ teaspoon dried basil or 2 teaspoons minced fresh
½ teaspoon dried oregano or 2 teaspoons minced fresh
¼ teaspoon freshly ground black pepper, or to taste
⅛ teaspoon ground cumin
Dash of hot pepper sauce, or to taste

GARNISH: corn, chopped scallions, raw cashews, shredded
  low-fat Cheddar or Monterey jack cheese, or a combination

In a medium-size saucepan over medium heat, heat the olive
oil. Add the carrot, bell pepper, celery, and onion; cook, stirring,
until the vegetables are tender, 4 to 5 minutes. Add the garlic;
sauté 30 seconds longer. Stir in the remaining ingredients (except the fresh basil and oregano, if using). Quarter the tomatoes.
Increase the heat to high; bring the mixture to a boil. Reduce the
heat to medium-low, cover, and cook until heated through,
about 5 minutes. (Add the fresh basil and oregano, if used, during the last minute or two.) Taste; adjust the seasonings. Ladle
into a soup bowl, garnish, and serve.

▼ ▼ ▼

ADVANCE PREPARATION
This will keep in the refrigerator for several days. The flavors
blend, and it reheats well.
Extra liquid may need to be
added when reheating.

▼ ▼ ▼

▼ When chopping an onion, cut it in half through the root, but don't cut the root end off. Place cut side down on a cutting board. Cut lengthwise slices to, but not through, the root. Then make crosswise cuts through the onion. Or an onion can be chopped quickly in a food processor. Refrigerated onions tend not to release the tear-producing vapors as much as those stored at room temperature.

▼ In Mexican markets, chili powder is simply a powdered form of ancho, pasilla, or other dried red pepper; however the domestic varieties often contain extra seasonings such as cumin, oregano, garlic, black pepper, and paprika. If you want to make your chili powder hotter, add cayenne pepper.

▼ Once open, refrigerate hot pepper sauce to retain the flavor and color.

▼ Cayenne pepper is the ground dried pod of the small, more pungent varieties of chili peppers. Use with restraint because it is very hot. Store it in a tightly closed container in the refrigerator.

1 serving: Calories 235 (22% from fat)/Protein 9.5g/Carb 36.3g/Fat 5.7g/Chol 0/Sodium 598mg/Calcium 92mg/Food Exchanges: Veg 2.8/Bread 1.2/Fat 0.9

VARIATIONS

▼ when sautéing, add other vegetables such as sliced mushrooms, zucchini, or 1 seeded and chopped jalapeño pepper; or when stirring in the tomatoes, add steamed broccoli florets, steamed potato cubes, corn, or canned diced green chilies

▼ substitute other beans such as pinto, garbanzo, or black beans

▼ for a hotter chili, add a dash of cayenne pepper or a pinch of crushed red pepper

▼ add 2 tablespoons raw cashews while the soup is simmering

▼ with the vegetables sauté 4 ounces boneless, skinless chicken breast, cut into ½-inch squares

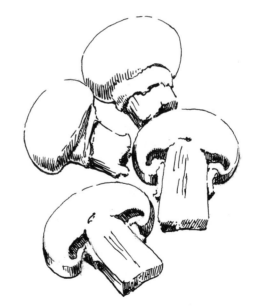

SALADS

Few foods have more visual appeal or alluring variations than salads. The possibilities are infinite, making them an easy solution to cooking for one. And, from a nutritional point of view, salads fill our need for eating uncooked fruits and vegetables high in fiber and vitamins.

Salads can be an excuse to use whatever is in season as you play with combinations of colors, textures, temperatures, and flavors. Salads can be an excuse to make an excursion to the local farmers' market, or they can be assembled from ingredients already on hand.

Some salads can be tossed quickly. Many can be prepared in advance and kept in the refrigerator until needed. Some can be stuffed into pita bread pockets for a "salad on the go" or can be packed in a container to make good take-along foods if you need to pack your lunch or want to go on a picnic. Or, salads can be "composed," as you arrange the ingredients with style on the plate. Let these creations bring out the artist in you!

Most of the salads in this chapter can be the focal point of your meal; or in smaller portions, they can serve as accompaniments. There are vegetable salads, grain salads, bean salads, and fruit salads. Some are warm—most are chilled. And remember, there is no need to limit them to summer dining.

The nutritional analyses in this chapter are provided for the total salads, including dressing, as well as separate figures for the salad dressings alone.

THE MIXED GREEN SALAD

The "mixed green salad" is one of the most misused and abused expressions in food terminology. In many homes and restaurants, it often means iceberg lettuce that is either slightly rusted or wilted, with perhaps the addition of a soft slice of tasteless cucumber or a pale tomato wedge. Dressings poured from a bottle are lacking in robust flavor, due to a high percentage of fat and the addition of preservatives.

There are really no firm rules for making a good salad combination. So here I present some practical guidelines for a proper and superb "mixed green salad."

THE GREENS

▼ If iceberg is the only type of lettuce you eat, you are consistently choosing the least nutritious member of a family of nutritional champions; and iceberg also is far less flavorful than many of the other greens. As a general rule, the darker green the leaves, the more nutritious the salad.

▼ By varying the greens in your salads, you can create a medley of different colors, textures, and flavors and boost the nutritional content at the same time. Many produce departments now sell a ready-made blend of mixed greens, usually sold in small bags ideal for the single gourmet.

SHOPPING TIPS

▼ Avoid wilted, limp, withered greens that have brown or yellow edges, dark or slimy spots, dirty leaves, or signs of insect damage.

▼ Salad greens should be crisp, fresh-looking, and vivid in color. Lesser quality can be masked in a cooked dish but not in a salad!

STORAGE AND PREPARATION

▼ Pick off any discolored leaves and store lettuce without washing. Wrap it in a plastic bag and place it in the refrigerator crisper, or in a plastic crisper container designed for the storage of greens.

▼ Soft-leaved lettuces do not keep as well as firm greens, such as romaine or iceberg. Iceberg should keep for up to 2 weeks, romaine for about 10 days, and butterhead and leaf lettuces for about 4 days. Delicate greens, such as arugula or watercress, are the most perishable; buy only enough for immediate use or keep them for no more than a day or two.

▼ Don't store greens near fruits because most give off ethylene gas as they ripen. The gas will cause the greens to develop brown spots and to decay rapidly.

▼ For loose-leaf lettuce, twist off the stem and wash the leaves separately in cool water. These greens are grown in sandy soil and require careful cleaning.

▼ Never allow greens to soak in water. After washing, dry them as thoroughly as possible using paper towels or a thin kitchen towel. Be careful not to crush or bruise the leaves. Or a salad spinner will dry them quickly and thoroughly.

▼ If necessary, greens can be washed a couple of hours before using. Refrigerate the leaves in a tightly closed plastic bag; put a paper towel in the bottom of the bag to absorb any excess moisture. If the greens are limp, wrap them in a damp paper towel or thin kitchen towel to crisp and refresh them.

▼ Tear, don't cut, greens to avoid bruising. Remove the rib and stem if they are thick or coarse.

THE EMBELLISHMENTS

▼ From this list of suggestions, choose other ingredients to toss into your salads to add texture, flavor, and visual appeal. Or use these ingredients as garnishes to top a bowl of greens. For variety, you can toss an assortment of these ingredients with your choice of dressing for a different sort of salad, eliminating the greens.

Alfalfa sprouts
Asparagus
Beans
Bean sprouts
Beets
Broccoli florets
Cabbage
Carrots
Cauliflower florets
Celery
Cheese
Croutons
Cucumber
Fresh herbs
Fruits
Grains
Green and red bell pepper
Green beans

Hard-cooked egg
Jicama
Leeks
Mushrooms
Nuts
Onions
Pasta
Pea pods
Peas
Potatoes
Radishes
Scallions
Seeds
Snap peas
Sunflower seeds
Tomatoes
Zucchini

BASIC SALAD DRESSINGS

Salads are rightly associated with healthful eating; but, unfortunately, many salads are spoiled by being drowned in high-fat dressings. Just 2 tablespoons of most supermarket dressings can increase a salad's calories by 150 and the fat by a high percentage. Store-bought low-fat versions seem to be watery and flavorless. Furthermore, most commercially prepared dressings are loaded with salt and preservatives. My dressings, which contain no salt or preservatives, are not only lower in fat but are so flavorful that only a small amount is necessary.

The secret to using a small amount of oil is to use high-quality, flavorful ingredients. For most salads, a fine olive oil is best. But, in some of my recipes, oil has been eliminated entirely. Fine vinegars, in all their various colors and tastes, play a great part in these dressings, as do herbs, and the aromatic flavors of Dijon mustard, garlic, and ginger.

Each week, when time permits, if you prepare one or two low-fat, salt- and preservative-free dressings, you'll have them on hand as staples to toss with your mixed green salad as the rest of your meal is cooking. The dressings are uncooked, requiring only whisking to combine; sometimes I place the ingredients in a jar (or a refrigerator container with a pour spout in the lid) and mix them by shaking. If any dried herbs are used, allow the dressing to sit a few minutes before using to hydrate the herbs. Be sure to whisk or shake the dressings again before adding them to your salads. Each recipe makes a small quantity; 1 tablespoon per serving is all you really need to dress most accompaniment salads, perhaps 2 tablespoons for a large salad. Be sure to add the dressing to your salad just before serving.

In addition, a number of dressings which are included as part of salad recipes or in other chapters can be used to dress your basic green salad:

- Light olive oil is pure olive oil with less than 5% extra-virgin content. It may have a lighter flavor and color, but it has the same calories as other olive oils.
- Oils can turn rancid at room temperature, but in the refrigerator they will keep for months. Safflower oil is usable direct from the refrigerator; but, when chilled, olive oil and dressings made from it will totally or partially turn cloudy and may solidify. Just let them warm up to room temperature or run the closed container under warm water.
- Vinegars infused with herbs (most often tarragon, basil, or garlic) are available in most supermarkets.
- Wine vinegars are made from red or white wine. They are mellow and full-bodied, and they retain the aroma of the wine from which they are made.

This can become your all-purpose dressing varied by using different vinegars and by adding herbs or Basil Pesto (page 25).

▼ ▼ ▼

Creamy Pesto Dressing (page 26)
Curried Yogurt Dressing (page 204)
Curry Vinaigrette (page 201)
Ginger-Soy Vinaigrette (page 196)
Honey-Mustard Dressing (page 190)
Lemon-Cinnamon Dressing (page 198)
Orange-Poppy Seed Dressing (page 205)
Raspberry Vinaigrette (page 204)
Sesame-Pepper Dressing (page 30)
Tomato Dressing (page 188)
Walnut Vinaigrette (page 203)

BASIC VINAIGRETTE
▼ ▼ ▼

MAKES ½ CUP
¼ cup red wine vinegar
2 tablespoons fresh lemon juice
1 tablespoon extra-virgin olive oil

Will keep, refrigerated, up to 2
weeks in a tightly closed container.

▼ ▼ ▼

TIPS

▼ Dijon mustard, which originat-
ed in France, is made from a
combination of husked and
ground mustard seeds, herbs,
spices, and white wine, making
it more flavorful, and more
expensive, than ordinary mustard. Some brands are available
unsalted.

▼ Vinegars do not require refrigeration and most will keep
about two years in a kitchen
cabinet.

1 teaspoon Dijon mustard
½ teaspoon minced garlic
⅛ teaspoon freshly ground black pepper, or to taste

In a small bowl, whisk together all the ingredients. Taste;
adjust the seasonings. Whisk or shake before serving.

1 tablespoon: Calories 19 (80% from fat)/Protein 0/Carb 0.9g/Fat
1.7g/Chol 0/Sodium 2mg/Calcium 1mg/Food Exchanges: Fat 0.3

VARIATIONS

▼ substitute other vinegars such as white rice or herbal vinegar
▼ add herbs or spices such as basil, celery seeds, chives, cilantro,
marjoram, paprika, parsley, tarragon, thyme (½ teaspoon
dried or 2 teaspoons minced fresh)
▼ for *Pesto Vinaigrette*, add Basil Pesto (page 25) to taste
▼ add a dash of honey for sweetness

This pairs well with greens, beans, grains, fish, and chicken.

▼ ▼ ▼

ADVANCE PREPARATION

If dried herbs are used, allow the dressing to set at least 15 minutes before using to hydrate them. Will keep, refrigerated, up to 2 weeks in a tightly closed container.

▼ ▼ ▼

TIPS

▼ Balsamic vinegar is an aged Italian red wine vinegar. The best are made in Modena, where the vinegar is transferred from red oak kegs to chestnut, mulberry, and juniper, each adding traces of flavor. Store in a cool, dark place for up to 6 months once opened. (Be aware that cheap imitations are made from wine with the additions of cane sugar, vanilla, licorice, and caramel flavoring.)

BALSAMIC VINAIGRETTE

▼ ▼ ▼

MAKES ½ CUP
¼ cup balsamic vinegar
¼ cup water
1 teaspoon extra-virgin olive oil
1 teaspoon Dijon mustard
2 teaspoons minced fresh basil or ¼ teaspoon dried
1 teaspoon light brown sugar
½ teaspoon minced garlic
⅛ teaspoon freshly ground black pepper, or to taste

In a small bowl, whisk together all the ingredients, stirring until the sugar is dissolved. Taste; adjust the seasonings. Whisk or shake before serving.

1 tablespoon: Calories 25 (61% from fat)/Protein 0/Carb 2.4g/Fat 1.7g/Chol 0/Sodium 6.4mg/Calcium 1.3mg/Food Exchanges: Fat 0.3

VARIATIONS

▼ omit the olive oil
▼ for the basil, substitute fresh or dried tarragon or thyme, fresh parsley, or cilantro (fresh coriander); a dash of ground cumin can also be added

HONEY-POPPY SEED DRESSING

▼ ▼ ▼

Both this sweetened dressing and its mint variation can be served over a fruit salad as well as a green salad. And one of my favorites is a mix of salad spinach, strawberries, and grapes tossed with this dressing.

▼ ▼ ▼

ADVANCE PREPARATION
Will keep, refrigerated, up to 2 weeks in a tightly closed container.

▼ ▼ ▼

MAKES ½ CUP
¼ cup white rice vinegar
3 tablespoons honey
2 tablespoons safflower oil
½ teaspoon poppy seeds
¼ teaspoon freshly ground black pepper, or to taste

In a small bowl, whisk together all the ingredients. Taste; adjust the seasonings. Whisk or shake before serving.

1 tablespoon: Calories 68 (47% from fat)/Protein 0.1g/Carb 9g/Fat 3.6g/Chol 0/Sodium 1mg/Calcium 6mg/Food Exchanges: Fat 0.6

VARIATIONS

▼ for *Honey-Mint Dressing*, omit the poppy seeds, substitute 1½ teaspoons minced fresh mint or ½ teaspoon dried

SESAME-GINGER DRESSING

▼ ▼ ▼

This dressing is the perfect topping for salads to accompany your oriental-theme meals.

▼ ▼ ▼

ADVANCE PREPARATION
Will keep, refrigerated, up to 2 weeks in a tightly closed container.

▼ ▼ ▼

TIPS
▼ Buy amber-colored, imported sesame oil rather than light-colored sesame oils which are not extracted from toasted sesame seeds and lack the distinctive strong flavor. Because its aromatics are quite volatile, sesame oil is usually added as one of the last steps in the cooking procedure; it is a flavoring oil, not a cooking oil.

MAKES ½ CUP
⅓ cup white rice vinegar
1 tablespoon low-sodium soy sauce
1 teaspoon dark sesame oil
1 teaspoon grated fresh ginger
1 teaspoon sugar
½ teaspoon minced garlic
½ teaspoon toasted sesame seeds (pages 30–31)
Dash of ground white pepper, or to taste

In a small bowl, whisk together all the ingredients, making certain the sugar is dissolved. Taste; adjust the seasonings. Whisk or shake before serving.

1 tablespoon: Calories 14 (53% from fat)/Protein 0.2g/Carb 1.4g/Fat 0.9g/Chol 0/Sodium 75mg/Calcium 7mg/Food Exchanges: Fat 0.1

VARIATIONS
▼ add ¼ teaspoon Chinese hot oil or a pinch of crushed red pepper

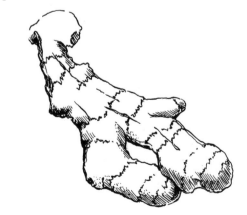

Besides using this dressing on your salads, think of it when you need a dip for raw or steamed vegetables.

▼ ▼ ▼

ADVANCE PREPARATION
Will keep for 3 days, refrigerated, in a tightly closed container.

▼ ▼ ▼

TIPS
▼ To keep brown sugar from becoming hard or lumpy, keep it in an airtight jar, preferably in the refrigerator or freezer. If it does become hard, enclose half an apple with it in a jar, seal tightly, and let it stand for 1 day; moisture from the apple will uncake the sugar.

CREAMY YOGURT DRESSING
▼ ▼ ▼

MAKES ½ CUP
⅓ cup low-fat plain yogurt
1 tablespoon fresh lemon juice
1 tablespoon white rice vinegar
½ teaspoon Dijon mustard
½ teaspoon light brown sugar
⅛ teaspoon minced garlic
⅛ teaspoon freshly ground black pepper, or to taste

In a small bowl, whisk together all the ingredients. Taste; adjust the seasonings. Whisk or shake before serving.

1 tablespoon: Calories 8 (16% from fat)/Protein 0.5g/Carb 1.2g/Fat 0.1g/Chol 0/Sodium 7mg/Calcium 18mg/Food Exchanges: 0

VARIATIONS
▼ add herbs or spices such as basil, dill, paprika, parsley, tarragon, or thyme (¼ teaspoon dried or 2 teaspoons minced fresh)

TORTILLA SALAD WITH TOMATO DRESSING

▼ ▼ ▼

FOR THE TOMATO DRESSING
1 small tomato, preferably peeled (pages 91–92), cut into ½-inch cubes (½ cup)
1 tablespoon red wine vinegar
¼ teaspoon minced garlic
⅛ teaspoon dried basil or ½ teaspoon minced fresh
⅛ teaspoon dried oregano or ½ teaspoon minced fresh
Dash of freshly ground black pepper, or to taste

FOR THE SALAD
½ cup broccoli florets
One 6- or 7-inch flour tortilla (white or whole wheat)
½ teaspoon olive oil
¼ cup low-fat cottage cheese
¼ cup drained and rinsed canned black beans
½ cup shredded salad spinach
1 tablespoon low-fat plain yogurt
½ scallion, chopped (green and white parts)
2 tablespoons seeded and chopped red bell pepper

GARNISH: *freshly ground black pepper, raw sunflower seeds, shredded low-fat Cheddar cheese*

Preheat the oven to 400° F.

Place the dressing ingredients in a food processor or blender; purée. Taste; adjust the seasonings. Set aside.

Place the broccoli in a small microwave-proof dish. Add a

▼ ▼ ▼

ADVANCE PREPARATION
The dressing may be made a day in advance and refrigerated. Assemble the salad just before serving.

▼ ▼ ▼

▼ When buying fresh spinach, look for springy, bright leaves and short stems. In general, the smaller the spinach leaves, the more tender and delicately flavored the vegetable will be. Before using, be sure to rinse the leaves under cold running water to remove any sand. Salad spinach, sold in most supermarkets, is tender spinach leaves that have been prewashed before packaging and are ready to use. Spinach will keep for only 2 to 4 days, so store it in a sealed plastic bag in the vegetable crisper and use it soon. If it seems wilted, wrap the leaves in moist paper towels and refrigerate to crisp.

▼ Select avocados that are very heavy for their size and free of bruises and dark sunken spots. Ripe ones will feel soft when pressed. Most require a few days of ripening. Ripen at room temperature; placing them in a pierced paper bag for a day or two will speed the process. When ripe, store in the refrigerator up to 5 days. To prevent the exposed flesh of avocados from discoloring, coat it with lemon or lime juice and add these juices to recipes containing avocado.

small amount of water, cover, and cook on high until crisp-tender, about 2 minutes, or steam in a vegetable steamer. Drain well. Rinse with cold water; drain again.

To toast the tortilla, lightly brush both sides with the olive oil. Prick the surface in several places with a fork. Place directly on the oven rack; toast until lightly browned, about 3 minutes. Flip; toast the other side until lightly browned, about 2 minutes. Watch closely! Remove from the oven, place on a serving dish, and allow to cool.

In a small bowl, stir together the cottage cheese and beans. Set aside. In another small bowl, stir together the spinach and yogurt.

To assemble the salad, spread the surface of the toasted tortilla with the cottage cheese-bean mixture. Top with the spinach-yogurt mixture. Sprinkle with the scallion. Drizzle with the dressing. Top with the chopped bell pepper and broccoli florets. Garnish and serve immediately.

Calories 245 (21% from fat)/Protein 14.6g/Carb 33.8g/Fat 5.7g/Chol 3mg/Sodium 579mg/Calcium 177mg/Food Exchanges: Veg 1.2/Bread 1.2/Meat 1.0/Fat 0.7

Tomato Dressing (entire recipe): Calories 22 (9% from fat)/Protein 0.6g/Carb 4.4g/Fat 0.2g/Chol 0/Sodium 6mg/Calcium 7mg/Food Exchanges: Veg 0.5

VARIATIONS

▼ rather than baking the tortilla, broil it 2 minutes on each side
▼ for the black beans, substitute other cooked beans such as kidney, great northern, or garbanzo beans
▼ add or substitute other vegetables such as chopped avocado, chopped green chilies, chopped marinated sun-dried tomatoes, chopped green bell pepper, or corn
▼ add a layer of shredded cooked chicken on top of the spinach-yogurt layer
▼ omit the tortilla; serve the salad stuffed in pita bread or mounded on a bed of greens

STEAMED VEGETABLE PLATTER WITH HONEY-MUSTARD DRESSING

▼ ▼ ▼

When I want to feel especially virtuous, I go for a run and work out—then feast on this heart healthy meal. Only 6 percent fat!

▼ ▼ ▼

ADVANCE PREPARATION
The dressing will keep, refrigerated, for 1 week. The vegetables may be steamed in advance and chilled; serve chilled or at room temperature. Drizzle the vegetables with the dressing just before serving.

FOR THE HONEY-MUSTARD DRESSING
2 tablespoons low-fat plain yogurt
1 tablespoon white rice vinegar
2 teaspoons Dijon mustard
1 teaspoon honey
¼ teaspoon minced garlic
Dash of ground white pepper, or to taste
Dash of hot pepper sauce, or to taste

FOR THE SALAD
5 asparagus spears
2 new potatoes, cut into ¼-inch slices
½ cup broccoli florets
½ cup cauliflower florets
1 medium-size carrot, cut into 2 by ¼-inch strips
3 leaves red leaf lettuce
1 plum tomato, cut into 6 wedges (preferably at room temperature)
¼ medium-size red bell pepper, seeded and cut into ¼-inch strips

GARNISH: *freshly ground black pepper and freshly grated Parmesan cheese*

In a small bowl, whisk together the dressing ingredients. Taste; adjust the seasonings. Set aside.

Place the asparagus, potatoes, broccoli, cauliflower, and carrot in a 1-quart microwave-proof dish. Add a small amount of water, cover, and microwave on high just until the vegetables

TIPS

▼ Red new potatoes are young potatoes harvested before maturity. They are thin-skinned, low in starch, and sweet in flavor. They cook quickly and retain their shape when boiled or steamed, making them ideal for potato salads.

▼ Loose-leaf lettuce comprises a number of varieties that don't form heads but consist of large, loosely packed leaves joined at a stem. Their crispness is between that of romaine and butterhead; their taste is mild and delicate. Oak leaf, red leaf, and green leaf are popular varieties.

are crisp-tender, about 4 minutes, or steam in a vegetable steamer. (The potatoes may take a minute or so longer.)

Meanwhile, arrange the leaf lettuce on a salad plate. When the vegetables are steamed, drain well. Artistically arrange them on the plate, along with the tomato and bell pepper. Drizzle with the dressing, garnish, and serve warm.

Calories 254 (6% from fat)/Protein 11.3g/Carb 48.1g/Fat 1.8g/Chol 2mg/Sodium 296mg/Calcium 193mg/Food Exchanges: Milk 0.1/Veg 5.0/ Bread 0.8

Honey-Mustard Dressing (entire recipe): Calories 47 (10% from fat)/ Protein 1.6g/Carb 9g/Fat 0.5g/Chol 2mg/Sodium 45mg/Calcium 55mg/ Food Exchanges: Milk 0.1

VARIATIONS

▼ use the Honey-Mustard Dressing on tossed green salads or as a dip for raw vegetables

▼ add or substitute other vegetables such as steamed zucchini strips, blanched snap peas, sliced mushrooms, strips of green bell pepper, bean sprouts, or blanched snow peas

▼ in addition to vegetables, add fish to the platter—drained, water-packed tuna or poached fish such as swordfish (poach for about 10 minutes in water to which lemon juice and pepper has been added)

▼ for the Honey-Mustard Dressing, substitute other creamy textured dressings such as Creamy Yogurt Dressing (page 187) or Curried Yogurt Dressing (page 204)

MARINATED VEGETABLES

▼ ▼ ▼

The five basic salad dressings in the beginning of this chapter (pages 182–87), as well as several which are included with other recipes, can be the flavoring for your marinated vegetable salads. Really, anything goes when making these salads—for the best results, try to keep the proportion about 2 cups vegetables to ¼ cup dressing.

▼ ▼ ▼

ADVANCE PREPARATION
The flavors will be the best if allowed to set for at least 8 hours; will keep in the refrigerator for 2 days.

▼ ▼ ▼

TIPS
▼ When buying broccoli, look for tight dark green heads on firm but pliable stalks; slender stalks will be more tender for eating. (If the stalks are coarse, peel the outer covering and use the tender interior for cooking.) Many markets sell only the florets, ideal for singles. Store unused

MAKES 2 SERVINGS
2 cups vegetables (any combination of broccoli and/or cauli-
flower florets, sliced carrot, sliced zucchini, cut green
beans, cut asparagus, snap peas)
1 tablespoon chopped scallion (both green and white parts)
1 tablespoon seeded and chopped red bell pepper
¼ cup dressing
Dash of freshly ground black pepper, or to taste
Fresh greens

Place your choice of vegetables in a small microwave-proof dish, and add a small amount of water. Microwave until crisp-tender, about 2 minutes; drain. Or steam in a vegetable steamer. Place the vegetables, scallion, and bell pepper in a bowl; add your choice of dressing and the black pepper. Toss gently to coat the vegetables. Taste; adjust the seasonings. Cover the container; refrigerate for about 8 hours. Toss the vegetables and dressing occasionally.

To serve, line a salad plate with greens. Using a slotted spoon, top with a mound of marinated vegetables.

Marinated Vegetables in Basic Vinaigrette: Calories 117 (30% from fat)/Protein 3.9g/Carb 16.6g/Fat 3.9g/Chol 0/Sodium 38mg/Calcium 77mg/Food Exchanges: Veg 2.7/Fat 0.6

VARIATIONS
▼ add cooked beans such as garbanzos, black beans, cannellini beans, or kidney beans
▼ other dressings to try are Honey-Mint Dressing (page 185), Walnut Vinaigrette (page 203), and Raspberry Vinaigrette (page 204)

broccoli in an open plastic bag or wrap in damp paper towels and store in the crisper drawer of your refrigerator; it will keep for 3 or 4 days.

BEAN SALADS

Legumes are plants that produce pods with edible seeds such as kidney beans, pinto beans, soybeans, garbanzo beans (chick peas), lentils, and peas (split and whole, yellow and green). They are a good source of soluble fiber (the kind that lowers blood cholesterol levels), complex carbohydrates, vitamins, and minerals; beans and peas are very low in fat and they are richer in protein than any other plant food. In fact, they are the least expensive way to fulfill your protein needs.

Beans serve as a main source of protein and a dietary staple for millions of people throughout the world, but here many people don't know how to prepare beans or what to do with them. Though it is simple to cook them from scratch, the larger and firmer beans require lengthy soaking before cooking, and for many beans, cooking time is hours. The best alternative for the 15-minute gourmet is to buy already cooked beans in cans or frozen packages. Canned beans are lower in sodium than most other canned vegetables, but it is still a good idea to drain and rinse them well under cool running water to remove the salty liquid before using. Some supermarkets also offer canned beans without salt. Extra cooked beans can be refrigerated for up to 5 days, or the drained beans can be frozen; they will soften slightly after thawing.

WARM BEAN AND SWEET PEPPER SALAD WITH BALSAMIC VINAIGRETTE

▼ ▼ ▼

1 tablespoon Balsamic Vinaigrette (page 184)
2 leaves romaine lettuce, shredded
4 leaves arugula
½ teaspoon olive oil
½ cup coarsely shredded carrot
¼ medium-size red bell pepper, seeded and cut into 2 by ¼-inch strips
2 tablespoons diced celery
1 tablespoon minced scallion (both white and green parts)
¼ teaspoon minced garlic
One 8-ounce can butter beans (about 1 cup), drained and rinsed

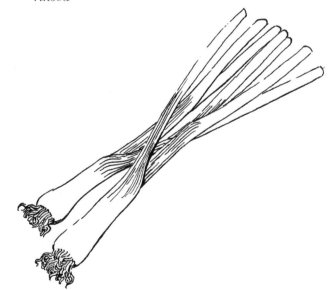

▼ ▼ ▼

ADVANCE PREPARATION
The salad may be made in advance, refrigerated, and served later the same day at room temperature.

▼ ▼ ▼

TIPS
▼ Arugula, also called roquette or "rocket," is rich in beta carotene and high in vitamin C compared to most greens. The leaves are long and spear-shaped, resembling dandelion greens; they have a spicy, peppery, mustardlike bitterness and aroma. The more mature the green, the stronger the flavor; select dark green leaves 3 to 5 inches long. Wrap the roots in moist paper towels and put them in a plastic bag; store briefly in the refrigerator.

Sorrel, a relative of rhubarb, has small, arrow-shaped leaves and a lemony tart taste that provides a good accent to salads. Paler leaves have a gentler flavor; the stems are tough and should be removed.

GARNISH: *freshly ground black pepper, crumbled mild feta cheese, an arugula leaf*

Prepare the vinaigrette; set aside.

Spread the lettuce in the center of a salad plate. Surround with the arugula leaves.

In a small skillet, heat the olive oil over medium heat. Add the carrot, red bell pepper, celery, and scallion; cook, stirring, about 1½ minutes. Add the garlic; sauté 30 seconds longer, retaining the crispness of the vegetables. Add the beans; stir for 1 minute to warm. Stir in the vinaigrette.

Spoon the salad mixture over the bed of romaine lettuce. Garnish and serve warm.

Calories 271 (14% from fat)/Protein 12.7g/Carb 45.1g/Fat 4.4g/Chol 0/Sodium 656mg/Calcium 107mg/Food Exchanges: Veg 1.4/Bread 2.3/ Fat 0.6

VARIATIONS

▼ for the romaine lettuce and arugula, substitute spinach leaves, watercress, or sorrel

▼ for the butter beans, substitute great northern beans or can- nellini

▼ to the salad mixture, add strips of cooked chicken

TERIYAKI SALAD WITH GINGER-SOY VINAIGRETTE

▼ ▼ ▼

Because this salad keeps well and improves in flavor as the vegetables marinate in the vinaigrette, I have doubled the recipe.

▼ ▼ ▼

ADVANCE PREPARATION
Refrigerated in a covered bowl, this will keep for 3 or 4 days. If possible, allow to set at room temperature for 15 to 20 minutes before serving.

▼ ▼ ▼

MAKES 2 SERVINGS
FOR THE GINGER-SOY VINAIGRETTE
2 tablespoons white rice vinegar
1 teaspoon safflower oil
1 teaspoon low-sodium soy sauce
½ teaspoon Dijon mustard
¼ teaspoon minced garlic
¼ teaspoon grated fresh ginger
⅛ teaspoon freshly ground black pepper or to taste
1 teaspoon sesame seeds

FOR THE SALAD
One 8-ounce can garbanzo beans (about 1 cup), drained and rinsed
1 cup sliced mushrooms (about 5 medium-size mushrooms)
1 plum tomato, cut into ½-inch cubes (½ cup)

▾ White rice vinegar, made in China and Japan, is smooth, mild, somewhat sweet, and has a low acid content.

▾ For many people, eating beans causes discomfort and flatulence, but you can minimize the problem: The human body adapts—eat beans more often. Eat only small amounts at any one time, and don't mix them with other gaseous vegetables like cabbage. Or stick to the beans less likely to produce gas, garbanzos, lentils, black-eyed peas, lima beans, and white beans.

¼ cup seeded and diced green bell pepper
1 scallion (both green and white parts), chopped
2 tablespoons minced fresh parsley
¼ pound firm or extra-firm tofu, cut into ½-inch cubes (⅔ cup)
2 leaves romaine lettuce

GARNISH: *red bell pepper strips*

In a small bowl, whisk together the dressing ingredients. Taste; adjust the seasonings. Set aside.

Place the beans, mushrooms, tomato, bell pepper, scallion, and parsley in a medium-size bowl; toss until well combined. Add the vinaigrette; toss. Add the tofu; gently toss again.

To serve, place the lettuce leaves on a salad plate. Arrange a mound of the salad on top; garnish and serve.

1 serving: Calories 271 (34% from fat)/Protein 16.2g/Carb 28g/Fat 10.4g/Chol 0/Sodium 656mg/Calcium 203mg/Food Exchanges: Veg 0.9/ Bread 1.5/Meat 1.2/Fat 0.8

Ginger-Soy Vinaigrette (1 serving): Calories 28 (75% from fat)/Protein 0.2g/Carb 1.5g/Fat 2.3g/Chol 0/Sodium 103mg/Calcium 3mg/Food Exchanges: Fat 0.4

VARIATIONS

▾ substitute other beans such as great northern or cannellini

▾ add or substitute other vegetables such as steamed cut green beans, steamed cut asparagus, or steamed sliced carrots

Once a food staple of the Incas, quinoa has only recently become widely available and popular in this country. Since it cooks quickly, it is an ideal grain for the 15-minute gourmet.

▼ ▼ ▼

ADVANCE PREPARATION
Refrigerate for up to 2 days and serve chilled, or remove from the refrigerator for 20 to 30 minutes and serve at room temperature. Refrigerate the salad and dressing separately; toss just before serving.

▼ ▼ ▼

TIPS
▼ Quinoa (keen-wah) is an ancient Peruvian grain which has been rediscovered in this country. Look for it in natural food stores, specialty food shops, and some large supermarkets. It has a distinctly sweet, nutty flavor and a light, fluffy texture.

QUINOA-COUSCOUS SALAD WITH LEMON-CINNAMON DRESSING

▼ ▼ ▼

¼ *cup quinoa*
½ *cup water*
¼ *cup hot water*
¼ *teaspoon vegetable stock powder*
¼ *cup couscous*

FOR THE LEMON-CINNAMON DRESSING
1 tablespoon lemon juice
1 teaspoon extra-virgin olive oil
1 teaspoon water
⅛ *teaspoon ground cinnamon*
2 drops hot pepper sauce, or to taste
Dash of freshly ground black pepper, or to taste
Dash of turmeric

TO COMPLETE THE SALAD
2 tablespoons chopped celery
½ *scallion (green parts), chopped*
1 tablespoon minced fresh parsley
1 tablespoon currants

GARNISH: *mandarin orange segments, toasted pine nuts (page 36)*

Rinse the quinoa thoroughly either by using a fine strainer or by running fresh water over it in a pan; drain.

▼ Rinsing quinoa before cooking removes saponins, a naturally occurring soaplike substance put in quinoa by nature to deter insects and birds. If not completely rinsed away, don't worry—it is not harmful to humans.

▼ Quinoa is considered to be one of the finest sources of vegetable protein. In fact, it is 16 percent protein; and, unlike some grains, the protein is complete, meaning that it contains all the essential amino acids. It also contains more iron than other grains and high levels of potassium and riboflavin.

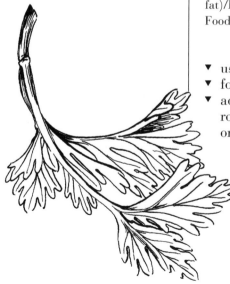

Place the quinoa and ½ cup water in a small saucepan. Bring to a boil over high heat. Reduce the heat to low, cover, and simmer until the water is absorbed, about 5 minutes. (When done, the grains will be translucent and the outer ring will separate.)

While the quinoa is cooking, in a medium-size bowl, dissolve the stock powder in the hot water. Stir in the couscous; cover and let stand until the liquid is completely absorbed, about 5 minutes.

In a measuring cup, whisk together the dressing ingredients. Taste; adjust the seasonings. Set aside.

When the couscous has softened, fluff it with a fork. Stir in the quinoa; toss in the celery, scallion, parsley, and currants. Add dressing and toss again. Allow the salad to cool or serve immediately; garnish.

Calories 410 (16% from fat)/Protein 12.1g/Carb 74g/Fat 7.3g/Chol 0/Sodium 29mg/Calcium 62mg/Food Exchanges: Fruit 0.5/Bread 4.3/Fat 1.3

Lemon-Cinnamon Dressing (entire recipe): Calories 47 (86% from fat)/Protein 0.1g/Carb 1.5g/Fat 4.5g/Chol 0/Sodium 0/Calcium 5mg/Food Exchanges: Fat 0.9

VARIATIONS

▼ use all couscous or all quinoa
▼ for the couscous, substitute cooked brown rice
▼ add other ingredients such as tomato cubes, finely diced carrot, or steamed cut asparagus, beans, cooked chicken cubes, or baby shrimp

Because this keeps well and is one of my favorites to have on hand, the recipe provides 2 servings.

▼ ▼ ▼

ADVANCE PREPARATION
Will keep for 2 days in the refrigerator; for a moister texture, add the vinaigrette just before serving.

▼ ▼ ▼

TIPS
▼ Green onions, also called scallions or spring onions, are delicately flavored members of the onion family. They come from the thinnings of immature onion bulbs as well as certain kinds of onions that produce long, thin stems. The leaves should be bright green and firm; the white bottom should be firm, unblemished, and free of soil; both parts may be used in recipes calling for scallions. As a rule, the more slender the bottoms, the sweeter the flavor. If fresh and hardy, green onions will keep for more than a week in a plastic bag in the refrigerator.

COUSCOUS AND BEAN SALAD WITH WALNUT VINAIGRETTE

▼ ▼ ▼

MAKES 2 SERVINGS
½ cup hot water
½ teaspoon vegetable stock powder
½ cup couscous
2 tablespoons Walnut Vinaigrette (page 203)
¼ cup small cauliflower florets
¼ cup finely diced carrot
1 tablespoon seeded and chopped green bell pepper
1 tablespoon seeded and chopped red bell pepper
½ scallion, chopped (both green and white parts)
¼ cup drained and rinsed canned great northern beans
1 tablespoon currants
½ cup shredded salad spinach

In a small bowl, dissolve the stock powder in the water. Stir in the couscous. Let stand, covered, until the liquid is completely dissolved, about 5 minutes.

Meanwhile, prepare the vinaigrette; set aside.

In a medium-size bowl, toss together the cauliflower, carrot, bell peppers, scallion, beans, and currants.

When the couscous has softened, fluff it with a fork. Toss the couscous into the vegetables. Add the vinaigrette and toss again. Spread the shredded spinach on a salad plate. Top with the couscous-bean mixture and serve.

1 serving: Calories 264 (10% from fat)/Protein 9.4g/Carb 50.3g/Fat 2.8g/Chol 0/Sodium 28mg/Calcium 59mg/Food Exchanges: Veg 0.5/ Fruit 0.2/Bread 2.8/Meat 0.1/Fat 0.4

VARIATIONS
- ▼ for the couscous, substitute 1 cup cooked rice or bulgur wheat
- ▼ add other vegetables such as tomato cubes
- ▼ substitute Basic Vinaigrette (page 182), Balsamic Vinaigrette (page 184), Sesame-Ginger Dressing (page 186), or Lemon-Cinnamon Dressing (page 198)
- ▼ substitute other cooked beans such as garbanzo, cannellini, black, or kidney beans
- ▼ in place of the beans, add strips of sautéed chicken breast

TOMATO-RICE SALAD WITH CURRY VINAIGRETTE

▼ ▼ ▼

FOR THE CURRY VINAIGRETTE
1 tablespoon white rice vinegar
1 teaspoon lemon juice
½ teaspoon extra-virgin olive oil
½ teaspoon curry powder, or to taste
¼ teaspoon minced garlic
Dash of freshly ground black pepper, or to taste

FOR THE SALAD
½ cup cooked rice—brown, white, basmati, or wild rice (pages 212–213)
1 plum tomato, cut into ½-inch cubes (½ cup)
½ scallion (green parts), minced
1 tablespoon minced fresh parsley
3 leaves Boston lettuce

GARNISH: *currants, unsalted sunflower seeds*

In a small bowl, whisk together the dressing ingredients. Taste; adjust the seasonings. Set aside.

ADVANCE PREPARATION
Will keep for 2 days refrigerated.

▼ ▼ ▼

▼ Shelled sunflower seeds are sometimes labeled sunflower kernels or nuts; they are available raw or roasted, salted or unsalted (the best choice being raw, unsalted). The seeds contain many important nutrients, including several B vitamins and vitamins A, D, and E, as well as calcium, phosphorus, and iron. Because the seeds derive 75 percent of their calories from fat, eat them in moderation. Store, refrigerated, in a tightly closed container to prevent rancidity; or keep them in the freezer for up to 1 year.

In a medium-size bowl, toss together the rice, tomato, scallion, and parsley. Add the vinaigrette and toss again. Taste; adjust the seasonings. Arrange the lettuce leaves on a salad plate. Top with a mound of the salad; garnish and serve.

Calories 197 (14% from fat)/Protein 4.8g/Carb 37.5g/Fat 3.1g/Chol 0/Sodium 202mg/Calcium 72mg/Food Exchanges: Veg 1.0/Bread 1.8/Fat 0.4

Curry Vinaigrette (entire recipe): Calories 31 (69% from fat)/Protein 0.2g/Carb 2.3g/Fat 2.4g/Chol 0/Sodium 1mg/Calcium 8mg/Food Exchanges: Fat 0.4

VARIATIONS

▼ for the Curry Vinaigrette, substitute Basic Vinaigrette (page 182), Sesame-Ginger Dressing (page 186), Balsamic Vinaigrette (page 184), or Walnut Vinaigrette (page 203)
▼ for the rice, substitute cooked orzo
▼ substitute or add other ingredients such as coarsely shredded or diced carrots, peas, steamed cut asparagus, chopped red or green bell pepper, baby shrimp, raw cashews, or cooked beans

FRUIT SALADS

You don't really need a recipe to make a fruit salad in the summer. Almost any combination of ripe juicy fruit is delicious with or without a dressing!

This section contains three recipes I have developed to inspire you when the choices of high-quality fruit may be limited to apples, pears, grapes, bananas, and citrus fruits. The dressings are so good, you may want to try them on summer fruit, too!

Additionally, I enjoy Honey-Poppyseed Dressing (page 185), Honey-Mint Dressing (page 185), and Raspberry Vinaigrette (page 204) on summer fruit and as variations to the recipes in this section.

APPLE AND BELGIAN ENDIVE SALAD WITH WALNUT VINAIGRETTE

▼ ▼ ▼

FOR THE WALNUT VINAIGRETTE
2 tablespoons red wine vinegar
1 teaspoon walnut oil
1 teaspoon lemon juice
½ teaspoon Dijon mustard
1 tablespoon minced fresh parsley
Dash of freshly ground black pepper, or to taste

FOR THE SALAD
1 small head Belgian endive
½ red Delicious apple, cut into ½-inch cubes (¾ cup)
1 tablespoon currants

GARNISH: *chopped walnuts, grated carrot*

To make the vinaigrette, in a small bowl whisk together the vinegar, oil, lemon juice, and mustard. Stir in the parsley and pepper. Taste; adjust the seasonings. Set aside.

Separate the Belgian endive leaves; wash and dry. Place 3 leaves in a pinwheel formation on a small salad plate. Cut the remaining leaves into slices 1 inch wide (about 1 cup); place in a bowl. Add the apple cubes and currants; toss.

Pour the vinaigrette over the salad mixture; toss. Mound the salad onto the center of the salad plate; garnish.

Calories 129 (34% from fat)/Protein 0.9g/Carb 20.8g/Fat 4.9g/Chol 0/Sodium 15mg/Calcium 33mg/Food Exchanges: Veg 0.1/Fruit 1.1/Fat 0.9

Walnut Vinaigrette (entire recipe): Calories 53 (78% from fat)/Protein 0.1g/Carb 2.7g/Fat 4.6g/Chol 0/Sodium 8mg/Calcium 8mg/Food Exchanges: Fat 0.9

▼ ▼ ▼

ADVANCE PREPARATION
The vinaigrette may be made in advance and refrigerated for 2 days. Assemble the salad just before serving.

▼ ▼ ▼

TIPS

▼ Walnuts contain 60% oil. The oil has a pleasant nutty taste, is high in iodine content, and is considered by the French to be one of the finest salad oils—not a cooking oil—particularly compatible with bitter greens like endive, chicory, and escarole. A little goes a long way. For the best taste, select a high-quality brand; and because it turns rancid quickly, refrigerate after opening.

▼ Belgian endive is an elegant pricey pale green vegetable whose somewhat bitter flavor makes an interesting addition to salads. Store in the refrigerator in a plastic bag for up to 5 days.

VARIATIONS

- ▼ in the Walnut Vinaigrette, for the walnut oil, substitute hazelnut oil or sesame oil
- ▼ for the Walnut Vinaigrette, substitute *Raspberry Vinaigrette*, made by substituting raspberry vinegar for the red wine vinegar, and safflower for the walnut oil
- ▼ for the apple, substitute ½ pear, cubed or thinly sliced

WINTER FRUIT SALAD WITH CURRIED YOGURT DRESSING

▼ ▼ ▼

FOR THE CURRIED YOGURT DRESSING
¼ cup low-fat plain yogurt
1 teaspoon fresh lemon juice
½ teaspoon honey
½ teaspoon curry powder, or to taste
Dash of ground cinnamon

FOR THE SALAD
6 to 8 spinach leaves
½ apple, cored and cut into ½-inch cubes (about ½ cup)
½ pear, cored and cut into ½-inch cubes (about ½ cup)
¼ cup halved seedless green grapes
1 tablespoon chopped celery

GARNISH: *chopped walnuts*

In a small bowl, whisk together the dressing ingredients. Set aside; let stand at room temperature to moisten the curry powder.

Arrange a layer of spinach leaves on a salad plate. In a small bowl, toss together the apple, pear, grapes, and celery.

▼ ▼ ▼

ADVANCE PREPARATION
The dressing may be made 1 day in advance and refrigerated. The salad should be served soon after being assembled.

▼ ▼ ▼

TIPS
- ▼ Shelled walnuts will keep in the refrigerator for about 3 months. Stored in an airtight container, they will retain their flavor in the freezer almost indefinitely. The flavor can be freshened by spreading the nuts on a baking sheet and heating them in a very low oven (150° F.) for a few minutes.

▼ There are two kinds of walnuts. Black walnuts are stronger in flavor than English (or Persian) walnuts.

Taste the dressing; adjust the seasonings. Add to the fruits; toss. Mound the salad on top of the spinach leaves. Garnish and serve immediately.

Calories 179 (9% from fat)/Protein 4.6g/Carb 36.2g/Fat 1.8g/Chol 3mg/Sodium 70mg/Calcium 157mg/Food Exchanges: Milk 0.3/Veg 0.2/ Fruit 1.8/Fat 0.1

Curried Yogurt Dressing (entire recipe): Calories 53 (17% from fat)/ Protein 3.1g/Carb 7.9g/Fat 1g/Chol 3mg/Sodium 40mg/Calcium 109mg/ Food Exchanges: Milk 0.3/Fat 0.1

FRUIT SALAD WITH ORANGE-POPPY SEED DRESSING

▼ ▼ ▼

FOR THE ORANGE-POPPY SEED DRESSING
1 tablespoon frozen orange juice concentrate, thawed
1 teaspoon white rice vinegar
1 teaspoon fresh lemon juice
1 teaspoon honey
¼ teaspoon poppy seeds
Pinch of dry mustard powder

FOR THE SALAD
6 leaves salad spinach
½ grapefruit, peeled and cut into ½-inch cubes (½ cup)
½ banana, cut into ¼-inch slices (¼ cup)
½ orange, peeled and cut into ½-inch cubes (½ cup)
3 strawberries, halved

In a medium-size bowl, whisk together the dressing ingredients. Set aside.

▼ ▼ ▼

ADVANCE PREPARATION
The fruit may be marinated, in the refrigerator, for 1 to 3 hours.

▼ ▼ ▼

▼ Grapefruit comes in white (actually yellow), pink, and red varieties—colors that refer to the peeling. All three types are similar in flavor and texture, and they all contain large amounts of vitamin C. In addition, the pink and red varieties contain beta carotene. Grapefruit is available year round, with the peak season extending January through June. Since it is not picked until fully ripe, you never have to worry about getting an unripe one. Grapefruit will keep at room temperature for about a week; they are the juiciest at room temperature. For longer storage, they should be stored in the refrigerator where they will keep for 6 to 8 weeks.

Line a salad plate with the spinach leaves. In a medium-size bowl, toss together the fruits. Add them to the dressing and toss. Using a slotted spoon, remove the fruit from the dressing and arrange on top of the spinach.

Calories 230 (4% from fat)/Protein 3.8g/Carb 51.4g/Fat 1.1g/Chol 0/Sodium 25mg/Calcium 96mg/Food Exchanges: Veg 0.2/Fruit 2.8

Orange-Poppyseed Dressing (entire recipe): Calories 76 (4% from fat)/Protein 0.8g/Carb 17.4g/Fat 0.4g/Chol 0/Sodium 1mg/Calcium 20mg/Food Exchanges: Fruit 0.7

VARIATIONS

▼ for the Orange-Poppy Seed Dressing, substitute Honey-Poppy Seed Dressing (page 185) or Honey-Mint Dressing (page 185)
▼ substitute or add other fruit such as pear or peach cubes or wedges, kiwi slices, grapes, raspberries, or blueberries

ACCOMPANIMENTS

▼ ▼ ▼

Although many of the 15-minute entrées in this book can stand alone, some can be made into a more complete and more interesting meal with the recipes and ideas in this chapter serving as enhancements. With more elaborate entrées, I usually just reheat plain rice or cook pasta; if the entrée is simply broiled fish or chicken, I invest my 15 minutes of meal preparation time on the accompaniment. Use your ingenuity to select the combinations which please you.

If you plan your menu, including many of these accompaniments will require no more time than preparing the entrée alone. Some, such as rice, can be made in a larger quantity in advance to be reheated during the week. Marinated Vegetables (page 192) can be prepared with leftover steamed vegetables and kept on hand several days. Others, like Baked Tortilla Chips (page 219), couscous, or steamed vegetables can be prepared while your entrée cooks.

Though I serve meals in courses when I entertain, I usually serve my simplified meals for one all at once. If you are a novice cook, following my suggestions will ensure that all the components of your meal will be ready to eat at the same time.

GRAINS AND STARCHES

In the sixties and seventies, many people tried to avoid grains and starches, thinking they were fattening. But today we know they are the very foundation of a well-balanced diet. Among the best sources of complex carbohydrates, grains and starches provide long-lasting energy. Yet despite advice from health professionals to increase complex carbohydrates in the diet,

Americans usually still fall short of the recommended 6 to 11 daily servings of grains, grain products, cereals, and pasta.

RICE

Instant rice will never have the texture or flavor of the real thing. And it is possible to cook perfect rice every time without ending up with a sticky mess! Once you have gained confidence in preparing rice, you will want to go beyond plain white rice to sample the many other varieties available in supermarkets, health food stores, and specialty markets. I always keep on hand at least four or five different kinds.

Rice is the main food for more than half of the world's population, which speaks well for its nutritional benefits. Rice contains only a trace of fat and no cholesterol.

TYPES OF RICES

Rices are labeled according to size: long-grain, medium-grain, and short-grain. They have different properties and different textures when cooked. Long- or medium-grain should never be substituted for short-grain rice in a recipe, and vice versa.

If properly cooked, long-grain rice will be fluffy and dry, with separate grains. This is the rice I most often use for accompanying my entrées.

Medium-grain rice cooks up moister and more tender than long-grain, but the two are interchangeable in recipes.

Short-grain rice, sometimes called pearl or round rice, may be almost oval or round in shape. Of the three types of rice, it has the highest percentage of amylopectin, the starch that makes rice sticky, or clump together, when cooked.

White and brown rice are variations of the same grain. Brown rice has only its husk removed during milling. Like white rice, it is available in long-, medium-, and short-grain. It has a richer flavor and chewier texture than white rice, and takes longer to cook.

Milling away the layer of bran and germ results in white, or

▼ The shelf life of white rice is a year or longer; keep it in a container with a tight-fitting lid in a dark, dry place. Brown rice should be stored in the refrigerator where it will keep for months.

▼ One-half cup of cooked white rice contains 132 calories and less than 1 gram of fat, about 2 percent. The same quantity of brown rice contains 108 calories and about 1 gram of fat, about 7 percent.

▼ One-half cup cooked wild rice contains 83 calories, about 3 percent from fat. Store wild rice a year or longer in a tightly closed container in a cool, dry place.

YIELDS OF COOKED RICE

1 cup white rice = 3 cups cooked rice

1 cup parboiled (converted) rice = 3 to 4 cups cooked rice

1 cup brown rice = 3 to 4 cups cooked rice

1 cup wild rice = 3 cups cooked rice

SERVING SUGGESTIONS

▼ Vary the flavor of any rice by cooking it in water seasoned

polished, rice. During this process, some protein and about half the vitamins and minerals in the rice are lost.

Enriched white rice has thiamin, niacin, and iron added after milling to replace some of the nutrients. As a result, it is higher in these nutrients than brown rice but lower in fiber.

Parboiled rice, also called converted rice, has been soaked and steamed under pressure, forcing some of the nutrients into the remaining portion of the grain so that they are not totally lost in the processing; sometimes it is also enriched. It takes longer to cook than regular white rice, but the grains will be very fluffy and separate.

Arborio, Italian short-grain rice, is a starchy white rice, with an almost round grain and a distinctive white spot on each one. Traditionally used for cooking Italian risotto, it absorbs up to five times its weight in liquid as it cooks, which results in grains of a creamy consistency.

Aromatic rices, such as basmati, jasmine, pecan rice, and wehani, are primarily long-grain varieties that have a toasty, nutty fragrance.

Glutinous rice (sweet rice) is a starchy, sticky, and resilient grain which is popular in Japan and other Asian countries. It turns translucent and cohesive when cooked, making it suitable for rice dumplings and cakes. It is not a substitute for the other rices used for entrée accompaniments.

Wild rice is not really rice but the seed of an aquatic grass that is native to America. It is harvested in areas where it grows wild, around the northern Great Lakes; and there is now some commercial production as well.

COOKING RICE

Including rice in your menu is easiest if it is cooked in advance when time permits. Reheat it during the last 5 minutes of your entrée preparation.

Rice cooking is not an exact science. The variables are the age of the rice, how it was treated, the weight and size of the with vegetable stock powder, in chicken stock, or in tomato juice.

▼ Add dried herbs and pepper as the rice cooks, or stir in dried or fresh herbs after the rice is done.

▼ To cooked rice, add a combination of steamed or sautéed vegetables, garlic, beans, chicken, shrimp, nuts, or bits of dried fruits, Parmesan cheese, or lemon juice.

▼ Toss cooked rice with Basil Pesto (page 25).

▼ For *Sesame Rice*, add to the rice sautéed mushrooms, frozen peas, toasted sesame seeds, minced parsley, soy sauce, and a dash of sesame oil and white pepper.

▼ For long-grain and medium-grain white rice, use 1¾ to 2 cups of cooking liquid per 1 cup of rice.

▼ For short-grain rice, use 1½ to 2 cups water per 1 cup of rice.

▼ For basmati rice, use 1½ cups water per 1 cup of rice.

▼ For parboiled (converted) and brown rice, use 2½ cups of liquid per 1 cup of rice, or 2¼ cups if you prefer a drier rice.

pan, and the cooking temperature; so use the suggested timings on your rice package only as a guideline.

Most important, make more rice than you need for a meal. Cooked rice will keep for 5 to 7 days in the refrigerator. To reheat rice on the stove, I usually use a nonstick pan. For each cup of rice, sprinkle with 2 tablespoons of liquid; cover the pan and place over low heat for 4 to 5 minutes. Or reheat the rice in the microwave in a covered container on high for 1 minute per cup of rice.

I rarely freeze rice because I think the flavor is altered. On the rare occasion that I do freeze some leftover rice, I add it to soup rather than using it on its own as an accompaniment.

It is not necessary to rinse domestic packaged rice before cooking nor is it necessary to add salt to the cooking water. If you want to perk up the flavor, you can squeeze some lemon juice over the rice near the end of the cooking time. I also think it is unnecessary to add butter or oil.

For stove-top cooking, combine the liquid and rice in a heavy 2- to 3-quart saucepan. Bring the mixture to a boil over high heat, stir it once or twice (stirring more will make the rice gummy), lower the heat to a simmer (low or medium-low), and cover the pan with a tight-fitting lid. Cook the mixture 15 to 20 minutes for long-, medium-, or short-grain white rice, 15 to 18 minutes for basmati rice, 20 to 25 minutes for parboiled rice, and 30 to 45 minutes for brown rice. Do not lift the lid while the rice is cooking; the steam helps to cook the rice. If all the liquid is not absorbed at the end of this time, cover the pan again and cook the rice a few minutes longer. If you want a fluffier, drier rice, fluff the cooked rice with a fork and let it stand, covered, for 5 to 10 minutes after you turn off the heat.

Microwave cooking of rice doesn't really save cooking time, but many people like the convenience. Since microwaves vary, it is probably best to check the manufacturer's directions. In general, put the rice and liquid in a covered glass container using the same proportions as for stove-top cooking. Microwave at maximum power for 5 minutes, then reduce to 50 percent

Note: When cooking quantities of less than 1 cup, less cooking time and more liquid may be necessary.

TIPS

▼ One half-cup of prepared couscous contains 100 calories, just 1 percent from fat.
▼ Couscous, in both white and whole wheat varieties, is found next to the rice in most supermarkets and health food stores. It keeps nearly indefinitely in a tightly closed container in a dark, dry place.
▼ Couscous can be served as is or drizzled with a hint of olive oil.
▼ The serving suggestions for rice (pages 211–212) also apply to couscous. I especially like it with the additions of diced carrots and minced parsley.

power for the next 15 minutes or so, until the rice is tender and the liquid absorbed. Let stand, covered, for 5 minutes.

Most often I cook my rice in a rice cooker, an electric appliance found in ethnic markets and gourmet shops, which cooks rice and then keeps it warm automatically. Rice to liquid proportions are the same; cooking instructions will accompany the cooker. The results are perfect with no need to check the progress as the rice cooks.

To cook wild rice, clean the rice by rinsing it under running water using a strainer or a bowl of water; drain. For each cup of rice, use 4 cups cooking liquid. Place the wild rice in a saucepan with the liquid. Bring to a boil over high heat, lower the heat, and simmer, covered, until the grains open and the texture is tender but not mushy, about 40 to 50 minutes. If any liquid remains, uncover the pot, and continue to cook the rice over low heat, stirring to dry the grains. Cooked wild rice will keep in the refrigerator for about a week.

The procedure for cooking arborio rice is included in Risotto Primavera (page 58). This basic recipe can be varied in innumerable ways.

COUSCOUS

Couscous, sometimes called Moroccan pasta, is actually a pasta made from semolina flour that has been rolled into tiny bead-like pellets. When prepared, it can be used as an alternative to rice.

This quick-cooking pasta is prepared by combining equal amounts of couscous and hot (nearly boiling) liquid. (Water is commonly used but vegetable stock, chicken stock, or even tomato juice will add flavor.) Then simply let it stand in a covered bowl until the couscous is tender and the liquid completely absorbed, about 5 minutes. (Couscous will double in volume as it absorbs the liquid.) Before serving, fluff it with a fork.

TIPS

▼ Bulgur wheat is found in supermarkets and natural food stores
near the rice or hot cereals.
Because of the precooked and
dried condition, the bulgur kernels are quite hard and may be
stored for longer periods than
regular wheat. Like most
grains, store it in a cool, dry
place in an airtight container.

▼ One-half cup of cooked bulgur
wheat contains 76 calories, just
2 percent from fat.

BULGUR WHEAT

Bulgur (or cracked wheat), a form of processed wheat, is a quick-to-prepare and nutritious grain. Its nutty flavor is created in the process of boiling wheat kernels, drying them, removing some of the bran layers, and finally cracking the kernels. Tender but chewy in texture, with a unique nutty flavor, it has been used in the Middle East for centuries as a staple food and is traditionally used in tabouli. Bulgur can be added to soups, stews, and casseroles; it can also be used as a side dish on its own as a substitute for rice.

Since it is already precooked, bulgur wheat can be hydrated by soaking the grain in liquid for a few hours. Or bulgur can be cooked: cover, bring to a boil, reduce the heat, and simmer for 15 minutes. With either method use 2 parts water, stock, or tomato juice to 1 part bulgur wheat.

PASTA

In addition to the entrée ideas in the Pasta chapter, don't over-look pasta as a side dish. In place of rice or potatoes, use plain cooked pasta to accompany highly flavored entrées; select fla-vorful pasta dishes to complement basic broiled fish or chicken.

Many of the ligher pasta entrées such as Parmesan Pasta with Herbs and Plum Tomatoes (page 22), Pasta Salad Primavera with Herbed Tomato Sauce (page 34), or Penne with Basil Pesto (page 24) can be served in smaller portions to accompany fish or chicken.

The Chinese traditionally use Chinese wheat noodles as an accompaniment. Serve the noodles after they are cooked and drained; or pat them dry and sauté in olive oil until lightly browned.

Nearly as quick and versatile as couscous or reheated rice is orzo (also called riso or rosa marina), a type of durum wheat pasta shaped like rice. Serve it alone as an accompaniment—or create orzo pilaf by adding cooked vegetables, olive oil, garlic, parsley, and herbs. All of the serving suggestions for rice (pages 211–212) also apply to orzo.

For variety, toss cooked noodles with olive oil; then toss in toasted wheat germ or bread crumbs.

VEGETABLE ACCOMPANIMENTS

When they are either a minor ingredient or absent in an entrée, vegetables make a healthful and visually appealing side dish.

There are literally hundreds of varieties available to us; pick a wide variety from the different categories:

- ▼ Leafy vegetables—spinach, salad greens, kale, watercress
- ▼ Flowers, buds, and stalks—celery, broccoli, cauliflower, asparagus
- ▼ Seeds and pods—snap beans, lima beans, peas, sweet corn
- ▼ Roots, bulbs, and tubers—onions, potatoes, beets, carrots, parsnips
- ▼ Fruit vegetables—eggplants, squashes, peppers, tomatoes

Buy high-quality fresh vegetables—shop frequently and use them as soon as possible. Though fresh is preferable, if necessary, choose frozen vegetables rather than canned. Many nutrients are destroyed by heat in the canning process and often large amounts of salt are added.

Wash vegetables carefully to remove pesticides; but never wash, chop, or slice vegetables until you are ready to use them. And do not soak them in water before cooking or you may lose water-soluble nutrients. Also, many nutrients are concentrated just beneath the skin, so, if possible, do not peel.

Use healthful methods to prepare vegetables using minimal liquid and fat, cooking them until they are crisp-tender. Long boiling reduces nutrients the most. Steaming and microwaving have been shown to preserve nutrients about equally. Cook the vegetables during the last 5 to 10 minutes of your entrée preparations, and your entire meal will be ready to serve at the same time.

TIPS

- ▼ Vegetables are "nutrient dense"—that is, their store of nutrients is relatively high for the number of calories they supply. And it is recommended that we eat them in generous quantities, 3 to 5 servings daily.
- ▼ Rather than using a single vegetable, serve mixed varieties like peas and carrots or broccoli and cauliflower.
- ▼ Serve steamed vegetables topped with a sauce such as Spicy Peanut Sauce (page 106) or Ginger Sauce (page 47).
- ▼ Toss steamed or sautéed vegetables with Basil Pesto (page 25) or Pesto Chevre Sauce (page 26). Serve warm or chilled.
- ▼ Serve chilled steamed vegetables with dressings such as Balsamic Vinaigrette (page 184) or Sesame-Ginger Dressing (page 186). See the recipe for Marinated Vegetables on page 192.

For steaming, use a steamer insert in a covered saucepan or a special steaming pan in which the vegetables do not come into contact with the water. For variety, top the vegetables with ginger or lime to add subtle flavor as they steam. Use your taste as a guide to timing.

To microwave vegetables, use a covered microwave-proof dish, adding just a small amount of water to the vegetables. Since microwaves vary in power and settings, check the manufacturer's suggestions for cooking vegetables. In general, take care not to overcook and keep in mind that small servings cook especially quickly.

For sautéed julienned vegetables, using a small amount of olive oil, quickly sauté vegetables like leeks and carrots. Stir in minced parsley; sometimes I also add a dash of honey or maple syrup. Julienne the vegetables when preparing the ingredients for your entrée; sauté them during the last few minutes of your entrée preparations.

Once cooked, serve vegetables promptly to minimize nutrient loss.

BRUSCHETTA

▼ ▼ ▼

In Italy, Bruschetta is traditionally a workman's midday snack. Sometimes I make it for lunch, but I also enjoy it as an accompaniment to soup, salad, or pasta.

Two ¾-inch-thick slices Italian bread or 4 slices French
 baguette
1 plum tomato, cut into ¼-inch cubes (½ cup)
½ teaspoon olive oil
¼ teaspoon minced garlic
⅛ teaspoon freshly ground black pepper, or to taste
4 large fresh basil leaves
1 tablespoon freshly grated Parmesan cheese

Adjust the oven broiler rack to 4 to 5 inches from the heating element; preheat the broiler. Place the bread slices on a baking sheet. Place under the broiler for about 1 minute to toast lightly.

In a small bowl, combine the tomato, olive oil, garlic, and pepper. Arrange the basil leaves on the toasted bread. Top with the tomato mixture; sprinkle with the Parmesan cheese. Broil for about 2 minutes to melt the cheese. Watch closely! Serve warm.

Calories 241 (17% from fat)/Protein 9.9g/Carb 40.3g/Fat 4.5g/Chol 5mg/Sodium 618mg/Calcium 137mg/Food Exchanges: Veg 1.1/Bread 2.0/Meat 0.3/Fat 0.5

TIPS

▼ For the cleanest cuts, use a serrated knife for slicing bread.

VARIATIONS

▼ to the vegetable topping, add chopped marinated sun-dried tomatoes
▼ for the basil, substitute fresh thyme, oregano, or rosemary
▼ for the Parmesan, substitute dollops of goat cheese (chevre); increase the broiling time to heat and lightly brown the cheese
▼ after it has been broiled, top the Bruschetta with matchstick strips of yellow, red, and green bell peppers and onion which have been sautéed in a small amount of olive oil

PITA CRISPS
▼ ▼ ▼

▼ ▼ ▼

ADVANCE PREPARATION
These are best when prepared just before serving. If you have extras, store for a day or two in a tin rather than a plastic container. They can be recrisped by heating on a baking sheet for about 5 minutes at 350° F.

▼ ▼ ▼

TIPS
▼ The flatness of pita or "pocket" bread may make you think it is unleavened, but it is made with yeast. The rounds of dough puff during baking and then deflate, leaving a hollow in the middle. Often the other ingredients are just flour and water, though some types have sweeteners or oil added. Pita bread is available in many varieties; white, whole wheat, and oat bran are found in most supermarkets.

*Half of a 6-inch pita bread (white or whole wheat) sliced
  horizontally*
½ teaspoon olive oil
¼ teaspoon dried oregano
1 teaspoon freshly grated Parmesan cheese

Set the oven rack 4 to 5 inches from the broiler heating element; preheat the broiler.

Using a pastry brush, spread the rough side of the pita bread with olive oil. Place on a baking sheet. Sprinkle with the oregano and Parmesan. Using kitchen shears, cut the pita into 6 wedges. Broil until the pita is lightly browned and the cheese is melted, about 2 minutes. Watch closely! Serve warm.

Calories 82 (35% from fat)/Protein 2.9g/Carb 10.4g/Fat 3.2g/Chol 2mg/Sodium 147mg/Calcium 45mg/Food Exchanges: Bread 0.7/Meat 0.1/Fat 0.5

VARIATIONS
▼ for the oregano, substitute other herbs such as dried basil, minced fresh chives, or minced fresh parsley
▼ omit the herbs and sprinkle with sesame seeds
▼ omit the herbs and spread the pita bread with Basil Pesto (page 25)
▼ add chopped marinated sun-dried tomatoes to the pita before broiling

BAKED TORTILLA CHIPS

▼ ▼ ▼

I like these chips as a low-fat snack, or as an appetizer, served with Strawberry Salsa and its variations (page 77).

▼ ▼ ▼

ADVANCE PREPARATION
May be made in advance and stored in an airtight container at room temperature for a few days.

▼ ▼ ▼

TIPS
▼ When buying baking sheets, select stainless steel instead of aluminum. With use, aluminum sheets will bend and buckle, giving an uneven surface.

One 6- or 7-inch flour tortilla (white or whole wheat)

Preheat the oven to 400° F.
Using kitchen shears, cut the tortilla into 6 wedges. Arrange in a single layer on an ungreased baking sheet. Bake until crisp, 5 to 7 minutes. (The chips will continue to become crisp as they cool.)

Calories 95 (17% from fat)/Protein 2.5g/Carb 17.3g/Fat 1.8g/Chol 0/Sodium no data/Calcium 46mg/Food Exchanges: Bread 1.0/Fat 0.2

VARIATIONS
▼ lightly brush each side of the tortilla with 1/4 teaspoon olive oil before cutting into wedges (calories 105—25 percent from fat)

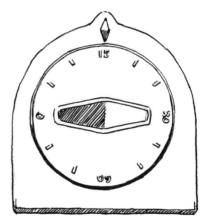

HERBED CROUTONS

▼ ▼ ▼

MAKES 2 SERVINGS
½ teaspoon olive oil
¼ teaspoon minced garlic
⅛ teaspoon dried basil
⅛ teaspoon dried oregano
1 slice whole wheat bread, cut into ½-inch squares

In a small skillet, heat the olive oil over medium heat. Add the garlic, basil, and oregano. Stir for about 30 seconds to soften the herbs.

Stir in the bread; cook, stirring, until browned and crisp, 3 to 4 minutes. (The croutons will become crisper as they cool.)

1 serving: Calories 44 (34% from fat)/Protein 1.3g/Carb 5.9g/Fat 1.7g/Chol 0/Sodium 80mg/Calcium 11mg/Food Exchanges: Bread 0.3/Fat 0.3

VARIATIONS

▼ for the basil and oregano, substitute curry powder, chili powder, or thyme
▼ croutons also can be made by toasting bread squares on a baking sheet at 350° F. until they are crispy and lightly browned, about 20 minutes

▼ ▼ ▼

ADVANCE PREPARATION

May be made 1 or 2 days in advance. Store in a tin at room temperature (they become soggy in a plastic container). To reheat, place on a baking sheet and heat for about 5 minutes at 350° F.

▼ ▼ ▼

TIPS

▼ Most breads are low in fat and a good source of complex carbohydrates, but the most nutritious are those that are the least refined; they contain more fiber, vitamins, and minerals. Make sure you're getting a true whole wheat bread by choosing one that lists one of the following first on the ingredient list: 100% whole wheat, stone-ground whole wheat flour, whole grain, rye, multigrain, or cracked wheat.

DESSERTS AND FRUITS

▼ ▼ ▼

▼ raspberries, blueberries, and strawberries drizzled with orange juice and garnished with fresh mint

▼ sliced banana and grapefruit sections sprinkled with brown sugar and lightly broiled

▼ fresh pears sprinkled with fresh ginger

▼ sliced apples with a dash of cinnamon or nutmeg

▼ a wedge of honeydew melon drizzled with fresh lime juice

▼ a cubed orange or pear tossed with maple syrup

▼ a Basic Omelet (page 67) topped with Strawberry Sauce (page 229) or Raspberry Purée (page 231)

Even when I'm eating alone, I feel that a good meal deserves a proper conclusion. And sometimes, after a quick and simple entrée, dessert becomes the most important part of the meal. A wonderful dessert does not have to be a rich, fattening, or complicated production; so we can look forward to this final touch without feeling guilty.

Because of the healthfulness, superb flavor, and ease of preparation, fruit is the base for most of these desserts. The only thing you need to remember is that fresh fruit is not at its sweetest until it is fully ripe.

I have used fruit in three forms: fresh, with sauces to make the most of fine in-season fruit; frozen, in pureed ice cream- and sorbetlike desserts without added fat; and cooked, which changes both the taste and texture of the fruit.

When it comes to artificial sweeteners, I avoid them. I prefer to use natural sweeteners—sugar, honey, and maple syrup—in moderation. To me it is of greater concern to avoid the high fat present in most desserts.

Much of the pleasure of desserts is visual, so create a happy ending by serving your dessert in an attractive dish with a simple garnish.

SEMISWEET FUDGE SAUCE

▼ ▼ ▼

MAKES ½ CUP
¼ cup firmly packed light brown sugar
3 tablespoons unsweetened cocoa powder
1 teaspoon instant coffee
½ teaspoon cornstarch
½ cup skim milk

In a small nonstick saucepan, stir together the sugar, cocoa, instant coffee, and cornstarch. Stir in the milk. Place the pan over medium heat. Cook, stirring constantly, until the sauce is smooth and thickened, about 5 minutes. Remove from the heat; allow to cool for a few minutes before using.

1 tablespoon: Calories 41 (5% from fat)/Protein 0.9g/Carb 8.8g/Fat 0.2g/Chol 0.2mg/Sodium 11mg/Calcium 28mg/Food Exchanges: 0

I believe in watching what I put into my body 98 percent of the time—the other 2 percent can be given over to life-enhancing foods like chocolate!

▼ ▼ ▼

ADVANCE PREPARATION
Will keep for 1 week in the refrigerator. Serve chilled or reheat gently.

▼ ▼ ▼

TIPS
▼ Chocolate is about 50 percent fat, mostly saturated. Cocoa, however, is chocolate with most of the fat (cocoa butter) removed.

Making your own granola is very easy and a good alternative to the supermarket varieties which are higher in sweeteners and fat. For dessert or breakfast, rather than consuming cupfuls with milk, try using just ¼ cup as a topping for low-fat yogurt.

▼ ▼ ▼

ADVANCE PREPARATION
Will keep for several weeks in the pantry or refrigerator in a container with a tight-fitting lid.

▼ ▼ ▼

TIPS

▼ "Old-fashioned" rolled oats are thicker than "quick-cooking" rolled oats, which are processed to cook faster when used to make oatmeal. Either can be used in this recipe.

▼ Toasted wheat germ should be kept in a tightly closed container in the refrigerator; keep raw wheat germ in the freezer to prevent rancidity.

ALMOND GRANOLA

▼ ▼ ▼

MAKES ABOUT 4 CUPS
2 cups rolled oats
½ cup bran
½ cup toasted wheat germ
¼ cup sliced almonds
¼ cup nonfat dried milk powder
¼ cup sesame seeds
2 tablespoons safflower oil
¼ cup honey
1 teaspoon ground cinnamon
1 teaspoon pure vanilla extract
1 tablespoon orange zest

Preheat the oven to 350° F.

In a large bowl, stir together the oats, bran, wheat germ, almonds, milk powder, and sesame seeds.

In a measuring cup, stir together the oil, honey, cinnamon, vanilla, and zest. Add to the dry ingredients, tossing until well combined. Spread the mixture evenly on a baking sheet. Bake, stirring frequently, until lightly browned, 8 to 10 minutes. Loosen from the baking sheet with a spatula; allow to cool. (The granola will become crisper as it cools.) Store in a tightly covered container.

1 tablespoon: Calories 49 (30% from fat)/Protein 2.2g/Carb 6.5g/Fat 1.6g/Chol 1mg/Sodium 12mg/Calcium 40mg/Food Exchanges: Bread 0.2/Fat 0.2

VARIATIONS

▼ add ¼ to ½ cup raw sunflower seeds
▼ for the honey, substitute maple syrup
▼ after baking, stir in ½ cup raisins or other dried fruits such as chopped apricots or prunes

PURÉED DESSERTS

For the best results I recommend making these puréed desserts in a food processor rather than a blender. The ingredients should be processed long enough to achieve a completely creamy or smooth consistency.

FROZEN BANANA-BERRY PARFAIT

▼ ▼ ▼

This is the most delicious low-fat alternative to ice cream when you crave a luxurious, voluptuous texture. And it is the perfect use for bananas that are past their prime. I always keep several bananas on hand in my freezer.

▼ ▼ ▼

TIPS

▼ Store honey at room temperature; refrigeration speeds up crystallization. If it does crystallize, stand the opened jar in a pan of hot water until it liquefies; or microwave 1 cup of honey at a time on high until the crystals dissolve, 2 minutes, stirring every 30 seconds.

1 medium-size banana
2 tablespoons low-fat plain yogurt
1 teaspoon honey
½ cup sliced strawberries or blueberries, or a combination

GARNISH: *whole strawberry, a grating of semisweet choco-late.*

In advance, peel the banana, wrap it in a plastic bag, and freeze it overnight.

At serving time, cut the banana into 1-inch slices while still frozen. Place it in a food processor with the yogurt and honey. Purée, pushing down the sides of the mixture several times with a rubber scraper; process until the mixture is the consistency of soft-serve ice cream. Spoon the mixture into a parfait glass, alternating with layers of fruit; or spoon into a bowl surrounded by the fruit. Garnish; serve immediately.

Calories 182 (6% from fat)/Protein 3.1g/Carb 39.6g/Fat 1.3g/Chol 2mg/Sodium 22mg/Calcium 70mg/Food Exchanges: Milk 0.1/Fruit 2.1

- ▼ add a dash of vanilla extract to the banana-yogurt mixture
- ▼ for a different flavor and pink color, add sliced strawberries (about ¼ cup) as you are puréeing the mixture
- ▼ top with Semisweet Fudge Sauce (page 224), Strawberry Sauce (page 229), or Raspberry Purée (page 231)

Virtually fat free, fruit sorbet can be made in minutes providing your fruit has been prefrozen.

▼ ▼ ▼

TIPS

▼ Fruits should be fully ripe to bring out the maximum flavor. Many fruits are ready to be used when purchased: apples, cherries, citrus fruits, strawberries, and grapes. Others often require additional ripening time: bananas, melons, mangoes, peaches, plums, pears, nectarines, and papayas. Hold them at room temperature until they reach the desired degree of ripeness or, to hasten the ripening process, keep the fruit in a brown paper bag or in a ripening dome at room temperature, checking daily. Then refrigerate after they are fully ripe. Refrigerate apples, blueberries,

FRUIT SORBET

▼ ▼ ▼

1 cup frozen 1-inch cubes ripe fresh fruit (strawberries, peach, pear, mango, papaya, kiwi, honeydew melon)
¼ cup orange juice
2 teaspoons honey

GARNISH: *almond slices, whole strawberry, sprig fresh mint*

In advance, prepare the fruit by peeling (if necessary), cutting, and wrapping the fruit in a plastic bag. Freeze overnight.

Ten minutes before serving, remove the fruit from the freezer to soften slightly. Just before serving, place all the ingredients in a food processor. Purée until smooth. Spoon into a serving bowl; garnish. Enjoy immediately.

Calories 210 (1% from fat)/Protein 1.1g/Carb 50.8g/Fat 0.3g/Chol 0/ Sodium 5mg/Calcium 22mg/Food Exchanges: Fruit 2.5

VARIATIONS

- ▼ rather than a single fruit, purée combinations such as strawberry-papaya, strawberry-honeydew, and kiwi-mango
- ▼ for the fresh fruit, substitute drained canned fruits such as pears, peaches, and mandarin oranges (use fruits canned in their own juice)

cherries, cranberries, grapes, raspberries, and strawberries. Refrigerate on preference: grapefruit, lemons, limes, oranges, tangelos, and watermelons.

▼ top with Strawberry Sauce (page 229) or Raspberry Purée (page 231)

FRESH FRUITS WITH SAUCES, TOPPINGS, AND DIPS

BERRIES WITH RICOTTA CREAM

▼ ▼ ▼

1 cup sliced strawberries
½ teaspoon sugar (optional)

FOR THE RICOTTA CREAM
¼ cup lite ricotta cheese
¼ teaspoon grated orange rind
1 tablespoon orange juice
1 teaspoon honey
⅛ teaspoon pure almond extract
1 teaspoon slivered almonds
1 teaspoon currants

GARNISH: *finely grated semisweet chocolate*

In a small bowl, toss together the strawberries and sugar. Spoon into a dessert bowl.

In a blender, whip together the ricotta cheese, orange rind, orange juice, honey, and almond extract. Stir in the slivered almonds and currants. Spoon the mixture over the strawberries. Garnish and serve.

Calories 201 (31% from fat)/Protein 8.7g/Carb 26g/Fat 6.9g/Chol

▼ ▼ ▼

ADVANCE PREPARATION
The cream may be made several hours in advance; refrigerate. Spoon over the fruit just before serving. (If allowed to set, the sugar will draw out some of the juice in the berries.)

▼ ▼ ▼

TIPS
▼ Extracts such as almond and vanilla are very intense in flavor. Use them sparingly. It's easy to overpour small quantities; to eliminate accidents, pour into the measuring spoon over the sink rather than over the bowl.

▼ Look for "pure vanilla extract" rather than "vanilla flavoring" or "artificial vanilla." "Vanilla essence," often used in Europe but infrequently found in the United States, is stronger in flavor.

▼ Chocolate must be cool and firm for grating; use a dry grater.

▼ ▼ ▼

ADVANCE PREPARATION
The sauce will keep for a day; cover and refrigerate. Assemble the dessert just before serving.

▼ ▼ ▼

TIPS
▼ Keep ripe kiwis in the refrigerator for several weeks. Since they do not discolor after being cut, kiwis are a good choice for fruit dishes, tarts, and salads. One large kiwi has more vitamin C than 1 cup of strawberries, a medium-size orange, or half a grapefruit.

19mg/Sodium 79mg/Calcium 201mg/Food Exchanges: Fruit 0.9/Meat 1.0/Fat 0.6

VARIATIONS
▼ substitute blueberries or raspberries, or a combination, or 1 sliced peach, 1 sliced pear, or about 1 cup cubed cantaloupe or honeydew melon; no need to add sugar
▼ into the Ricotta Cream, stir 1 tablespoon semisweet chocolate chips

KIWI IN STRAWBERRY SAUCE
▼ ▼ ▼

½ cup low-fat vanilla yogurt
*1 kiwi, peeled and cut in half lengthwise, each half cut into
    ¼-inch slices*

FOR THE STRAWBERRY SAUCE
¼ cup sliced strawberries
1 tablespoon orange juice
½ teaspoon honey
Dash of ground nutmeg

GARNISH: *sprig fresh mint, strawberry fan (page 230)*

Spoon the yogurt into a dessert bowl. Arrange the kiwi slices over the yogurt.
Place the strawberry slices, orange juice, honey, and nutmeg in a food processor or in a blender; process until smooth. Pour over the kiwi and yogurt. Garnish and serve.

Calories 154 (13% from fat)/Protein 7g/Carb 26.4g/Fat 2.3g/Chol 7mg/Sodium 84mg/Calcium 234mg/Food Exchanges: Milk 0.7/Fruit 0.9/ Fat 0.3

▼ To make a *strawberry fan*, choose a firm, red, ripe strawberry. Place it, hull down, on a cutting board and make parallel cuts in the berry, from the bottom nearly to the leaves, taking care not to slice all the way through. (The number of cuts will depend on the size of the berry.) Hold the strawberry gently and twist so that the slices fan out. The hull can be left intact or be removed and replaced with a sprig of fresh mint.

▼ ▼ ▼

ADVANCE PREPARATION
To serve chilled, refrigerate several hours until serving time. (Cover the dessert bowl with plastic wrap after the sauce has cooled.)

▼ ▼ ▼

TIPS
▼ To peel an orange, immerse it in boiling water for 5 minutes, cool for a few minutes, then peel; the white membrane which often gives a bitter flavor will be removed more easily using this method.

Strawberry Sauce (entire recipe): Calories 29 (5% from fat)/Protein 0.3g/Carb 7.1g/Fat 0.2g/Chol 0/Sodium 1mg/Calcium 7mg/Food Exchanges: Fruit 0.2

VARIATIONS
▼ after the Strawberry Sauce has been puréed, stir in ½ teaspoon minced fresh mint
▼ in the Strawberry Sauce, for the strawberries, substitute other fruit such as chopped nectarine, peach, or kiwi

GLAZED ORANGE
▼ ▼ ▼

1 large seedless orange
Zest from 1 orange
2 tablespoons frozen pineapple juice concentrate, thawed
1 teaspoon fresh lemon juice

GARNISH: *sprig fresh mint*

Using a zester (or potato peeler), strip the rind from the orange; set aside. Remove the remaining peeling with a knife; discard. Place the whole peeled orange in a dessert bowl.

Place the concentrate and orange zest in a small saucepan. Bring to a simmer over medium heat, stirring constantly, until the zest is softened and the juice reduces and darkens slightly, about 1 minute. Remove from the heat; stir in the lemon juice.

Pour the sauce over the orange, arranging some of the rind in a mound on top of the orange as a garnish. Top with a sprig of mint. Serve immediately with the sauce warm or cover the bowl with plastic wrap and refrigerate at least 10 minutes to cool. Serve with a serrated knife and fork.

Calories 136 (1% from fat)/Protein 1.7g/Carb 31.7g/Fat 0.2g/Chol 0/Sodium 1mg/Calcium 67mg/Food Exchanges: Fruit 1.9

- Thick-skinned oranges are the easiest to peel. (For squeezing, thin-skinned oranges will give more juice.)
- Store oranges at room temperature for up to 1 week, or refrigerate up to 1 month.

Not only delicious with breakfast, this sometimes _is_ breakfast! The splendid sauce also can turn a bowl of uncooked fruit or frozen yogurt into a luxury.

▼ ▼ ▼

ADVANCE PREPARATION
The pear may be cooked up to 1 day in advance, chilled in the purée, and assembled with the yogurt at serving time.

▼ ▼ ▼

VARIATIONS

VARIATIONS
- rather than leaving the orange whole, cut it into ½-inch cubes
- substitute other juice concentrates such as orange, pineapple-orange, pineapple-grapefruit, or tropical blends such as pineapple-passion fruit-banana

COOKED FRUITS

PEAR IN RASPBERRY PURÉE

▼ ▼ ▼

1 pear (preferably at room temperature), peeled, cored, and halved

FOR THE RASPBERRY PURÉE (MAKES ¼ CUP)
¼ cup frozen slightly sweetened raspberries, thawed
1 tablespoon honey
2 tablespoons water
Pinch of ground nutmeg

TO COMPLETE THE DISH
¼ cup low-fat vanilla yogurt

GARNISH: _Almond Granola (page 225), toasted sliced almonds (page 232), and a few fresh raspberries, if available!_

Place the pear halves in a small microwave-proof baking dish. Set aside.

Pour the raspberries with juice, honey, and water into food processor or blender; purée. Pour the puréed mixture into a strainer, place over a small bowl, and stir to press the liquid through. Stir in the nutmeg.

▼ To toast almonds, place them on a baking sheet in a 375° F. oven or in a dry skillet on the stove, stirring frequently until they are lightly browned. Or they can be sautéed in a small skillet in a small amount of oil.

▼ Buy pears when they are firm, but not rock-hard, and ripen them on your kitchen counter in a paper bag; this can take 2 to 7 days. Most pears do not show ripeness with a color change; they ripen from the inside out. Once they are ripe, they will keep for 3 to 5 days in the refrigerator. Slightly under-ripe pears are best for cooking and baking.

Pour the purée over the pear halves. Cover the baking dish tightly with plastic wrap. Cook in the microwave on high for 2 minutes. Uncover and allow to cool for about 5 minutes.

To serve, spread the yogurt onto the bottom of a serving bowl. Arrange the pear halves on top; top with the warm purée. Garnish and serve.

Calories 230 (6% from fat)/Protein 4.1g/Carb 49.7g/Fat 1.6g/Chol 3mg/Sodium 41mg/Calcium 132mg/Food Exchanges: Milk 0.3/Fruit 2.7/ Fat 0.1

Raspberry Purée (entire recipe): Calories 194 (4% from fat)/Protein 1.1g/Carb 45.7g/Fat 0.8g/Chol 0/Sodium 1mg/Calcium 28mg/Food Exchanges: Fruit 2.7

VARIATIONS

▼ substitute a peach or nectarine

▼ rather than cooking in the microwave, the pear can be poached: Bring water or orange juice to a boil over high heat; reduce heat to medium, add the pear halves (or a whole, peeled pear), cover, and cook until tender, about 10 minutes. Prepare the purée; drizzle over the pear when assembling the dessert.

▼ Instead of the Raspberry Purée, the poached pear can be drizzled with Semisweet Fudge Sauce (page 224)

▼ Raspberry Purée is delicious on low-fat plain or vanilla yogurt, frozen yogurt, waffles, pancakes, hot cooked cereal, or poured over other fruit such as fresh pineapple or peach slices.

▼ For Peach Melba, drizzle Raspberry Purée over vanilla frozen yogurt and peach slices.

CURRIED PEACH

▼ ▼ ▼

½ teaspoon olive oil
1 tablespoon orange juice
1 teaspoon honey
1 teaspoon curry powder, or to taste
½ teaspoon grated fresh ginger
1 peach (preferably at room temperature), peeled and cut
into 1-inch cubes
¼ cup low-fat vanilla yogurt

GARNISH: *chopped walnuts or pecans, or toasted wheat germ*

In a small saucepan, heat the olive oil over medium heat. Stir in the orange juice, honey, curry powder, and ginger. Cook, stirring occasionally, until the mixture is bubbly and smooth, about 2 minutes.

Stir in the peach; cover and cook, stirring occasionally, until the fruit is heated through and tender, about 5 minutes.

To serve, spoon the yogurt into a dessert bowl, top with the warm peach and sauce; garnish.

Calories 200 (17% from fat)/Protein 4.6g/Carb 37.2g/Fat 3.7g/Chol 3mg/Sodium 42mg/Calcium 104mg/Food Exchanges: Milk 0.7/Fruit 1.3/ Fat 0.6

VARIATIONS

▼ substitute pineapple juice
▼ for the honey, substitute light brown sugar
▼ substitute a nectarine, 2 apricots, a pear, or an apple (an apple may require a longer cooking time)
▼ substitute 1 cup drained canned fruit such as pineapple chunks, mandarin oranges, or a combination
▼ add about 1 tablespoon raisins or currants

▼ ▼ ▼

ADVANCE PREPARATION

May be made in advance and served chilled later the same day. Assemble with the yogurt just before serving.

▼ ▼ ▼

TIPS

▼ Choose peaches that are firm to slightly soft with a yellow or creamy skin color. The red "blush" of a peach is not a good indication of ripeness because it varies with the variety. Leave at room temperature for 2 to 3 days or place in a paper bag with an apple to speed up ripening. When fully ripe, keep peaches in a sealed bag in the refrigerator and use within a few days.

▼ To peel a peach, immerse it in boiling water and let it stand for 1 minute; then drop into cold water. Peel with a firm downward pull. After peeling, cook or eat promptly to prevent browning, or coat the exposed flesh with an acidic ingredient such as lemon juice.

BAKED BANANA WITH ORANGE-RAISIN SAUCE

▼ ▼ ▼

FOR THE ORANGE- RAISIN SAUCE

¼ cup orange juice
1 tablespoon raisins
1 teaspoon chopped pecans

TO COMPLETE THE DISH

1 banana, peeling left on

Preheat the oven to 400° F.

Place all the sauce ingredients in a small saucepan over medium heat. Cook, uncovered, until the raisins are plumped and the orange juice reduced and darkened, about 10 minutes. Remove from the heat; cover to keep warm.

While the sauce is cooking, place the banana on an unoiled baking sheet. Using a sharp knife, prick the skin on all sides. Bake the banana for 4 minutes; turn and bake until the skin has blackened completely, an additional 4 to 6 minutes. Allow to cool 5 minutes.

To serve, slit the skin with a knife and flip the banana into a serving bowl. It will have an almost puddinglike consistency. Serve warm topped with warm sauce.

Calories 191 (11% from fat)/Protein 2.1g/Carb 40.8g/Fat 2.2g/Chol 0/Sodium 3mg/Calcium 19mg/Food Exchanges: Fruit 2.7/Fat 0.2

VARIATION

▼ use the Orange-Raisin Sauce to top pancakes, waffles, or hot cooked cereal
▼ substitute Strawberry Sauce (page 229), or Raspberry Purée (page 229)

▼ ▼ ▼

TIPS

▼ Bananas are rich in potassium, magnesium, and many other minerals. They contain vitamins A and B complex and have twice as much vitamin C as apples. They are high in carbohydrate but low in fat and protein.

▼ ▼ ▼

APPLE IN PARCHMENT

▼ ▼ ▼

1 tablespoon pure maple syrup
1 tablespoon orange juice
Dash of ground cinnamon
1 apple (preferably at room temperature), cored and cut into
    ¼-inch wedges
1 tablespoon raisins
1 teaspoon chopped walnuts

GARNISH: *dollop low-fat vanilla yogurt, Almond Granola
    (page 225), toasted wheat germ*

SPECIAL EQUIPMENT: *1 sheet baking parchment, about 16
    inches in length*

Preheat the oven to 425° F.

For an illustration of the parchment procedure, see page 93. Fold the parchment paper in half and cut into the shape of a half-circle; set aside.

In a measuring cup, stir together the maple syrup, orange juice, and cinnamon.

Place the apple wedges, raisins, and walnuts in a small bowl; toss. Add the syrup mixture; toss again. Open the parchment circle; place the apple mixture on one half of the paper. Close the flap. Seal the parchment packet by starting at one end; fold the cut edges toward the packet contents, creating many small overlapping folds.

Place the packet on a baking sheet; bake for about 8 minutes. To serve, open the packet and spoon the warm contents into a dessert bowl. Garnish.

Calories 204 (9% from fat)/Protein 1.3g/Carb 45g/Fat 2g/Chol 0/Sodium 23mg/Calcium 20mg/Food Exchanges: Fruit 1.9/Fat 0.2

▼ ▼ ▼

ADVANCE PREPARATION

The apples may be baked earlier on the day they are to be served. Remove from the packet, place in a bowl, cover, refrigerate, and serve chilled.

▼ ▼ ▼

TIPS

▼ My favorite baking apples are Rome Beauty. Others that cook well are Golden Delicious, Granny Smith, Haralson, Braeburn, and Winesap. Avoid using Red Delicious and Jonathan, which are rather tender for cooking and lack the acidity that gives apple dishes their characteristic flavor.

▼ Pick apples with firm, unblemished skin and stems attached. They can be kept for 2 weeks in the refrigerator in a perforated plastic bag.

▼ ▼ ▼

ADVANCE PREPARATION

If you would prefer serving the pear chilled, cook it at least 1 hour in advance and refrigerate.

▼ ▼ ▼

TIPS

▼ Like other nuts, shelled almonds should be refrigerated or frozen to prevent rancidity.

▼ Dried cranberries, sometimes sold as "craisins," are becoming commonly available with the dried fruits in supermarkets. They are delicious as a snack, colorful as a garnish, and can be used as an alternative to raisins if you bake muffins, breads, or cookies.

VARIATIONS

▼ rather than baking the apple in parchment, use a small, covered baking dish

▼ substitute a pear; baking time should be reduced to about 6 minutes if quite ripe

▼ for the raisins, substitute currants or dried cranberries

GINGERED PEAR WITH ALMOND STUFFING

▼ ▼ ▼

1 pear (preferably at room temperature)
1 teaspoon finely chopped sliced or slivered almonds
1 teaspoon raisins, about 10
2 teaspoons honey
¼ teaspoon grated fresh ginger

GARNISH: *dollop low-fat vanilla yogurt, toasted wheat germ, Almond Granola (page 225)*

Core the pear to within ½ inch of the bottom. Place in a microwave-proof dish. Set aside.

In a small bowl, mix together the almonds, raisins, and 1 teaspoon of the honey. Stuff the cored pear with this mixture.

In a measuring cup or small bowl, combine the remaining 1 teaspoon honey and the ginger; drizzle over the pear. Cover the dish tightly with plastic wrap. Microwave on high for 2 minutes.

Transfer the pear to a serving bowl; spoon the sauce over it, garnish, and serve warm.

Calories 202 (9% from fat)/Protein 1.5g/Carb 44.3g/Fat 2.1g/Chol 0/ Sodium 2mg/Calcium 31mg/Food Exchanges: Fruit 2.1/Fat 0.2

▼ for the raisins, substitute dried cranberries
▼ remove the pear from the baking dish with a slotted spoon; top with Raspberry Purée (page 231), or Semisweet Fudge Sauce (page 224)

BROILED PINEAPPLE WITH VANILLA YOGURT

▼ ▼ ▼

One ½-inch-thick slice fresh pineapple, cored and peeled
1 tablespoon honey
Dash of ground cinnamon
¼ cup low-fat vanilla yogurt

GARNISH: *fresh strawberry or fresh raspberries, sprig fresh mint*

Place the oven broiler rack about 4 to 5 inches from the heating element. Preheat the broiler.

Lay the pineapple ring on a baking sheet. In a small bowl or measuring cup, combine the honey and cinnamon. Drizzle over the pineapple. Broil until it is heated and the sauce is bubbly, about 3 minutes.

▼ ▼ ▼

ADVANCE PREPARATION
Broil the pineapple in advance and serve at room temperature or chilled.

▼ ▼ ▼

TIPS
▼ A ripe pineapple can be mostly yellow to orange; the inner leaves at the crown will pull out easily. Smell the bottom; it should have a fresh and sweet pineapple aroma—no aroma means little flavor! Fresh pineapple is at peak perfection for only a day, but it can be refrigerated for 3 to 5 days.

▼ Pineapple is high in carbohydrate and is a source of vitamin A, B complex, and C; it also contains an enzyme called bromeline which can aid indigestion. One cup of pineapple contains 52 calories.

Meanwhile, spread the yogurt on a serving plate. Using a spatula, lay the broiled pineapple, bottom side up, on top of the yogurt. Garnish and serve while still warm.

Calories 170 (7% from fat)/Protein 3.3g/Carb 36.3g/Fat 1.3g/Chol 3mg/Sodium 42mg/Calcium 90mg/Food Exchanges: Milk 0.7/Fruit 0.6/Fat 0.1

VARIATIONS

▼ omit the yogurt
▼ top the broiled pineapple with thawed lightly sweetened frozen raspberries, Raspberry Purée (page 231), or Strawberry Sauce (page 229)

INDEX

▼   ▼   ▼

Accompaniments, 209–20
Alfalfa sprouts, as garnish, 51, 67
Almond-Currant Sauce, 88–89
Almond extract, 228
Almond Granola, 225, 231, 235, 236
Almonds, 236
  in curried chicken, 138
  in dessert stuffing, 236
  as garnish, 121, 138, 140, 227, 228, 231
  with sole, 76–77
  toasting of, 232
Apple and Belgian Endive Salad with Walnut Vinaigrette, 203–204
Apple in Parchment, 235–36
Apples, 223, 235
  in curried chicken, 137
  in desserts, 233, 235–36
  in salad, 204
Apple sauce, sea scallops in, 79
Apricot-Glazed Chicken, 127–28
Apricots
  with curried chicken, 118–19
  in dessert, 233
  dried, in granola, 225
  yogurt, in chicken with chutney, 120
Artichoke hearts
  in omelets, 64
  as pasta addition, 33
Arugula, 194
  in salad, 194–195
Asparagus, 68
  in fish dishes, 96–98
  guacamole, 67–69, 124
  in omelets, 64
  in pasta, 24, 26–27, 30–31, 35
  in rice dishes, 57
  in risotto, 59
  in salad, 141, 190, 192, 197, 199, 202
  in soup, 155
  in stir-fry with chicken, 121–22

Asparagus-Leek soup, 162–63
Avocados, 189
  in California Rolls, 109–10
  in rolling tortillas, 124
  in salad, 189

Baked Banana with Orange-Raisin Sauce, 234
Baked Salmon with Goat Cheese, 90–91
Baked Tortilla Chips, 170, 219
Baking, 89
Baking sheets, 219
Balsamic Vinaigrette, 184
  for pasta, 33, 36
Bamboo shoots, in spring rolls, 114
Bananas, 76, 234
  in desserts, 223, 226, 234
  in salad, 205–206
  in seafood dishes, 76–77, 80–81
  in soup, 151
Barley, 168
  soup, 168–69
Basic Omelet with Asparagus Guacamole, 67–69
Basil, 28–29, 125
  Goat Cheese Pizza with, 43–44
  lemon chicken with, in pita bread, 124–25
Basil Pesto, 25, 44, 218
Basting, 130
Beans, 197
  black
    with bulgur, 61
    in omelets, 66
    as pizza topping, 46
    in rice dishes, 57–58
    in salad, 188–89, 192, 201
    in soup, 103, 164–65, 169, 171, 173
    in Spicy Peanut Sauce, 108
    in tostada, 52
    in Veggie Burger, 54–55

butter, in salad, 194–95
cannellini
  in salad, 192, 195, 197, 201
  in soup, 165, 167, 169
garbanzo (chick peas), 170
  with bulgur, 61
  in curry, 50
  in guacamole, 69
  in omelets, 66
  in salad, 36, 38, 189, 192, 196–97, 201
  in soup, 103, 167, 169, 170, 173
  in tostada, 52
great northern
  in rice dish, 58
  in salad, 189, 195, 197, 200
  in soup, 167, 169
green
  Chunky Tomato Sauce on, 136
  in curry, 50
  in fish dishes, 96, 98
  with pasta, 27, 33
  in salad, 192, 197
  in soup, 167, 169
kidney
  with bulgur, 61
  in omelets, 66
  as pizza topping, 46
  in rice dish, 58
  in salad, 189, 192, 201
  in soup, 103, 165–67, 171, 172
  in tostada, 52
navy, in soup, 167
pinto, in soup, 171, 173
Bean sprouts, 140
  in salad, 141, 191
  in spring rolls, 114
Bean threads, in spring rolls, 108
Belgian endive, 203
Berries with Ricotta Cream, 228–29
Black Bean Soup, 164–65

Blanching, 141, 143
Blueberries
    in desserts, 223, 226, 229
    in salad, 206
Bok choy, 113
    in Chinese Chicken Salad, 140–41
    in rice dishes, 56
    in spring rolls, 113
    in stir-fry, 47–48
Breads, 217–20
Broccoli, 192
    in curry, 50, 95–96
    in omelets, 64, 66
    with pasta, 27, 31, 34–35, 38
    in pesto, 26
    in rice dishes, 57
    in salad, 188–191
    in soup, 155, 163, 167, 169, 173
    in stir-fry with chicken, 122
    in tostada, 52
Broiled Pineapple with Vanilla Yogurt,
        237–38
Broiled Salmon with Lime-Ginger
        Marinade, 83–84
Broiling, 81–82, 126
Bruschetta, 217
Bulgur wheat, 102, 214
    in salad, 201
    in soup, 167, 169
    Spanish-style, 60–61
Buttermilk, 150, 152

Cabbage
    Chinese, 140–41
    in Tandoori Chicken pita bread,
        132
Calcium, 155
Calcutta Curry, 49–50
California Rolls, 109–12
Cantaloupe
    in desserts, 229
    in soup, 151
Capers
    in Caponata, 54
    Greek snapper with, 91–92
    in pasta, 32–33
Caponata, 53–54
Caprini, 44

Carbohydrates, 12, 19, 193, 209–10,
        220, 238
Caribbean Sole, 76–77
Carrots, 49–50
    with bulgur, 60
    in curry, 49, 95–96
    in omelets, 64, 66
    with pasta, 30–31, 35, 38
    in pizza, 44
    in rice dishes, 56, 58–59
    in salad, 141, 190–92, 194, 197, 199,
        200, 202, 203
    with shrimp, 92–93
    in soup, 104–105, 154–55, 158–59,
        165–68, 172
    in Spicy Peanut Sauce, 108
    in spring rolls, 114
    in stir-fries, 47–48, 122
    in sushi, 112
    in tostada, 51–52
    in Veggie Burger, 54
Cashews, 117
    with bulgur, 61
    in curry, 50
    as garnish, 47, 121, 138
    in salad, 202
    in soup, 167, 173
    in Stir-Fried Rice, 57
Cauliflower, 96
    in curry, 50, 95–96
    in omelets, 64
    with pasta, 35
    in rice dishes, 57
    in salad, 190–92, 200
    in soup, 167
Cayenne pepper, 173
Celery
    in curry, 49, 138–39
    in pizza, 44
    in rice dish, 58
    in salad, 141, 194–95, 198–99,
        204–205
    with shrimp, 92–93
    in soup, 149, 154–55, 157–59, 168,
        170–71, 172
Cheese
    Cheddar, 45
        as garnish, 51, 160, 170, 172, 188

    in omelets, 66
    in pizza, 44, 46
    cottage, in tortilla salad, 188–89
    feta, 33
        baked salmon with, 91
        as garnish, 195
        Greek snapper with, 91–92
        in mostaccioli, 32–33
        in rolling tortillas, 124
    goat, 44
        in bruschetta, 217
        in pizza, 43–44
        salmon baked with, 90–91
        See also Chevre Cream
    Monterey Jack
        in omelets, 66
        as topping or garnish, 46, 170, 172
    mozzarella
        with pasta salad, 36
        in pizza, 44
    Parmesan, 24
        in baked chicken, 134–36
        in bread, 217, 218
        as garnish, 24, 27, 28, 35, 51, 99,
            101, 166
        in omelets, 63, 65–66
        Parmesan Cream, 157, 159
        in pasta, 22–23
        in pesto, 23–24, 26
        in pizza, 45–46
        in risotto, 58–59
        in soup, 155, 157, 168
    ricotta, 27
        in Fettucine Almost Alfredo, 26–27
        in omelets, 64, 69
        Ricotta Cream, 228–29
    Romano, 24
        in soup, 155
Chevre Cream, 159
    baked salmon with, 91
    in pasta, 26, 28
    in rolling tortillas, 124
    See also Cheese—goat
Chicken, 117–18, 126
    baked, Parmesan, 134–36
    chutney-yogurt, 120
    in curry, 50
    Ginger Sauce for, 48

glazed, 127–29
lemon-basil, in pita bread, 124–25
in omelets, 66
as pasta addition, 24, 27, 29, 31, 33, 36, 38
in pizza, 44
rice with, 58, 59
salad. *See* Salads—chicken
in soup, 161, 167, 171, 173
in spring rolls, 114
in Stir-Fried Rice, 57
tandoori, 131–32
Chicken-Asparagus Stir-Fry, 121–22
Chicken Fajitas, 123–24
Chicken Kabobs with Tomato-Soy Marinade, 133–34
Chicken with Curried Fruit, 118–19
Chick peas. *See* Beans—garbanzo
Chiffonade, definition of, 152
Chili, vegetarian, 172–73
Chilies, 65, 164–65
as garnish, 46, 52
in omelets, 65–66
in rice dish, 58
in salad, 189
in soup, 161, 170–71, 173
Chili powder, 173
Chilled Cucumber-Spinach Soup, 152
Chilled Melon-Lime Soup, 151
Chilled Strawberry-Mint Soup, 150
Chinese Chicken Salad with Sesame-Ginger Dressing, 140–41
Chives, 29
as garnish, 28, 149, 152
Chocolate, 224, 229
as garnish, 226
Chunky Garden Gazpacho, 148–49
Chunky Tomato Sauce, 134–36
Chutney, 50, 79
sea scallops in, 79
Chutney-Yogurt Chicken, 120
Chutney-Yogurt Cucumber Slices, 132
Chutney-Yogurt Dressing, 138–39
Cilantro, 78
Cinnamon, 223
Cinnamon and lemon dressing, 198–99
Cioppino, 100–101
Clam sauce, creamy, 99–100

Cocoa, 224
Cod, 101
almandine, 78
Caribbean, 77
in Cioppino, 100–101
orange poached, 87
Cookware, 10, 12
Coriander, 78
Corn, 160
with bulgur, 60–61
in omelets, 64
as pizza topping, 46
in soup, 155, 160–63, 165, 169, 172, 173
in tostada, 52
Cornstarch, 50
Couscous, 213
in salads, 36–38, 198–201
in spring rolls, 108
Couscous and Bean Salad with Walnut Vinaigrette, 200–201
Crab strips, imitation, 107, 109–110, 112
Cranberries, dried, 236, 237
Creamy Clam Sauce, 99–100
Creamy Pesto Dressing, 26
Creamy Potato-Carrot Soup, 154–55
Creamy Yogurt Dressing, 187
Crepes, Chunky Tomato Sauce on, 136
Croutons. *See* Herbed Croutons
Cucumber, 152
in California Rolls, 109–10
in Chinese chicken salad, 141
with pasta, 38
slices with chutney and yogurt, 132
in soup, 148–49, 152
in spring rolls, 106–108
in Tandoori Chicken pita bread, 132
Cumin, 65
Currant-almond sauce, 88–89
Currants, 137
in curried chicken, 137–38
in desserts, 228, 233, 236
in salad, 198–201, 203
Curried Chicken in Parchment, 137–38
Curried Chicken Salad with Mango, 138–39

Curried Corn and Pepper Chowder, 160–61
Curried Peach, 233
Curried Shrimp with Banana, 80–81
Curried Sweet Potato Soup, 156–57
Curried Yogurt Dressing, 204–205
Curry, 118–19
Calcutta, 49–50
chicken with fruit, 118–19
sauce, orange, 95–96
in soup, 152, 162–63
Curry Vinaigrette, 201–202

Desserts, general comments on, 223
Dijon mustard, 183
Dill, 105
as garnish, 152
Dressings
creamy pesto, 26
sesame-peanut, 36–38
sesame-pepper, 30–31
See also Salad Dressings

Eggplant, 33
in Caponata, 53
in pasta, 32–33
Eggs, 56–57, 61–69, 134–36
as garnish, 152, 164
English muffins, topping for, 52

Fajitas, Chicken, 123–24
Fettucine Almost Alfredo, 26–27
Fiber, 13, 19, 193
Fish, 73–75, 87
Ginger Sauce for, 48
as pasta addition, 33, 38
rice with, 58, 59
in wrappers, 105–109
See also specific types of fish
Five-spice powder, 113
Flounder, 77
in Cioppino, 102
Foccacia bread, 44
Food processors, 12, 226
Frittata, Italian, 63–64
Frozen Banana-Berry Parfait, 226–27
Fruits, 227–28, 234

Fruit Salad with Orange-Poppy Seed Dressing, 205–206
Fruit Sorbet, 227–28
Fusilli with Creamy Clam Sauce, 99–100

Garlic, 8, 13, 57–58, 149
Gazpacho, 148–49
Ginger, 47–48, 111, 112
   in curried chicken, 137
   in desserts, 223, 233, 236
   in marinades, 83–84, 130–32
   in salad dressing, 186
   in sesame sauce, 121–22
   in soup, 157
   in Spicy Peanut Sauce, 108
Gingered Pear with Almond Stuffing, 236–37
Ginger Sauce, 47–48
Ginger-Soy Vinaigrette, 196–97
Ginger Steamed Red Snapper with Lemon-Sesame Sauce, 97–98
Glazed Orange, 230–31
Goat Cheese Pizza with Fresh Basil, 43–44
Gourd strips, in sushi, 112
Granola, 225
   almond, 225, 231, 235, 236
Grapefruit, 206, 223
   in salad, 205
   salsa, 78
Grape juice, in soup, 150
Grapes, in salad, 204–205, 206
Greek Snapper with Feta Cheese, 91–92
Grouper, in Cioppino, 102
Guacamole, asparagus, 67–69, 124

Halibut
   almandine, 78
   Caribbean, 77
   with marinades, 84, 85
   steamed, 95–96
Hazelnuts, 142
Hazelnut Vinaigrette, 204
Herbed Croutons, 220
   in various soups, 149, 154, 157, 159, 168
Herbed Tomato Sauce, 34–36

Herbs, 35–36, 53, 55, 99, 135, 167
   fresh compared to dry, 8–9, 25, 35
   Parmesan pasta with plum tomatoes and, 22–23
   as salt substitute, 8, 12–13
Hoisin sauce, 107
Honeydew melon, in desserts, 223, 227, 229
Honey-Mint Dressing, 185
Honey-Mustard Dressing, 190–91
Honey-Poppy Seed Dressing, 185
Horseradish, Japanese. See Wasabi powder
Hot Chicken Salad with Walnut Vinaigrette, 142–43
Huevos Rancheros, 65–66

Imitation crab strips, 107, 109–10, 112
Italian Frittata, 63–64
Italian Omelet, 69

Jams and jellies, 127
Jicama
   in Chinese chicken salad, 141
   in rice dishes, 57

Kabobs
   chicken, 133–34
   tuna-vegetable, 84–85
Kitchen equipment, 11–12
Kiwi in Strawberry Sauce, 229–30
Kiwis, 229
   in desserts, 227
   as garnish, 150
   in salads, 206
   salsa, 78
Knives, 11, 91, 112, 217

Labeling, package, 9
Leeks, 162
   with shrimp, 92–93
   in soup, 162–63
Legumes, 193
Lemon-Basil Chicken in Pita Bread, 124–25
Lemon-Cinnamon Dressing, 198–99

Lemon juice, 8, 13, 125
   in guacamole, 67–68
   in salads, 139, 187
   in seafood dishes, 76, 78, 96, 99–100
   in soup, 150, 151
Lemons, 97
Lemon-Sesame Sauce, 97–98
Lettich, 142
Lettuce
   Boston, 201–202
   in chicken salad, 138–39, 143
   in chicken with pita bread, 124–25, 132
   chiffonade of, 149, 152
   iceberg, 178
   loose-leaf, 191
   in rice paper spring rolls, 106
   romaine
      in salad, 141–43, 194–95
      spring rolls, 113–14
   shredded, 51, 124, 141
   in soup, 152
Lime-Ginger Marinade, 83–84
Lime juice, 123, 125
   in Basil Pesto, 26
   in curried chicken salad, 138–39
   in desserts, 223
   in guacamole, 69
   in seafood dishes, 77–78, 80, 83
   in soup, 150, 151
Limes, 97, 123
   as garnish, 77

Macaroni, in soup, 166–67
Mangoes, 138
   curried dishes with, 81, 138–39
   in desserts, 227
   salsa, 78
   sole with, 77
Maple-Soy Marinade, 84–85
Maple syrup, 85, 223
   in granola, 225
   in marinade, 130–31
   in soup, 151
Marinades, 81–82
   apricot, 127–28
   lime-ginger, 83–84
   maple-soy, 84–85

plum, 128–29
Tandoori, 131–32
teriyaki, 130–31
tomato-soy, 133–34
Marinated Vegetables, 192
Mediterranean Mostaccioli, 32–33
Melons, 151
Mexican Rice, 57–58
Mexican Taco Soup, 170–71
Mexican Tortilla Pizza, 45–46
Microwaves, 10, 215, 216
Minestrone Soup, 166–67
Mint, 132
  in desserts, 230
  as garnish, 127, 128, 131, 227, 229, 230, 237
  in salad dressing, 185
  in soup, 150, 151
  for spring rolls, 106–108
Mirin, 84–85, 130
Mixed Green Salad, 178–80
Montrachet, 44
Mushrooms
  with bulgur, 60
  in Caponata, 53
  in chicken kabobs, 134
  in curry, 49
  in omelets, 63
  with pasta, 23, 27, 30–33, 35, 102
  in pizza, 44
  in rice dishes, 56, 58–59
  in salad, 141, 191, 196–97
  in soup, 158, 162–63, 169, 173
  in spring rolls, 114
  with steamed red snapper, 97–98
  in stir-fries, 47–48, 122
  in tostada, 51–52
Mustard cabbage. See Bok choy

Nectarines
  in desserts, 230, 232
  sole with, 77
Noncholesterol egg product, 56–57, 61–69, 134–36
Nonstick cookware, 10, 12
Noodles, in spring rolls, 108
Nutburgers, 54

Nutmeg, 157, 223
  in soup, 151

Oats, rolled, 225
Oil and fat, 10, 12, 13–14, 63, 149, 181–82, 186, 203
Olive oil, 181–82
Omelets, 61, 67
  with Asparagus Guacamole, 67–69
  Chunky Tomato Sauce on, 136
  Italian, 63–64, 69
  Oriental, 69
  with Huevos Rancheros sauce, 65–66
  Vegetarian Tostada filling for, 52
Onions, 173
  with bulgur, 60
  in Caponata, 53
  in chicken dishes, 123, 134
  in Cioppino, 100–101
  in curry, 49
  green. See Scallions
  in omelets, 64
  in pizza, 44, 46
  in rice dish, 57
  in seafood dishes, 84–85
  in soup, 163, 166–68, 170, 172
  in stir-fry, 47–48
  in tostada, 51–52
Orange Curry Sauce, 95–96
Orange-Glazed Chicken, 128
Orange juice
  in desserts, 223, 227–29, 233–35
  in salad dressing, 205
  in seafood dishes, 78
  in soup, 150
Orange Poached Walleye, 87
Orange-Poppy Seed Dressing, 205–206
Orange roughy
  with Almond-Currant Sauce, 89
  orange poached, 87
Oranges, 230–31
  to accompany curry, 50
  in chicken kabobs, 134
  in desserts, 223, 227, 233
  as garnish, 37, 51, 67, 87, 198
  glazes, 230–31
  in salad, 140, 205
  yogurt, in chicken with chutney, 120

Oriental Omelet, 69
Orzo, 102, 202
  in minestrone, 167

Pak choy (pak choi). See Bok choy
Pancakes, Raspberry Purée on, 231–32
Papaya
  curried shrimp with, 81
  in desserts, 227
  salsa, 78
Paprika, 160
Parchment
  apple in, 235–36
  curried chicken in, 137–38
  pear in, 236
  shrimp in, 92–93
Parfait, Frozen Banana-Berry, 226–27
Parmesan Chicken with Chunky Tomato Sauce, 134–36
Parmesan Cream, 157, 159
Parmesan Pasta with Herbs and Plum Tomatoes, 22–23
Parsley, 53, 88
  Chinese, 78
  as garnish, 65, 76, 77, 79, 80, 87, 88, 90, 91, 99, 102, 120, 128, 131, 135, 149, 154, 156, 157
  in omelets, 69
  in Orange Curry Sauce, 95–96
  in pesto, 23–24, 26
  in salad, 142–43, 196–99, 201–203
  in seafood with pasta, 99–101
  in soup, 102–103, 166–68, 170–71
  in Veggie Burger, 54
Pasta, 19–21, 214–15
  Chunky Tomato Sauce on, 136
  fettucine, almost Alfredo, 26–27
  fusilli, with clam sauce, 99–100
  linguine, in Cioppino, 100–102
  mostaccioli, Mediterranean, 32–33
  penne
    Parmesan, 22–23
    with pesto, 24–25, 28–29
  rainbow rotini, 23–24
  reheating of, 20
  rotini and rotelle, 34, 35

Pasta (*cont.*)
  salad
    with couscous, 36–38
    with Herbed Tomato Sauce, 34–36
  spaghetti
    in minestrone, 167
    with Sesame-Pepper Dressing,
      30–31
  spinach ribbon noodles, in salad,
    36–37
  warm *vs.* chilled, 34
  See also Couscous
Pasta and Couscous Salad with Sesame-
    Peanut Dressing, 36–38
Pasta Primavera with Sesame-Pepper
    Dressing, 30–31
Pasta Salad Primavera with Herbed
    Tomato Sauce, 34–36
Peaches, 233
  with curried chicken, 118–19
  in desserts, 229, 230, 232, 233
  in salad, 206
  sole with, 77
  yogurt, in chicken with chutney, 120
Peach Melba, 232
Peanut butter, 37
Peanuts
  dry roasted, 37, 50, 138
  as garnish, 30, 106
  spicy sauce, 106–109
Pear in Raspberry Purée, 231–32
Pears, 232
  with curried chicken, 119
  in desserts, 223, 227, 229, 231–32,
    236
  in salad, 204, 206
  yogurt, in chicken with chutney,
    120
Pear sauce, sea scallops in, 79
Peas, 157
  in omelets, 64
  with pasta, 27, 30–31, 34–35, 38
  in risotto, 58–59
  in salad, 141, 202
  in soup, 104–105, 157–58, 169
  See also Snap peas; Snow peas
Pea Soup, 157–58
Pecans, in dessert, 234

Penne with Basil Pesto, 24–25
Penne with Triple Tomato Pesto, 28–
    29
Pepper, 29, 90, 157, 173
Peppers, 31, 164–65
  jalapeño
    in Chicken Fajitas, 123
    as garnish, 52
    in rice dish, 58
    in soup, 164–65, 173
  red and green bell
    in Bruschetta, 217
    with bulgur, 60
    in Caponata, 53
    in chicken dishes, 123–24, 134
    in kabobs, 84–85, 134
    minced, in tomato pesto, 29
    in omelets, 63–66
    with pasta, 24, 27, 30–31, 33,
      35–37, 100–101
    in pizza, 44
    in rice dishes, 55–58
    in salad, 141, 143, 188–92,
      194–97, 200, 202
    in soup, 148–49, 160–61, 164–67,
      169, 170–72
    in stir-fries, 47–48, 121, 122
    in Veggie Burger, 54–55
  yellow bell, in kabobs, 84–85
Perch
  almandine, with fruit salsa, 78
  Caribbean, 77
Pesto
  basil, 25, 44, 218
  broccoli, 26
  creamy, 26
  parsley-walnut, 23–24
  spinach-parsley, 26
  triple tomato, 28–29
  vinaigrette, 36
Pesto-Chevre Sauce, 26
Pesto Vinaigrette, 36, 183
Pignoli nuts. *See* Pine nuts
Pineapple juice, in dessert, 233
Pineapple, 237–38
  to accompany curry, 50
  in chicken kabobs, 133–34
  with curried chicken, 119

  in desserts, 232, 233, 237–38
  as garnish, 37
Pine nuts, 22–23
  in Basil Pesto, 25
  in pastas, 22, 24, 35
  as pizza topping, 44
  toasted, 36, 140, 142, 198
Piñons. *See* Pine nuts
Pita bread, 218
  curried chicken-mango mixture in, 139
  in Goat Cheese Pizza, 43
  lemon-basil chicken in, 124–25
  salad served in, 189
  spring-roll mixture, 114
  Tandoori Chicken in, 132
Pita Crisps, 218
Pizza, 42
  goat cheese, 43–46
  Mexican tortilla, 45–46
Plum-Glazed Chicken, 128–29
Plums
  paste, in sushi, 112
  sauce, Chinese, 113–14, 128–29,
    141
Poaching, 86, 232
Poppy seed and orange dressing,
    205–206
Poppy seeds in salad dressing, 185
Potatoes, 153, 191
  baked, Chunky Tomato Sauce on, 136
  in curry, 50
  in omelets, 63
  in salad, 190–91
  in soup, 104–105, 154–56, 160–63,
    173
  in Tuna-Vegetable Kabobs, 85
Prawns, definition of, 74
Protein, 12, 60, 74, 155, 193, 199
Prunes, dried, in granola, 225

Quinoa, 198–99
Quinoa-Couscous Salad with Lemon-
    Cinnamon Dressing, 198–99

Radish, in sushi, 112
Rainbow Rotini with Parsley-Walnut
    Pesto, 23–24
Rainbow trout with goat cheese, 91

Raisins
    to accompany curry, 50
    in desserts, 233–36
    in granola, 225
Raspberries
    in desserts, 223, 229, 231–32, 237,
        238
    in salad, 206
Raspberry Purée, 231–32
Raspberry Vinaigrette, 204
Red snapper, ginger steamed, 97–98
Rice, 210–13
    arborio, in risotto, 58–59
    in California Rolls, 109–12
    Mexican, 57–58
    in omelets, 64
    in salad, 199, 201–202
    in soup, 102–103, 159, 165, 167, 169
    in spring rolls, 106–108
    stir-fried, 56–57
Rice Paper Spring Rolls with Spicy
    Peanut Sauce, 106–109
Ricotta Cream, 228–29
Risotto Primavera, 58–59
Rolls
    California, 109–112
    See also Spring rolls
Romaine Spring Rolls, 113–14
Rosemary, 90–91

Salad dressings, 181–82
    chutney-yogurt, 138–39
    creamy yogurt, 187
    curried yogurt, 204–205
    honey-mint, 185
    honey-mustard, 190–91
    honey-poppy seed, 185
    lemon-cinnamon, 198–99
    orange-poppy seed, 205–206
    sesame-ginger, 186
    tomato, 188–89
    See also Vinaigrette
Salads, 177
    bean, 193
    chicken
        Chinese, 140–41
        with couscous, 201
        curried with mango, 138–39

    glazed, 128, 129
    hot, with vinaigrette, 142–43
    lemon-basil, 124–25
    with quinoa and couscous, 199
    teriyaki, 131
    with tortilla, 189
    warm, with beans and peppers,
        195
fish
    glazed, 128
    teriyaki, 131
fruit, 202–206
marinated vegetable, 192
mixed green, 178–80
pasta
    with couscous, 36–38
    with Herbed Tomato Sauce, 34–36
shrimp
    Chinese, 141
    glazed, 128
    with quinoa and couscous, 199
    with tomato and rice, 202
spring-roll mixture, 114
steamed vegetable, 190–91
teriyaki, 196–97
tomato-rice, 201–202
Salmon, 14, 74, 91
    apricot-glazed, 128
    baked with goat cheese, 90–91
    broiled, 83–84
    creamy sauce, 100
    steamed, 96
Salsa, fruit, 77–78
Salt, substitutes for, 8–9, 12–13
Sauces
    almond-currant, 88–89
    almost Alfredo, 26–27
    Chinese plum, 113–14, 128–29, 141
    chunky tomato, 134–36
    creamy clam, 99–100
    fudge, semisweet, 224
    ginger, 47–48
    herbed tomato, 34–36
    lemon-sesame, 97–98
    orange curry, 95–96
    orange-raisin, 234
    pesto-chevre, 26
    sesame-ginger, 121–22

    spicy peanut, 106–109
    strawberry, 229–30
    taco, 45, 65, 67
    teriyaki, 85
Sautéing, 10, 75–76, 80, 121–22, 216
Scallions, 200
    curls, 47, 48
    as garnish, 131, 172
    in omelets, 63
    in salad, 35, 138–40, 143, 188–89,
        192, 194–95, 196–202
    with seafood, 93, 95–98
    in soup, 104–105, 148–49, 152
    in spring rolls, 113
    in Stir-Fried Rice, 56
    in sushi, 112
Scallops, 75, 79
    in chutney, apple, and pear sauce, 79
    ginger steamed, 98
    with marinade, 84, 85
    in parchment, 93
Scrod, 101
Sea Scallops in Chutney, Apple, and
    Pear Sauce, 79
Seaweed, 110
Semisweet Fudge Sauce, 224
Sesame-Ginger Dressing, 186
Sesame-Ginger Sauce, 121–22
Sesame oil, 186
Sesame-Peanut Dressing, 36–38
Sesame-Pepper Dressing, 30–31
Sesame seeds, 30
    as garnish, 30, 47
    in granola, 225
    in Pita Crisps, 218
    toasted, 30–31, 95, 109–12, 140
    in vinaigrette, 196
Sesame Vinaigrette, 204
Shallots, 154–55
    in pasta, 32–33
    in risotto, 58–59
    in seafood dishes, 90–92
    in soup, 103, 105, 154–61
Shellfish, 73–76
Shrimp, 74–75, 80, 103
    apricot-glazed, 128
    in Cioppino, 100–101
    in curry, 50, 80–81

Shrimp (*cont.*)
  with Lime-Ginger Marinade, 84
  as pasta addition, 31
  in pizza, 44
  with risotto, 59
  salad. *See* Salads—shrimp
  in soup, 149
  in spring rolls, 113
  in stir-fries, 48, 57
  Tandoori, 132
  teriyaki, 131
Shrimp and Rice Soup, 102–103
Shrimp in Parchment, 92–93
Skewers, 133
Snap peas
  in curry, 50
  in fish dishes, 96, 98
  with pasta, 31, 38
  in salad, 191, 192
  in stir-fry with chicken, 122
Snow peas, 143
  with Ginger Steamed Red Snapper, 98
  with pasta, 31
  in salad, 140, 143, 191
  in stir-fry with chicken, 122
Sole, 77
  Caribbean, 76–77
  orange poached, 87
Sole Almandine with Strawberry Salsa, 77–78
Sole with Almond-Currant Sauce, 88–89
Sorbet, fruit, 227–28
Sorrel, 195
Soups, 12, 147–48, 153
  black bean, 164–65
  chilled
    asparagus-leek, 162–63
    cucumber-spinach soup, 152
    gazpacho, 148–49
    melon-lime soup, 151
    strawberry-mint soup, 150
  chowders
    curried corn and pepper, 160–61
    tuna, 104–105
  chunky, 166
  Cioppino, 100–102
  creamy potato-carrot, 154–55

  curried sweet potato, 156–57
  minestrone, 166–67
  pea, 157–58
  shrimp and rice, 102–103
  spicy tomato-carrot, 158–59
  taco, 170–71
  vegetable-barley, 168–69
  vegetarian chili, 172–73
Sour cream, 65
  as garnish, 65, 67
  in rolling tortillas, 124
Soy sauce, low-sodium, 130
Spanish Bulgur, 60–61
Spices, 9, 13, 29, 51, 65, 113
Spicy Peanut Sauce, 106–109
Spicy Tomato-Carrot Soup with Chevre Cream, 158–59
Spinach, 189
  in pasta, 31
  in pesto, 24, 26
  in pizza, 44
  in salad, 141, 143, 188–89, 195, 200, 204–206
  in soup, 103, 152, 155
  in Tandoori Chicken pita bread, 132
Spring rolls
  rice paper, with Spicy Peanut Sauce, 106–109
  romaine, 113–14
Squash, in soup, 157, 169
Steamed Halibut and Vegetables with Orange Curry Sauce, 95–96
Steamed Vegetable Platter with Honey-Mustard Dressing, 190–91
Steaming, 94, 97, 215–16
Stir-Fried Rice, 56–57
Stir-fry, 121–22
  chicken-asparagus, 121–22
  vegetable, with tofu, 47–48
Strawberries, 150
  in desserts, 223, 226–30, 237
  fan, 229, 230
  in salad, 205–206
  in soup, 150, 151
Strawberry Salsa, 77–78
Strawberry Sauce, 229–30
Sugar, 12, 13, 187

Sunflower seeds, 202
  as garnish, 156, 188, 201
  in granola, 225
Sushi, 109–12
Sweet potatoes, 156
Swordfish
  kabobs, with Tomato-Soy Marinade, 134
  with steamed vegetables, 191

Taco sauce, 45, 65, 67
Tandoori Chicken, 131–32
Tarragon, 142, 163
Teriyaki chicken, 130–31
Teriyaki Salad with Ginger-Soy Vinaigrette, 196–97
Teriyaki sauce, 85
Thyme, 159, 187
Tofu, 48
  with pasta salad, 36, 38
  vegetable stir-fry with, 47–48
Tomato Dressing, 188–89
Tomatoes, 91–92, 101, 159
  canned, 103
    with bulgur, 60
    in Cioppino, 100–102
    in pesto, 28–29
    in salmon with goat cheese, 90
    in soup, 102–103, 159, 166–67, 169, 170–72
  cherry
    in chicken kabobs, 134
    in Tuna-Vegetable Kabobs, 85
  cubed
    in Chunky Tomato Sauce, 135
    in Greek Snapper with Feta Cheese, 91–92
    in salad, 199, 201–202
    in soup, 158–59, 168
  marinated sun-dried, 43
    in bread, 217, 218
    in Caponata, 54
    in Chunky Tomato Sauce, 135
    in omelets, 64, 66
    as pasta addition, 24, 33
    in pizza, 43, 45–46
    in risotto, 59

in salad, 189
in soup, 102, 169
in Triple Tomato Pesto, 28–29
plum (Italian, Roma), 44
  in Bruschetta, 217
  in Caponata, 53
  in curry, 50
  in pasta, 22–25, 30–33
  in pesto, 28–29
  in pizza, 43
  in rice dish, 57
  in salads, 35, 142–43, 190–91, 196–97, 201–202
  with shrimp, 92–93
  in soup, 148–49
  in tostada, 51–52
Tomato Pistou, 23
Tomato-Rice Salad with Curry Vinaigrette, 201–202
Tomato-Soy Marinade, 133–34
Tortillas, 123
  baked chips, 170, 219
  for Chicken Fajitas, 123
  omelets with, 65–66
  in pizza, 44, 45–46
  in soup, 171
  for Vegetarian Tostada, 51–52
Tortilla Salad with Tomato Dressing, 188–89
Tostada, Vegetarian, 51–52
Tuna, 104
  in Cioppino, 102
  creamy sauce, 100
  with Lime-Ginger Marinade, 84
  with steamed vegetables, 191
Tuna Chowder, 104–105
Tuna-Vegetable Kabobs with Maple-Soy Marinade, 84–85

Vanilla extract, 227, 228–29
Vegetable-Barley Soup, 168–69
Vegetables, general comments on, 215–16
Vegetable Stir-fry with Tofu and Ginger Sauce, 47–48
Vegetable stock powder, 147
Vegetarian Chili, 172–73
Vegetarian Tostada, 51–52
Veggie Burger, 54–55
Vinaigrette, 182–83
  curry, 201–202
  ginger-soy, 196–97
  walnut, 200
  See also Balsamic Vinaigrette; Walnut Vinaigrette
Vinegar, 110, 128, 182–84, 197

Waffles, Raspberry Purée on, 232
Walleye
  with Almond-Currant Sauce, 89
  almandine, 78
  Caribbean, 77
  orange poached, 87
Walnuts, 203–205
  in dessert, 235
  as garnish, 118, 119, 156, 203, 204
  in parsley pesto, 23–24
  in pasta, 31
Walnut Vinaigrette, 142–43, 200–201, 203–204
Warm Bean and Sweet Pepper Salad with Balsamic Vinaigrette, 194–95
Wasabi Cream, 151
Wasabi powder, 41, 110

Water chestnuts
  in Chinese chicken salad, 141
  in rice dishes, 56
Watercress
  in salad, 195
  in soup, 152
Wheat germ, 225
  as garnish, 235, 236
  in Parmesan Chicken, 134–36
  with pasta, 22
  in Veggie Burger, 54
Winter Fruit Salad with Curried Yogurt Dressing, 204–205

Yogurt, 120, 125
  to accompany curry, 50
  in Chevre Cream, 159
  with cucumber and chutney, 132
  in desserts, 226, 229, 231–33, 237
  in dressings, 26, 37, 138, 187, 190, 204
  as garnish, 65, 67, 149, 151, 152, 156, 164, 235, 236
  in sauces, 95–96, 106–108
  in soup, 151, 152
  in Tandoori Marinade, 131–32
  on tortillas, 124, 188–89

Zesting, 83, 230
Zucchini, 51
  in kabobs, 85, 133
  in omelets, 63, 66
  in pasta, 30–35
  in pizza, 44
  in risotto, 58–59
  in salad, 191, 192
  in soup, 149, 155, 166–68, 173
  in tostada, 51–52